Training Your Brain To Adopt Healthful Habits:

Mastering The Five Brain Challenges

By:
Jodie A. Trafton, Ph.D.
William P. Gordon, Ph.D.
& Supriya Misra, M.A.

Published by:
Institute for Brain Potential (IBP)

This book is not intended as a substitute for the medical recommendation of physicians or other healthcare providers. It reflects the experiences, studies, research and opinions of the authors. Neither the authors nor the publisher shall be liable or responsible for any health, welfare or subsequent damage allegedly arising from the use of any information contained in this book.

The authors have made every effort to ensure the accuracy of the information herein, particularly with regard to treatments. However, appropriate information sources should be consulted, especially for new or unfamiliar drugs or procedures. Authors, editors and the publisher cannot be held responsible for typographical or content errors found in this publication.

Library of Congress Cataloging-in-Publication Data
Training Your Brain To Adopt Healthful Habits: Mastering The Five Brain Challenges
ISBN: 978-0-9832465-0-3 Library of Congress Control Number: 2011900511

Institute for Brain Potential (IBP) is a non-profit organization dedicated to providing advances in Behavioral Medicine through publications and conferences. IBP is a 501(c)(3) organization (tax identification number 77-0026830) founded in 1984 as Institute for Cortext Research and Development. The Institute has trained over one million health professionals in the neurobehavioral sciences and has published books in the fields of Neuropsychology and Behavioral Medicine including the three-volume series, *Best Practices in the Behavioral Management of Chronic Disease*.

Printed in the United States of America

Table of Contents

PREFACE

One of the most difficult challenges in life is learning to make healthful decisions, whether it is about how we eat, exercise, take prescribed drugs and illicit drugs, drink, smoke or manage our emotions. There is convincing evidence that the majority of people know what they should be doing but fail to heed the recommendations of their physicians and other caregivers.

Why is it so hard to maintain healthful habits? This book will explain successful processes to initiate and maintain change from a neuroscience perspective. Specifically, we will examine five key brain challenges that underlie many of the most effective cognitive, behavioral and pharmacological strategies for changing health behaviors and maintaining healthful practices. The neuroscience is presented simply and focused on the practical. Each of the brain challenges is followed by exercises to target the brain processes, encouraging you to change your brain responses as you learn about them. Research has consistently shown that behavior change requires active participation rather than just passively learning concepts. As such, this text will walk you through activities as you learn how and why they work.

It is remarkable that the brain circuits that participate in self-destructive drug-dependence and substance misuse, including nicotine, alcohol, cocaine, amphetamines and heroin, can also encourage self-benefiting practices that we will call healthy pleasures (e.g., eating healthy foods, engaging in stimulating physical activity, thinking calming thoughts, fostering genuine friendships and collaborations, and driving productive activities). Just as use of addictive substances can become automatic and compulsive, we believe that positive behaviors can be acquired and become habit-forming. Once learned and supported in your everyday life, both negative and positive habits can be performed without much conscious effort. However, acquiring a health-promoting habit takes a good deal of effort and focused attention. We will show you how.

Many books purport to enable their readers to make changes that are quick and easy. The overwhelming evidence is that changing habits is neither quick nor easy. Making real change requires making thoughtful decisions everyday and deferring immediate gratification even when you are stressed or in a hurry. Moreover, making real change normally involves the need to reinstate the behavior multiple times. Lapses and relapses are a normal part of the process of achieving positive health habits, just as they are part of the process of overcoming self-destructive behaviors such as drug-dependence. Read the chapters, participate in the exercises, and put them into practice, and you will have an excellent chance to create meaningful and lasting change. We challenge you to try and try again to continually come closer to realizing your optimal health. Your goal should be to continue to work on optimizing your health rather than to attain a specific weight or level of fitness. Health is a process, a state of being, and an ongoing activity rather than a specific outcome or marker of achievement.

Your odds of adding years to your life and life to your years are greatly increased if you avoid tobacco and illicit drugs, maintain a healthy weight, eat healthful foods, do not drink to excess, and avoid infections, toxic agents, and risky use of firearms, sexual behavior, or motor vehicles. You already know this. However, what is less understood is that over half of all deaths in the United States and the industrialized world are related to self-destructive behaviors and habits (Mokdad et al., 2004). The top three causes of U.S. deaths are tobacco use (18.1%), poor diet and physical activity (16.6%), and alcohol use (3.5%). Motor vehicle crashes, firearm accidents and incidents, unsafe sexual behaviors and drug use are also large contributors to mortality. However, it is very difficult to stop smoking, drinking, over-eating, under-exercising, emotionally over-reacting, and other seemingly intractable habits. The table below provides some statistics demonstrating the impact of these risks.

TABLE: Top Causes of Mortality in the United States (after McGinnis & Foege, 1993)

Disease Associated with Death		**Behavioral Causes of Death**	
Heart Disease	720,000	Tobacco	400,000
Cancer	505,000	Diet/Inactivity	300,000
Stroke	144,000	Alcohol	100,000
Accidents	92,000	Infection	90,000
Lung Disease	87,000	Toxic Agents	60,000
Pneumonia/Influenza	78,000	Firearms	36,000
Diabetes	48,000	Sexual Behavior	30,000
Suicide	31,000	Motor Vehicles	25,000
Liver Disease	26,000	Drug Use	20,000
HIV	25,000		

Legend: This table provides the number of people per year who die in the United States based on (1) the top diseases that contributed to their death or (2) the top behaviors that contributed to their death.

Conclusions About Changing Health-Related Habits

* *Information alone is rarely sufficient to meaningfully alter behavior.* Information about why to change a behavior may be necessary to motivate change, but practice and support for new behaviors are needed to create enduring health-related habits.

* *Learning "how" to change a behavior is of much greater value than learning "why" a behavior should be changed.* We offer more than a lecture about why you should change and what behaviors you should adopt. We help you take positive steps to discover what works for you and to make these new behaviors an ongoing part of your life. We show you how to initiate action, learn from mistakes and refine healthful behavior.

* *Chronic interventions are more effective than acute interventions.* Learning to convert a health behavior into a habit often requires chronic interventions from health professionals and coaches. Chronic interventions to promote behavioral change work

best for chronic conditions but most interventions provided by physicians and allied health professionals are provided in an acute care setting. We will show you how to build an environment and support structure that will help you achieve chronic health, using tools such as automatic reminders, scheduling, environmental modification, networking, and revaluation of health-related choices.

* *Relapse is the norm rather than the exception. Therefore, it is very helpful to build in back-up strategies at the start.* We show you how to reinstate healthful behaviors by identifying what worked previously and evaluating what went wrong.

* *Daily or frequent self-monitoring is immensely valuable in helping you focus on what you are trying to achieve, the obstacles to change and everyday problem-solving.* We show you several ways to institute self-monitoring. We also provide you with forms so that you can easily review your progress.

* *A support system is extremely helpful for maintaining changes.* We will show you how to recruit family, friends and health professionals who can encourage, remind or participate in what you seek to change. We will also show you how to recognize when family or friends unwittingly sabotage your efforts to institute and maintain change.

* *Defer immediate gratification.* We will explain why your brain is biased toward seeking short-term pleasure at the expense of long-term health. We go into substantial detail to describe how the part of the brain that drives automatic behavior to get immediate rewards (the limbic reward system) can overwhelm other higher brain centers (the prefrontal executive system) that facilitate the ability to delay gratification.

* *Make healthful habits automatic through practice and reinforcement.* A habit requires little conscious effort whereas a conscious behavior requires short-term memory and initiating or reminding events. We will show you how to convert healthful conscious behaviors into habits, this time focusing on the basal ganglia, the part of the brain that learns and retains new habits even when your short-term memory does not function well.

* *It is possible to acquire more than one health-related habit at a time. If you want to try this program, be bold as you work for meaningful results.*

What Is New About This Book

1. To our knowledge, this is the first book to break health behavior change into specific neural processes, describing first the underlying brain activity that needs to be changed and then providing exercises to help you alter these processes. You will learn how to reprogram your reward circuits and prefrontal cortex to achieve your health objectives.

2. We draw our recommendations based on the totality of evidence from our three-volume series, *Best Practices in the Behavioral Management of Chronic Disease*, the single largest compilation of data on behavioral health interventions ever made available to health professionals.

3. We explain how the addiction-related reward circuits of the brain can be reprogrammed to help people acquire and maintain healthful habits. Emphasis is placed on the three health-related habits of greatest interest to health professionals:
   a) Changing preference for healthful food to achieve a healthy weight,
   b) Changing a sedentary lifestyle to include regular and rewarding physical activity,
   c) Changing the way emotions and emotion-driven thoughts are managed.

4. We provide interactive exercises for the learning components of this book. We invite the readers who have completed the exercises to contact the authors to help us update the

exercises based on what works, what is confusing and what is unhelpful. Therefore, we seek to improve the book on a regular basis. We invite you to participate.

About The Authors

Jodie Anne Trafton, Ph.D., William P. Gordon, Ph.D. and Supriya Misra, M.A. are behavioral neuroscientists deeply interested in both the neural mechanisms underlying change and also the psychological processes needed to facilitate meaningful health-related change. They are committed to creating a clear, practical resource for health professionals, clients and anyone who seeks to change health-related behaviors.

Both Drs. Trafton and Gordon are actively involved in research and training to develop methods of creating meaningful, enduring change in health behaviors, and to design books and programs to help others achieve these objectives. Their goal is to not only spur initial attempts to reach a health objective, but also to encourage reinstatement of the behavior until it becomes an enjoyable lifelong habit. They have edited the three-volume series, *Best Practices in the Behavioral Management of Chronic Disease*, the most comprehensive set of evidence-based reviews of the best behavioral interventions for modifying health-related behaviors. Written by experts in the management of all major chronic disorders throughout the lifespan, these findings can be adopted and adapted to create enduring and meaningful change for most chronic disorders. In this book, they apply the key principles embodied in three-volume, 1500-page, 52-chapter series.

Disclaimer To Neuroscientists

In order for us to explain many of the neurobiological processes important for encouraging healthful behavior change in a clear, concise manner, we are forced to oversimplify systems and particularly their underlying cell biology quite a bit. Neuronal systems rarely do only one thing and have layers and layers of modifiers, regulatory processes and feedback loops that keep behavior both flexible and stable. Trying to discuss all that we know about these systems, their detailed and changing connections, and the chemical interactions that modify cellular activity over short and longer time scales, would take an encyclopedia, confuse all but the most dedicated neurobiologists, be extremely dull in many places, and, most importantly, is not necessary to understand the key elements of how to change our health behaviors. There are places in this text where we oversimplify the neurobiology to the point that the details are not exactly correct: a few neurons in a circuit are missing, effects are ascribed to a single neurotransmitter or receptor system when many are involved with much more intricate interactions and regulatory effects, or we leave out the effects and processes occurring in whole brain regions. Although the broader literature is exciting and may contribute greatly to our understanding, there is just too much to discuss. So please forgive us in places where the details are fudged for the sake of simplicity. We have purposely chosen to focus on the broader concepts and processes that guide these neurobiological systems. Apologies to the neurobiologists whose decades of work are summarized in a sentence, have been stripped of their subtleties or are ignored all together. We have sacrificed the detail of your work in an attempt to make it accessible to those with a day rather than a decade to understand it.

INTRODUCTION

Imagine how vastly we could improve the health of people in the industrialized world simply by changing their habits. The top contributors to disease in these countries are all unhealthful behaviors. It would seem that no new medications, medical devices, diagnostic tests and machines or surgical techniques are needed to eliminate the biggest contributors to disease and death in our population. But then why have not most people altered their health behaviors? Education cannot be the main problem. Who does not know that smoking, drinking, taking drugs, eating unhealthful food, not exercising, playing with guns, driving too fast or when intoxicated, and having unprotected sex are bad for you? So why do so many of us do these things anyway? Why is it so hard to make healthful choices and act on them consistently?

Immediate Gratification: The Deadly Trade-Off

One major problem is that these unhealthful behaviors can seem fun and rewarding at the time. While cookies and a soda might make a pretty lousy lunch in terms of nutrition, they still taste good, and the sugar and caffeine are highly rewarding to our brains. In the moment, risky sex, fast driving, substance use, gun play, or laying around watching TV can all seem exciting, relaxing, thrilling or enjoyable, even if they make us feel bad, get sick or risk injury later. In order to behave healthfully, we need to control our actions and keep ourselves safe when these quick pleasures present themselves. And that can be a very difficult thing to do.

In order to make good choices that lead to long-term wellness, we need to be able to forgo immediate gratification at least some of the time. Shortsighted decisions keep us from reaching our health potential. In this book, we explore the brain circuits that influence our search for immediate gratification. We discuss how we learn bad habits and why we favor bad habits over more objectively rewarding behaviors. We describe how feeling helpless, stressed and out of control make it difficult to make good choices. We demonstrate why not recognizing opportunities in your life can make you impulsive. We explain how unrealistic expectations, social pressure and media exposure can lead our brain to overvalue quick fixes. Most importantly, by revealing how these systems work, we provide techniques for shaping these circuits to support your quest for long-term health and happiness. Lastly, we offer exercises to help you practice these important psychological techniques.

To focus our exploration of the neurobiological and psychological basis of good health choices, we have broken the process of health behavior change into five steps or challenges. These steps map onto a simplified brain circuit that processes information to guide your behavior. These steps are as follows:

Challenge #1: Learning to highly value behaviors that promote wellness and devalue behaviors that lead to poor health.

When we make decisions, our brains weigh options and consider the expected benefits, including immediate gratification, of one action versus another. If you expect big benefits from behaviors that lead to poor health, then you will make self-destructive choices. If you expect healthful behaviors to be boring, painful or unpleasant, then you probably will not do them. For example, if I think of a big five-scoop ice cream sundae as a delicious reward then I will probably want to eat it. If I instead think of the stomachache that it will likely produce shortly after, I probably will not. If I think of how much my legs will hurt while I go running, I probably will not go running. If I think of the warm glow I will experience after I run, I probably will. Altering our expectations about the benefits of behaviors can lead to big changes in health.

Challenge #2: Enriching your life to tame the need for immediate gratification.
Our brains keep track of opportunities to improve our lives. When opportunities are rare, our brains will drive us to habitually take advantage of these rare opportunities, even when the benefits may be short-lived and the negative consequences may be relatively great. If you spend your days feeling neglected and deprived, you will find it hard to turn down the quick pleasure presented by the cookies at the convenience store. Conversely, when our brains recognize that we have many opportunities, they slow down and consider options more thoughtfully and deliberately. If you have a rich life with lots of positive interactions with people and choices about what to eat and how to spend your time, you will find it easier to turn down a quick reward and stick to your long-term goals. Learning to recognize and take advantage of more opportunities in your life can help you make decisions with greater long-term benefits. Learning to recognize problems as an opportunity to make your life better can be a helpful step.

Challenge #3: Enhancing resiliency to new threats and chronic stressors.
Threats to our well-being cause us to favor quick fixes over potentially better or more durable solutions. When we feel threatened, it feels so important to do something to make things better immediately, that we may not even consider other options that would provide much greater long-term benefits. Feeling endangered brings out bad habits, and inhibits careful, purposeful problem-solving. When we reduce stress in our lives and feel in control of our fate, we are more likely to be able to make good choices that lead to excellent health. As we will show, by increasing the predictability of unpleasant events and increasing your sense of control over them, you will become resilient both emotionally and physically. Eating, smoking and drinking are common responses to feeling unsafe and are well-known health-related risks. By learning ways to keep your physiology in balance and change your response to threatening situations, you can avert self-destructive choices in trying times. The key is to create life patterns and responses that promote safety and confidence.

Challenge #4: Training your addiction circuits to make health behaviors habitual.
It is much easier to do behaviors regularly when they become habits. But to make a behavior habitual, we have to first learn it and then practice it a lot. Finding ways of learning new behaviors, encouraging practice and rewarding good behavior is key to learning new habits that will keep us healthful as we age. We will show you first how to efficiently learn a new behavior. We will then teach you how to convert behaviors into habits by introducing monitors and rewards for your attempts. For example, if you want to consistently walk half an hour a day, it is very helpful to keep a log of your daily physical activity and find a buddy to check your log and praise your successful efforts.

Challenge #5: Making flexible decisions to empower your brain to make healthful choices.

Even with the best health habits, life provides us with challenges that we cannot resolve with quick, easy answers. In these situations, you need to be able to imagine new responses, think through the long-term consequences of your choices, and plan novel and potentially complex solutions. For example, it is very helpful to think out ways of handling problems you are apt to encounter before you try something, rather than waiting until an emergency arises. Pre-planning solutions to problems you are likely to encounter can help you avoid relying on quick fixes that save you in the moment, but generate more problems later. We show you techniques for making creative, flexible, future-focused plans and generating more adaptive long-term solutions to obstacles.

What You Take Away

In sum, you will learn to reduce the tendency to make impulsive and self-destructive actions while acquiring strategies to help you progress towards your long-term goals. At the end of each challenge we include exercises to help you practice what you learn. Feel free to modify or adapt these to meet your needs. In the final section, we will combine the five challenges into a single case study entitled "The Example of Weight Loss". We will walk back through each of the sections of the book with a specific consideration for how we can apply what we have learned to the specific health behavior goal of losing weight. This understanding will go beyond eating healthfully and exercising consistently to tackle the underlying behaviors we need to undertake to value health, enrich our lives, develop stress resilience, train good habits, and improve problem-solving in our combined efforts to lose weight or reach other health behavior goals.

In this book, we present these processes from a brain-based perspective. We will discuss findings from neuroscience, but these are presented to help you understand why specific behavior change processes work. We have attempted to keep the concepts simple and understandable for readers without a detailed knowledge of neuroscience – it is not crucial that you know and remember the neuroanatomical structures or understand the detailed cellular mechanisms, as long as you grasp the behavior change processes. Nevertheless, we expect that some readers will want to understand the neurobiology more explicitly so we have included appendices that provide more information about the brain structures we mention (Appendix 1), and more information about the cellular processes involved in learning (Appendix 2). Additionally, Appendix 3 contains an alternative conceptualization of three different circuits of the brain that have to do with the acquisition, retrieval or modification of habits. If you find the sections on neurobiology difficult to conceptualize, we suggest starting with the Appendices 1 and 2 first. These are not necessary reading, but we hope they will be helpful to those more curious about the neurobiological mechanisms of the health-related processes we describe.

To make best use of this book, it is helpful to take an honest inventory of your own health behaviors before proceeding. With your own risks and habits in mind it will be easier to relate the processes to your life and make effective use of the included exercises. On the next page, complete the checklist of risk factors. You can refer back to it as you work through the book and identify your specific health goals for the various exercises.

What Are My Health Risks?

Risk Factor	Check if you have this risk	Personal Notes
High Level of Stress		
Low Level of Life Satisfaction		
Chronic Anxiety or Depression		
Easily Angry or Upset		
High Cholesterol		
High Blood Pressure		
Exercise <30 Minutes Daily		
Body Mass Index over 27.5		
Smoke Tobacco or Cannabis		
Harmful Alcohol Use*		
Use Illicit Drugs		
Failure to Use Safety Belts		
Unsecured Gun in the Home		
Have Unprotected Sex		
Excessive TV Viewing**		
Take Too Much or Too Little Prescribed Medication		
Sleep <6 hours Nightly		
Work >50 hours per week		
Absenteeism		
Other (specify):		
Other (specify):		

*For men: greater than 14 standard drinks per week or more than 4 in a sitting; for women: greater than 7 standard drinks per week or more than 3 in a sitting.

**For our purposes, defined as more than 2 hours of TV viewing a day.

With these risks in mind, we encourage you to explore the key neurobiological challenges to reshaping your lifestyle and decisions, and begin and repeat the exercises and practices that will make healthful choices and actions habitual.

Brain Challenge #1

Learning to Highly Value Behaviors that Promote Wellness and Devalue Behaviors that Lead to Poor Health

Challenge Introduction

You are dining with friends and are served an extra large piece of hot apple pie with a huge scoop of vanilla ice cream. You know this is not good for you, but ah, the aroma, the sight of it, the encouragement of the host; it's her special recipe and you do want to please, right? How can you possibly stick to your diet when everything and everyone is encouraging you otherwise?

Your health-related decisions depend upon your brain's perception of the value of your options. When you make a decision to do something, you are inevitably choosing not to do something else. In deciding between two or more actions, you want to pick the choice that improves your life the most. To do this, you must estimate how much each of the possible actions will help you. Should you eat the apple pie and ice cream or finish your meal with a cup of tea instead? The answer depends on what you expect eating the pie or drinking the tea will do for you. Will the apple pie or tea taste better? Will the people around you approve of you more or make you feel a part of the group if you choose the pie versus the tea? Will your host be upset if you turn down her pie? Your brain carefully calculates and keeps track of estimates and expectations about the outcomes of your possible actions based upon your past experiences and observations about each option. Using a well-developed system, you automatically assign a value to every behavior you know how to do in a given situation. You then use these estimates to choose between options available at any given time. Thus, your expectations about the value or results of a behavior are hugely important in determining what you choose to do over time. If you highly value or expect greater benefits from healthful behaviors, you will generally choose healthful behaviors over other options. If you have strong expectations that doing unhealthful behaviors will better your life, improve your social status or make you feel good, then you will tend to do those unhealthful behaviors rather than make more healthful choices. This can lead you down a path towards chronic health problems.

Your brain will consider many factors when estimating the benefits of an action. Your previous experiences will shape your estimations. Your perception of how others close to you will react to the behavior will strongly color your estimates. If doing a behavior gains you immediate approval from people important to you, you will learn to expect social rewards for that behavior in the future. Your own expectations about the results of the action, objectively accurate or not, will strongly influence your estimates. Your expectations may be strongly influenced by cultural stories about the meaning or results of a behavior. You may have learned to associate the behavior with other good or bad things through advertising, entertainment or interactions you have seen. Your current emotional or physiological state may drastically affect your judgments about the value of an action. For example, you will probably expect the benefits of eating apple pie to be greater when you are hungry than when you are not. The impact of the action on your long-term goals may change your estimates. If you use addictive substances, you will overestimate the benefits of using these substances because of the pharmacological effects of the substances on your brain. On the next page is a checklist of possible factors that may lead you to over- or undervalue options when you are making a decision.

Factors that can influence our evaluation of the benefits of health options

- Previous experiences
- Beliefs and expectations
- Social norms
- Social approval
- Associations
- Physiological state
- Emotional state
- Long-term goals
- Drugs of abuse

In Challenge #1, we will examine each of these influences on your estimates of the benefits of your potential actions. In Chapter 1.1, we discuss how your brain, and specifically your dopamine neurons, generates value estimates so your brain can weigh options when making health-related decisions. In Chapter 1.2, we reveal how opportunities for reward can get overvalued through social pressure, expectations and advertising. In Chapter 1.3, we explain additional social factors that contribute to this overvaluation and how that can sabotage your health. In Chapter 1.4, we specifically address how addictive substances can hijack the brain's reward system. In Chapter 1.5, we suggest ways in which you can learn to correct your value estimates and assess the true value of a reward.

Because there are so many factors that contribute to your judgment of the value of doing a behavior, there are many ways in which your estimates can become harmfully inaccurate. Beliefs, social pressures, learned associations, and unpleasant emotional states can lead you to overvalue unhealthful behaviors and undervalue healthful ones. Correcting these inaccurate estimates can help you make more healthful choices.

<u>Chapter 1.1:</u> How Your Brain Weighs Options When Making Health-Related Decisions

In this chapter, we discuss how the brain calculates and keeps track of expectations of the outcomes of our health choices. We will provide examples of ways in which actions can become over or undervalued. We then discuss effective psychological techniques for changing our expectations. Throughout, we provide exercises to encourage these changes in ourselves and in others.

What parts of your brain calculate the value of an opportunity?
Our brains contain an intricate network of neurons that provide ongoing assessment of opportunities in the environment. These neurons generally contain the chemical messenger dopamine, a neurotransmitter that has been associated with disorders of habit and impulsivity. Firing of these neurons encodes the expected value of an opportunity: the greater your expectations about the benefits afforded by an opportunity, the faster these neurons fire. This firing encourages you to repeat the behavior, regardless of how you feel when you are doing it. These dopamine neurons are important for understanding why we make self-destructive versus healthful choices, particularly when tempted by the promise of quick pleasures.

It is important to note that our reward system is not a pleasure system, although many things that are rewarding are also pleasurable in the moment. The reward system motivates behavior, rather than setting mood. While feelings of pleasure may occur around the same time as firing of these neurons, they are neither the cause nor the outcome of it. A reward is something that 1) improves your immediate, if not your long-term, well-being, and 2) encourages learning such that you try to repeat the experience whenever an opportunity presents itself. You will gravitate toward and attend to situations, thoughts and behaviors that previously led to activation of your reward system regardless of whether the situations, thoughts or behaviors provided benefits, happiness and health or hassles, stress and disease over the long-term. Thus, the dopamine neurons do not signal pleasure but identify opportunities and estimate their potential value.

Neurobiologists have found that these dopamine neurons fire both tonicly and phasicly. In the languages of the brain, tonic refers to an ordinary, stable rate of nerve firing and phasic refers to quick bursts of nerve firing that occur at the time of an event. In this system, dopamine neurons fire slowly and consistently (tonicly) in the absence of an opportunity. When your brain has not identified any particular prospects for making life better, your dopamine neurons calmly plod away, firing slowly and steadily. However, when your brain detects a chance to improve on your current state, dopamine neurons come to attention, firing a burst of nerve impulses (phasic firing) to indicate the presence and value of that opportunity. The intensity of firing during these brief bursts tells our brain systems our expectations about the benefits of the present opportunity. Encoded in that burst of dopamine neuron firing is our anticipation of benefits awaiting us if only we take action to claim them. How big of an incentive is that apple pie? The intensity of that burst of dopamine neuron firing when your host offers you the apple pie will determine how strongly you are driven to take it. The more you find the pie enticing, the more rapidly your dopamine neurons will fire. If you are having trouble visualizing how these dopamine neurons work, think of them like a Geiger counter for radiation or a metal detector for metal objects. Your dopamine neurons beep slowly (fire tonicly) until you come near a known opportunity for immediate gratification or relief. When you come near an opportunity, they start to beep faster with the speed of the beeps indicating how big an opportunity you have just encountered (phasic firing).

Because brains are adaptive, your dopamine neurons do not just relay signals about your expectations; they also constantly learn and update expectations based on the near-term outcomes of your chosen actions. This learning happens within a single experience, as part of the process. The brain estimates, makes a decision and then adjusts its estimations for next time after it experiences the near-term result of the decision. Perhaps you just took a bite of pie, driven to action by the anticipatory burst of phasic dopamine neurons firing generated by your hosts offer. Was it what you expected? If so, your dopamine neurons are done. Their predictions were great, and their work is finished. But if they were wrong, they will send feedback about their mistakes. How big was the error? Was the pie much better than you anticipated? Was it worse?

In the case that the outcome was worse than expected, tonic firing becomes important. Because these dopamine neurons still fire when no opportunities are present, they are able to slow down below their normal, tonic firing rate to indicate when they made a mistake, such as when an opportunity that they predicted would be present does not pan out. For example, suppose your host was not such a good cook after all, and her beautiful looking pie tasted terrible. Your brain would need some way of warning you not to get so excited about *her* apple pie in the future. Because your dopamine neurons can both speed up or slow down from their resting state, they can provide both positive and negative feedback about your expectations. This slow, constant firing allows these neurons to damp down their expectations when they overestimated the benefits at the outset. Thus, the rate at which dopamine neurons fire provides two pieces of information for every decision: (1) they make a prediction about the benefits to be had before the choice is made, and (2) they provide feedback about the accuracy of their prediction after the choice occurs.

How do our dopamine neurons come up with their estimates?

Our dopamine neurons get information from all over the brain. These other brain regions provide information about what we are currently observing, what we have experienced in the past, and what our goals are for the future. Each of the brain regions that talk to the dopamine neurons can slow down or speed up the rate at which the dopamine neurons fire. Thus, the information they provide shapes the firing patterns of the dopamine neurons to provide an estimate of the value of a given behavioral choice.

To get a sense of all the things that shape our expectations about our options, it may be helpful to briefly explore some of the neuroanatomy that underlies the predictions made by our dopamine neurons. The dopamine neurons that make these predictions originate in part of our reward circuits, in a brain region called the ventral tegmental area (VTA) (see the Figure on page 21 and Appendix 1 for further details). These reward circuits are a highly conserved and ancient computational system, similar throughout mammalian and reptilian species, and are crucially important for long-term survival. These dopamine neurons receive input from a number of other brain regions that strongly influence their firing patterns, each of which can alter estimations of the value of an opportunity. So what are some of these brain inputs and what do they contribute to our expectations? We need to know what is going on if we are going to create expectations about possibilities in our immediate future. First, we need sensory information. But information about our environment is not enough. We need this information in a personal context. We need to know about our current environment in terms of our past experiences and current goals. Let's go back to that apple pie example. There are a wide variety of sensory cues being observed by various parts of the brain, including the smell and sight of the pie and the sound of the pie being removed from the oven. If this is not your first exposure to apple pie, your memories of these smells, sights and sounds, and things you have learned in eating apple pie previously, will influence how you interpret these sensory experiences.

Additionally, we need information about your current state and goals. For example, if you are hungry and looking for something to eat, that will change how you perceive the pie. The prefrontal cortex keeps track of our goals and our intentions, and inputs from this region can also influence the amount these dopamine neurons fire (Del Arco & Mora, 2008). From these prefrontal cortex inputs, information about long-term goals and expectations contribute to the influences on the dopamine neuron firing patterns and thus our valuation of an option.

This is a lot of complicated information, but fortunately, a part of our brain with the virtually unpronounceable name of pedunculopontine tegmentum (PPTg) pulls all of it together to send to our dopamine neurons. The PPTg integrates sensory information from the auditory, visual and somatosensory (sound, sight, touch and other forms of body-awareness) systems with information from the limbic system (including our emotional memory and reward circuits) and prefrontal cortex (conscious problem-solving and decision-making), which can then change dopamine neuron firing (Grace et al., 2007). This allows the PPTg to combine information about what we are hearing, seeing and feeling with information about our emotional state and long-term goals. The PPTg uses this combined information to guide our dopamine neurons as they estimate the value of opportunities, like a piece of pie, that we encounter. All of this happens while you are sitting at the table, perhaps even before you realize that you are making decisions about whether or not to eat the pie.

Moreover, a part of your brain called the hippocampus helps recall conscious memories and provides information to dopamine neurons about the novelty of a situation. Our brain finds new options more exciting and motivating. Instead of the usual apple pie, if you are served French apple pie, the hippocampus will help amplify dopamine neuron firing to let you know that this is a new option (Grace et al, 2007). When an opportunity is novel, your brain will inflate its estimates of the benefits to be gained through these circuits, encouraging you to test out a situation that you have not experienced before.

Together, the inputs to your dopamine neurons provide information about what we are encountering, our knowledge or experience with similar situations in the past, our current state and goals are for the future, and the novelty of the experience. Thus, all these elements will color your valuation of a choice.

FIGURE: Projections of the dopamine reward neurons

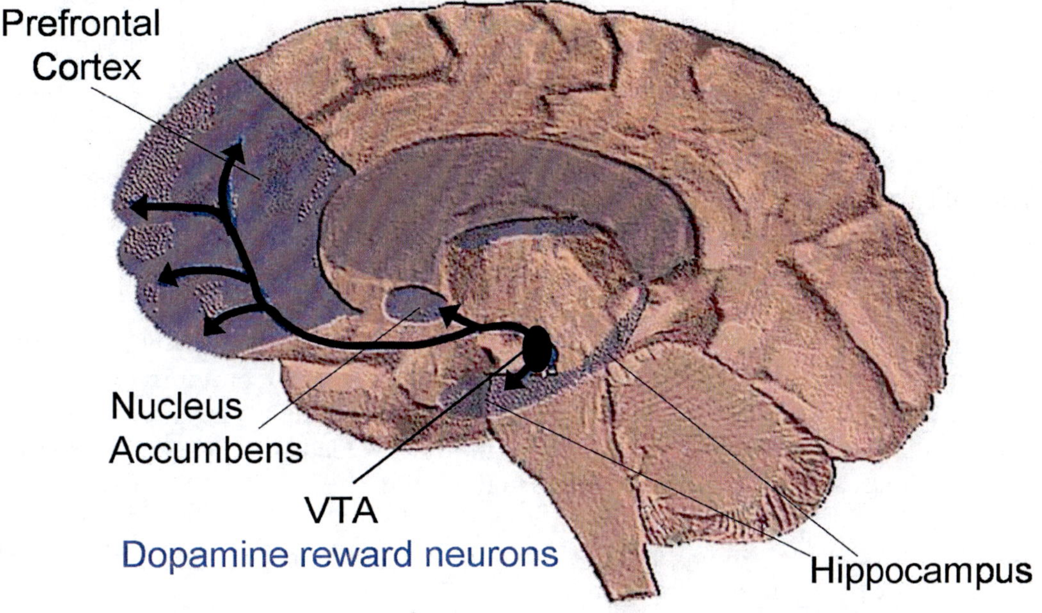

Legend: Reward circuit dopamine neurons originate in the VTA (black oval). They receive inputs from and project back to regions throughout the brain (black arrows). In particular, inputs to the VTA are consolidated in a region of the brain known as the PPTg (not shown). This combines information from the limbic reward system, including the hippocampus, and the prefrontal cortex. The hippocampus provides memories of what we experienced in the past and helps alert us when we encounter something new. The neurons use this consolidated information to predict – based on our previous experience, current states, and future goals – how much we might gain from doing a behavior in our current setting. The dopamine neurons then send outputs back to the limbic reward system and the prefrontal cortex. The prefrontal cortex can modify these predictions based upon additional information about our long-term goals.

What does your brain do with the value estimates that the dopamine neurons provide?

Some of the same regions that provide inputs to the dopamine neurons also receive the outputs. The main targets of these dopamine neurons are the limbic reward circuit and the prefrontal cortex, which use this information to make decisions about how to respond to opportunities. Dopamine neurons provide both brain regions with similar information. In both brain regions, the phasic firing of these neurons represents the expected value of the reward that will be obtained by doing a behavior. The faster the dopamine neurons fire, the greater the expected value of the reward. This firing rate is used to guide the choice of habitual behaviors. This has been observed directly in the nucleus accumbens, part of the limbic reward system (Abler et al., 2006), and in the orbitofrontal cortex, a part of the prefrontal cortex (Roesch & Olson, 2004).

For both short and long-term decisions, the brain must compare between the expected benefits of one choice versus another. Both the limbic reward circuit and the prefrontal cortex must make these choices based on the firing rate of the dopamine neurons.

The limbic reward circuit uses this information to decide whether to carry out well-learned, habitual behaviors to meet an immediate need or desire. It focuses on habits and the NOW! The limbic reward circuit uses the estimates from dopamine neurons to ask, "Can I make my life better this very moment by doing a well-practiced behavior to get something nice or get rid of something unpleasant?"

The prefrontal cortex uses the estimates from dopamine neurons to make broader decisions about behavior. It focuses on new behaviors and the LATER. It asks, "Will this opportunity help me reach a long-term goal? Do I need to do a new or less trained behavior to get the most out of this opportunity? Do I need to do something special because of the unique social or environmental context of this opportunity? Can I solve a complex, multi-part problem with this opportunity?"

Thus, dopamine neuron information is used simultaneously to answer two questions to plan behavior: (1) The limbic system determines if this opportunity can provide immediate gratification—the NOW. Will it provide immediate pleasure or relief? (2) The prefrontal cortex determines if this opportunity can lead to longer-term benefits or goals—the LATER. Will it make life better in the future?

The battle between the "here and now" of the limbic reward circuit and the "what could be" of the prefrontal cortex

To a substantial extent, these two brain regions make their decisions in parallel rather than collaboratively. They can be considered to compete for control over your behavior. When the limbic reward circuit predominates, you will tend to favor behaviors that benefit you right now, the hot apple pie moments of life, regardless of their effect on your future. When the prefrontal cortex predominates, you will tend to favor behaviors that benefit you in the future, even if they involve delay of immediate gratification in the moment or denial of pleasure for the foreseeable future.

The competition between these two brain circuits for control over behavior is influenced by the speed at which they make their choices. The limbic reward circuit tends to make faster decisions than the prefrontal cortex. This reflects the more complex processing that the prefrontal cortex carries out. The limbic reward circuit tends to follow a pretty standard calculation for picking between options whereas the prefrontal cortex can use a variety of logic or decision-making rules in making its choices. This flexibility is crucial for making wise long-term decisions. However, not having clearly set decision-making rules like the limbic reward circuit can slow down choices (Saling & Phillips, 2007). This means that the limbic reward circuit can beat out the prefrontal cortex in controlling behavior, simply by directing a behavior to be carried out before the prefrontal cortex had a chance to make a decision. Once this limbic-driven behavior is started, other better choices that the prefrontal cortex was planning may no longer be possible. For example, if your limbic system already directed you to eat the pie, you can no longer choose to search for a more healthful dessert. To keep the limbic system from constantly preempting decisions, the prefrontal cortex has connections with the limbic reward circuit that can inhibit limbic decisions from being carried out. Overall, the prefrontal cortex has some ability to stall or override limbic decisions both while it completes its analysis and if it comes up with a better behavioral plan. However, when you strongly overvalue a habit or have a powerful drive for immediate gratification, your prefrontal cortex will find it difficult to delay behaviors, and your limbic decisions will start to win out over your more careful long-term plans.

EXAMPLE: How do you develop expectations about the value of an opportunity? How much is pie worth to you?

At an early age, one of the author's (W.G.) dopamine neurons linked the smell, taste, and sight of apple pie with positive memories of sweet, satisfying food and a caring family. My overindulgent little grandmother loved to bake tasty apple pies. From that point on, I have been compelled to attend to suggestions of apple pie. The smell of pie reorients my attention, distracts me from what I am doing and sends me searching for the source. I have learned to highly value apple pie, and these learned cues get my dopamine neurons firing rapidly. How did I become so driven by the smell of apple pie? How did my experiences shape the firing patterns of my dopamine neurons? Scientists have worked out how our expectations about the benefits of a choice are calculated and modified over time. We will walk through this process step by step to help illustrate how the reward system works.

As we have stated, dopamine neurons use a feedback system to learn and update estimates of the value of an opportunity. Dopamine neurons use this feedback system to guide learning of cues that predict opportunities in the environment. My wonderful experience eating grandma's apple pie induced learning, so that on my next visit to grandma's house, my dopamine neurons were happily firing awaiting the next opportunity. Once cues that predict an opportunity are learned, our brains pay more attention to and alert us to their presence. These cues become emotionally important to us. Apple pie becomes linked with love, caring, and grandma. We notice these cues among the myriad of other things in our environment, and consider changing our behavior in response. For each of these cues, our dopamine neurons learn and update an estimate of the value of responding to the cue or opportunity. Whining about how hungry I am is apt to produce bigger rewards if I whine during my visit with grandma, rather than on the car ride over. My dopamine neurons recognize this and their anticipatory firing at grandma's house encourages my brain to begin doing things that might get me pie when I arrive. The estimates provided by our dopamine neurons help our brain to decide whether an opportunity is worth responding to in comparison to other possibilities. To help clarify how our dopamine neurons develop this estimate, let's walk through an example of this feedback system in action.

EXAMPLE: How do dopamine neurons learn to identify opportunities?

Another author (J.T.) recalls how dopamine neurons can even train behavior in graduate students studying dopamine neurons. In particular, I describe the example of training neurobiologists to attend science seminars. Let's consider how my graduate program trained my classmates and me to regularly attend optional seminars from invited guest speakers using cookies as bait. At each point in the learning process, I will illustrate how dopamine neurons fire to guide decision-making and learning.

When starting graduate school, I had no expectations for seminars beyond the seminar itself. My dopamine neurons fired only to indicate my expectations of the benefit I would receive from hearing the speaker. For simplicity's sake – and reflecting my generally burned out and overwhelmed state as a graduate student – let's assume I didn't consider it much of an opportunity at all and pretend my dopamine neurons didn't change their firing rates at all. Nevertheless, I was good at following orders and compliantly went to the seminar. Once there, I was quick to notice the free cookies and juice offered at the back of the room. This offer of free sugar was quickly detected by my dopamine neurons, which increased their firing rate to signal that I could head to the back of the room for a snack should I so desire.

Thus, at my first seminar experience, my dopamine neurons fired as in line A (see diagram below). There was no dopamine neuron firing at the time I saw the seminar announcement. But when I entered the seminar and got a cookie, my dopamine neurons increased their firing by one cookie's worth. My dopamine neuron firing after I entered the seminar signaled my brain to try to find and learn cues that predicted the availability of cookies in a room. Putting my expensively trained intellect to work, it didn't take long for me to guess that the free cookies were part of the seminar series.

The next time I saw a posting for a neuroscience seminar, my dopamine neurons predicted that this indicated an opportunity for free cookies. The posting elicited a cookie's worth of dopamine firing, alerting of my brain of this nutritional resource. Having made this prediction, my dopamine neurons then expected the cookies when I got there. When the cookies were there as predicted, my dopamine neurons didn't respond any further. They had already let me know of the opportunity and done so accurately so the presence of the cookies didn't elicit anything new. There was nothing else to learn, and no corrections to make. My dopamine neurons fired as in line B.

Thinking I had figured out the seminar/cookie connection, I started noticing flyers for other seminars around campus. Feeling particularly hungry one day, I saw a flyer for a seminar for medical doctors put on by a well-known drug company. My dopamine neurons dutifully increased their firing by a couple of cookies' worth to let me know of the opportunity presented by this seminar. To my surprise and delight, this seminar was stocked not only with cookies, but also with freshly made sandwiches and salad. My dopamine neurons had underestimated the opportunity this seminar provided, and quickly started firing again (a sandwich's and salad's worth of firing to be exact) to indicate the additional opportunity that this presented. This notified my brain of the original error in my prediction, and told me that there was more to learn. I guessed that pharmaceutical company seminars are better funded, and my brain quickly learned to distinguish between pharmaceutical-related seminar flyers, worth a full meal plus dessert, and neuroscience-program-related seminar flyers, worth only cookies. Thus, I increased my dopamine neuron firing more when pharmaceutical-related seminar flyers were identified. In this situation, my dopamine neurons fired as in line C.

I began to favor seminars about new pharmaceuticals. When I saw a flyer for a seminar targeting pharmacy students, my dopamine neurons fired a full meal's worth and I headed expectantly to the talk. I entered and, to my shock, there was no food at all at the back of the room. My dopamine neurons slowed their firing well below their stable rate and fired as in line D. They had made a mistake. There was no meal, no cookies. Something was wrong with the prediction, and I needed to learn new cues to stop me from making that mistake again. I had confused pharmaceutical-related with pharmaceutical-company-related. The pharmacy school was even poorer than the neuroscience graduate department. Not only did they not provide lunch, they did not even provide cookies. My brain quickly noted this contingency and from then on was very careful to distinguish between pharmaceutical-company-funded seminars (a meal's worth of dopamine neuron firing) and pharmacy school seminars (no change in dopamine neuron firing).

FIGURE: Dopamine neuron firing rate

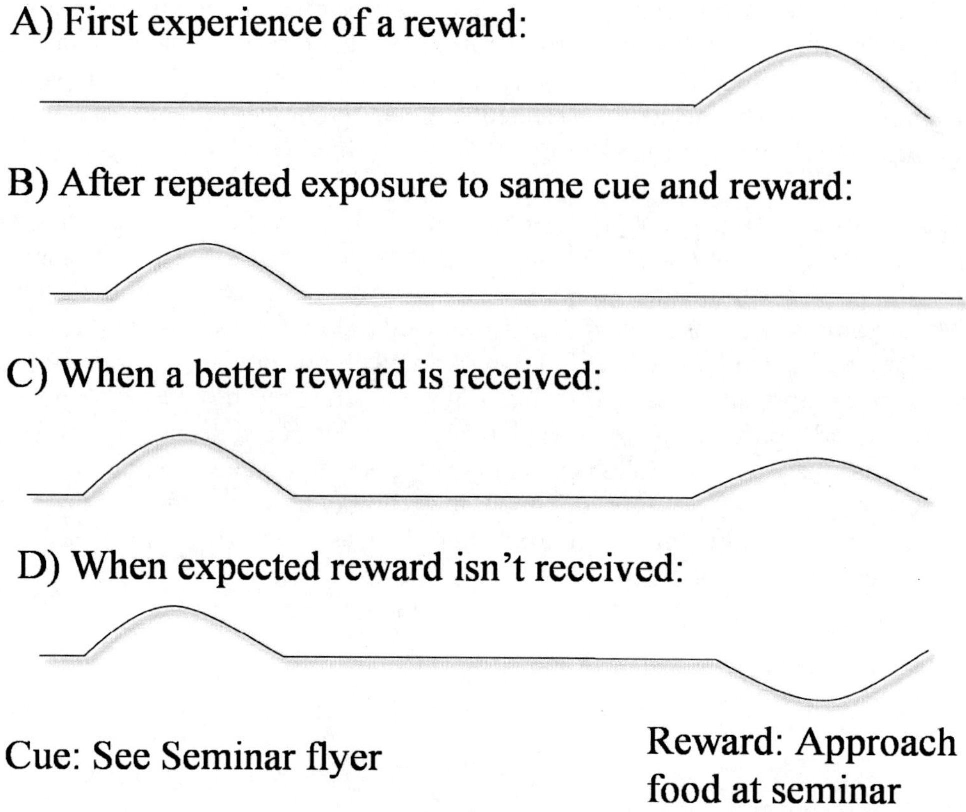

A) First experience of a reward:

B) After repeated exposure to same cue and reward:

C) When a better reward is received:

D) When expected reward isn't received:

Cue: See Seminar flyer

Reward: Approach food at seminar

Legend: A) The rate of dopamine neuron firing following the first unexpected experience of a reward in the form of cookies, B) After repeated exposure, considering going to a seminar that should have cookies brings about dopamine neuron firing even before the cookies are encountered, C) Attending a seminar with sandwiches and salads instead of cookies provides an even better reward than expected, leading to increase in dopamine neuron firing, and D) attending a seminar with no cookies – the expected reward is not received – results in a decrease in the rate of dopamine neuron firing.

What this set of lines signifies is the process by which the brain develops predictions about rewards it could seek. The technical name for this form of learning is called an "error signal learning model". Specifically, learning is guided by a process of prediction and correction based on the accuracy of the prediction. In other words, the error signal is the difference between the prediction and the actual occurrence at the time the predicted reward is expected to materialize. The rate at which dopamine neurons fire during the prediction encodes the predicted reward value. The actual value of the encountered reward is the combination of (1) the firing during the prediction and (2) the error signal firing at the time of the predicted reward. Errors in the original prediction trigger learning of new cues and contingencies. In other words, dopamine neuron firing at time the reward should be encountered encourages new habit learning. Scientists have observed this process in both monkeys using intercellular recording (Schultz, 1998; Tobler et al., 2005), and humans using fMRI during learning exercises (e.g., Rodriquez et al., 2006).

The concept of the predicted "value" of a reward might seem a bit abstract, particularly when we are talking about the value of relief from a bad mood or the solution to a distressing problem. It may help to think of it in more concrete terms like the "value" of a specific purchase. Our brain uses the same process to make fast decisions in the realm of personal economics, and dopamine neurons guide our shopping decisions. The quick choices that we make regarding what to purchase – our impulse buying – depend on the value predictions of the dopamine neurons that provide input to our nucleus accumbens.

For example, a study examined how we make decisions about what to purchase by having people shop while being monitored in an fMRI machine, a device capable of recording images of ongoing brain activity (Knutson et al., 2007). People were shown items, then a price, then given 4 seconds to choose whether or not to purchase the product. The investigators found that the amount of activity in the nucleus accumbens during the time that people were shown the items predicted whether or not they would choose to buy them. This was a better predictor of whether they would purchase the product than what they *said* was their preference for the product. As we mentioned earlier, dopamine neurons that indicate predicted reward value are the major input to the nucleus accumbens so this study shows that the brain uses these reward predictions to guide rapid decisions about the worth of an opportunity, even when someone may not realize it. In this case, the decision was about whether it was worthwhile to spend money, a form of stored work, on an opportunity. In every day life, we buy things based on our dopamine neurons' estimates of the reward value of objects all the time. If we overvalue certain products, because of advertising, perceptions that the product will improve social status, the addictive nature of the product, or stress (see Challenge #3), our shopping cart may get filled with these immediate-gratification items.

Chapter 1.2: Great Expectations: How Do Opportunities for Reward Get Overvalued?

When reward appraisal works optimally, we create realistic expectations about our options and our limbic reward circuit and prefrontal cortex work together to ensure that we are both taken care of in the moment and on-track to achieve our long-term goals. However, there are many ways in which our estimates can become biased and cause us to favor behaviors that do not objectively help us, or more ominously, are self-destructive – for example, addictions of all kinds.

Social factors, artificially connected rewards and drugs of abuse are just a few of the things that can fool these brain regions into overvaluing unhealthful behaviors. We will discuss some of the most common and well-understood ways in which the process of learning reward value can get manipulated to favor thoughts and behaviors that make us unwell. Dopamine neurons that talk to brain region known as the nucleus accumbens play an important role in this process by relaying our expectations about the immediate benefits of doing habit behaviors. Notably, you do not need to understand the neurobiology of dopamine neurons to effectively shape behavior. In fact, external parties such as social groups and advertisers often use these techniques to their advantage to manipulate the behavior of those around them. Being aware of these influences is a first step towards preventing others from manipulating your expectations to the detriment of your health.

Social reinforcement and peer pressure

What we hear from others about the effects or importance of a health-related choice can greatly influence our calculation of reward value, even changing how we respond to the opportunity when we encounter it. We learn a lot about how certain behaviors, products or experiences are supposed to make us feel by watching or talking to others, or seeing them in the media. Our brains use these social observations and rumors to set up expectations about the value or effect of various behaviors, often long before we have ever experienced their effects ourselves. Our observations of the effects and rewards of a behavior on other people get factored into our estimates of reward value. In other words, our interpretations of other peoples' experiences influence our value estimates just like our own experiences do.

Rumors can change peoples' behaviors by altering their expectations about the risks and benefits of a health-related choice, even when they are not true. Because we cannot always have our own experiences ahead of time, we often rely on information from others without always knowing or confirming its validity. For example, the uproar over the risk of autism resulting from vaccines containing trace amounts of mercury unduly scared parents from vaccinating their children. Media-driven fears reduced the expected value of the vaccines, thus making them a less appealing option. This had a significant effect on vaccination rates, even though the vaccines had proven beneficial effects on health and the single report suggesting a risk was shown to be incorrect. Similarly, the social buzz around fad diets, though not evidence-based, often drives people to alter choices about what to eat, demonizing hamburgers one month and then buns the next.

What we hear about certain foods can change our predictions about how good they are for us, and change what we eat. Because of this, the human brain is more likely to base choices on social norms than objective realities. Because our expectations are so vulnerable to suggestion, our choices often reflect opinion more than true experience. Objectively, vaccination has overwhelmingly positive benefits, reducing suffering related to infectious disease. But our brains have no way of knowing this ahead of time, so we rely on what we hear from others, though it may be highly evidence-based or complete fabrication. By altering our expectations about the value of specific health choices, what we hear and observe can change how we react to things, even when we have not experienced them ourselves.

This process can lead whole groups or cultures of people to harbor beliefs about the effects of a certain behavior that may have no objective basis in fact. Are dogs a tasty treat or a disgusting horrible thing to eat? It depends on what those around you tell you and how they react when offered dog meat—it depends on whether your neighbors walk the dog or wok it. Will crystals prevent you from picking up other people's bad moods or negative energy? It depends on what you have been told, how others react when you wear the crystals, and how you interpret your own behavior while you are wearing them. The stories we create around behaviors and objects will shape our expectations about their effects, color our observations and interpretations of their actual effects, and even change our responses to experiences. We tend to act the way we think we are supposed to in response to opportunities even if there is no real objective reason to do so. Someone of European heritage may throw up their dinner after learning that they just ate dog, even though the dinner was in no way poisonous or less healthful than their typical dinner of pig. They are responding to their expectations about eating dog rather than the actual effects of eating dog on their physiology. In other cultures, a dinner of dog is considered a luxury. It is not uncommon for cultures or groups to develop expectations about behaviors or objects that lead to unhealthful or even dangerous behaviors. Recognizing these expectations and working to correct these false beliefs can be very helpful for changing behavior in a more healthful direction.

EXAMPLE: The impact of expectation on behavior

To illustrate the impact of expectation on behavior (in this case dietary choice), one of us (J.T.) will share another story from her graduate school years. Having both a horrendous family history of heart disease and allergies to dairy products, I followed a vegan diet (no meat, eggs, and dairy products). My lab-mates were all very aware of my diet, as it provided endless opportunity for mocking, taunting, and teasing during lab outings and meals. So, when I was assigned the duty of picking up bagels for our 7:00 am lab meetings, I felt perfectly justified in buying the soy-based imitation cream cheese that they sold at the bagel shop. Because few other people bought the fake cream cheese by container, the store had to repackage their giant container of soy-cheese into smaller plastic containers that didn't have any labels. So I brought soy cream cheese in unmarked containers to lab meeting.

I never explicitly announced that I was purchasing soy cream cheese for the meetings, but I also never hid the fact that I was smearing large quantities of the stuff all over my bagels, and assumed that anyone who gave it a thought would know it was not really cream cheese. No one ever complained and everyone in the lab ate lots and lots of soy cream cheese with their bagels each week. So all was fine and I was very happy breakfasting vegan for a full year and a half. But then the bagel shop decided they were selling enough packaged soy cream cheese to keep smaller containers on hand. Now, the soy cream cheese package boldly announced the fact that it was imitation, non-dairy, vegan cream cheese. But, no worries, I thought, everyone has been happily eating the stuff for 18 months.

Boy, was I wrong. The minute I put the soy cream cheese package on the table, there were complaints, vocal, outraged, angry complaints. There was no way the rest of the lab was going to eat weird soy-products on their bagels, and how dare I bring this to the lab meeting. When I pointed out that this was exactly what I had been bringing for the last year and a half, just without the fancy lid, and everyone liked it just fine before, I completely infuriated one of our senior scientists. She scowled, saying that she knew that there was something wrong with the cream cheese all that time, and that it was disgusting and horrible. I noted that she had nevertheless put it on and ate it with at least two bagels each Monday morning for the last 78 weeks, without ever once mentioning her concerns. But that was the end of her experience with soy. She never again ate a bit of the soy cream cheese, and I was forced to buy additional tubs of real cream cheese to appease my lab-mates who had distaste for things that say "soy" on the cover.

In exchange for having the senior scientist hate me for a few days and suspiciously examine the cream cheese during lab-meetings for the next few weeks, I got a great demonstration of the power of expectation. While she thought the soy cream cheese was real cream cheese, our senior scientist ate it with gusto. If she didn't like it, she didn't show it, and ate it whenever offered and without complaint. When she thought it was soy, her expectations changed completely. She would no longer even taste the stuff, refused to eat it, and told anyone who asked how nasty it was. Her expectations completely changed her thoughts and behaviors about soy cream cheese, and never once did it get valued highly enough for her to eat it knowingly, at least at any of our lab-meetings.

To counter scientific illiteracy promoted by the commercial media and unreliable online sources, we urge you to draw inferences directly from evidence-based sources when making health-related decisions. For example, if you want to review research on mercury in vaccines, go to the publicly available National Library of Medicine through Pub Med at www.ncbi.nlm.nih.gov/sites/entrez and enter key terms, read the abstracts, perhaps review articles or read reviews of scientific studies. We shamelessly promote our *Best Practices* series as but one source of worthy information about changing health-related behavior at www.indiseasemanagement.org.

The power of suggestion: Placebo and nocebo effects

Expectations about an experience or treatment can have a huge effect on the perceived outcome. The effect of expectations can be positive, in which case they may produce a placebo effect or benefits beyond those produced by pharmacological or objective actions alone. But expectations of bad outcomes can be negative, in which case they produce harmful effects such as worsening of symptoms, medication inefficacy, or side effects. These are called nocebo effects.

Scientists interested in pain have studied placebo and nocebo effects in depth. Suggestion has large effects on the feelings, thoughts, and behaviors produced by a potentially painful stimulus. When people fear something or expect it to be particularly painful, they find it to be particularly painful. Often, peoples' expectation about how painful something will be is a better predictor of reported pain following the experience than the actual intensity of the painful stimulus itself.

These expectations work in the opposite direction as well. When people expect something to hurt less, it will. This was shown in a brain imaging study that used a fake "analgesic cream" (Wager et al., 2004). The researchers caused a painful sensation by heating up volunteers' forearms, then told the volunteers they were applying an analgesic cream that would reduce but not eliminate pain. The researchers then repeated the study with the same cream but told the volunteers it was just the base for the analgesic medication. In both cases, the heat stimulus was the same and the cream had no medication in it. All that differed was what they were told was in the cream. However, when told that they had received an analgesic cream, clients reported less pain and brain imaging showed less brain activity in regions that represent emotion and regions that transmit information about potentially damaging stimuli (i.e. things that might cause pain). Their expectations had changed how they experienced the heat sensation, and how their brains responded.

Another brain imaging study observed people when they were expecting a painful stimulus rather than during the painful stimulus itself (Koyama et al., 2005). They showed that expectation alone altered brain activity in the cortical brain regions involved in the experience of pain (anterior cingulate cortex, insula cortex), judgment of the value of responding to potential rewards or punishments (prefrontal cortex), and the gating or filtering of sensory information to cortical brain regions (thalamus). Expecting that a painful stimulus was coming set up the brain to respond to the pain, including starting to feel the experience in advance, preparing itself for the possible need to escape, and activating pain control regions to either amplify or dampen the impending painful signal. In other words, guessing how much an upcoming stimulus would hurt changed activity in brain regions that generate behavioral and emotional responses. This guess set up the brain to respond to the expectation when the stimulus actually arrived.

Lastly, a brain imaging study observed how a certain region of the brain that receives information from dopamine neurons (the nucleus accumbens) responded when people were given a placebo painkiller (Scott et al., 2007). Using positron emission tomography (PET) to view changes in the amount of dopamine released (by seeing how many D2 dopamine receptors were dopamine-free), they showed that being told you were given a painkiller increased dopamine release in the nucleus accumbens when people were anticipating a painful stimulus. In other words, if you knew a painful experience was coming, just thinking you had been given a painkiller made your reward circuits expect a reward (e.g. relief from pain). The amount of dopamine release was related to how much pain relief the individuals expected to experience when they were given the placebo "drug"; greater expected pain relief was associated with greater dopamine release.

Moreover, expectations and the amount of dopamine release during anticipation of the pain stimulus predicted how much pain relief participants experienced when the painful stimulus was actually applied. The researchers also looked at activity in the nucleus accumbens of these same participants when they anticipated receiving a monetary reward. They found that the people who expected larger pain relief and released more dopamine in anticipation of the painkiller also showed greater dopamine release when anticipating a monetary reward. Thus, placebo expectations and responses may be related to how much your reward system anticipates rewards in general. This study clearly demonstrates that the dopamine-based process of reward learning in the nucleus accumbens is involved in generating our expectations and responses to opportunities both when we can get something nice or escape something unpleasant. It also shows that expectations, rather than true reality, change how our brain responds and thus shape our behavior. Lastly, it shows that individual differences in the brain's responsiveness to rewards have meaningful effects on how people react to opportunities and expectations.

While the effects of expectation have been studied extensively as they relate to the experience of pain, the clinical impact of expectation-driven placebo and nocebo effects are much broader. As Fabrizio Benedetti describes in detail in his book, *Placebo Effects: Understanding the Mechanisms in Health and Disease* (2008), expectations of clinical improvement can have a substantial effect on symptoms for a wide variety of disorders. For insomnia, placebos can induce behavioral and electroencephalographic (a measure of neuronal firing patterns) changes. In depression, the rate of improvement in placebo groups is high and has increased over the past years, presumably in part because of advertising touting the virtues of antidepressant medications. In addiction, tobacco smoking and nicotine intake reveal large placebo effects, perhaps because expecting a drug of abuse may make using it more pleasurable. Sexual function may improve after placebo and worsen after nocebo. Cough is powerfully reduced by placebo treatments, as is bronchial hyper-reactivity in asthma. Reduction of gastrointestinal symptoms is common in clients who receive placebos for gastrointestinal and genitourinary disorders including irritable bowel syndrome. Reduction of subjective lower urinary tract symptoms is greater than objective symptoms in placebo groups. Placebo surgery is associated with clinical improvement at high rates, even in those who incorrectly believe they have received organ transplantation.

Expectation may also induce unpleasant side effects in clients receiving inert medications. Such nocebo effects are common in control groups in cardiovascular trials. Nocebos can even mimic the depressant effects of narcotics on breathing rate in respiratory disorders. As the above series of studies show, our expectations about the effects of treatments modify the reward estimates of our dopamine neurons. These differences in dopamine neuron firing influence activity in the nucleus accumbens and alter our body's choice of habit responses – thereby changing the physiological effects of the treatment.

To practice creating positive expectations and examples of how to make use of placebo in clinical practice, see Exercise 1A (page 60).

TIPS FOR HEALTH PROFESSIONALS:
Using expectation to improve pain management and treatment effects

1. *Talk about wellness, not pain.* Clients' pain intensity ratings are consistently and significantly lower after verbally reinforcing "well talk" in contrast to verbally reinforcing pain talk (White & Sanders, 1986); therefore a focus on wellness and recovery more meaningfully reduces pain than a focus on the pain itself. When treating clients with pain or mood disorders, focus on what will lead to wellness, not the pain. Focusing directly on the pain itself can heighten the pain; focusing on recovery may reduce it.

2. *Model positive outcomes.* Clients can learn a placebo effect by social observation. For example, when people observed someone else not respond in pain to a procedure they expected would be painful, they found it less painful (Colloca & Benedetti, 2009). Help your clients learn positive outcomes by watching other clients. Expose your clients who are too scared to try activities like exercise and physical therapy to your clients who have used these methods with good results. Seeing that these clients weren't hurt by these activities may reduce their expectations of pain and increase pain tolerance. Seeing that these clients benefited from treatment may help them to believe that they will benefit too.

3. *Provide hope.* Helping clients feel hopeful about their life and treatment can improve mood and amplify the effects of analgesics, antidepressants and other treatments that target emotions and emotional behavior. Even simple exposure to a sunny day can reduce the need for pain management. For example, clients recovering from spinal surgery who stayed on the on the sunny side of a hospital unit used 22% less analgesic medication per hour and had lower perceived stress (Walch et al., 2005).

Expectancy and alcohol: Thinking you are drinking when you are not

Many research studies have examined the effects of having both strong positive and negative expectations about the effects of alcohol. The most famous and creative versions of these studies asked people about their expectations about the effects of alcohol and then observed them in a simulated bar environment while they drank "alcoholic" beverages. The bar was actually a lab staffed by researchers and equipped with cameras and two-way mirrors. Some participants were actually given alcoholic drinks; others were given placebo non-alcoholic drinks that were made to smell and taste like typical cocktails. Additionally, some participants were told they were drinking alcohol and some were told they were not. These studies allowed researchers to separate the effects of actually drinking alcohol from the effects of thinking you are drinking alcohol.

Not surprisingly, this type of study showed that drinking alcohol had effects on both physiology and behavior. For example, actually drinking alcohol impaired motor performance and information processing, and improved mood (Hull & Bond, 1986). However, these studies also showed that thinking that you are drinking alcohol had significant effects on social behaviors. For example, people who thought they were drinking alcohol but actually were not still showed significantly increased sexual arousal to erotic stimuli, drank more "alcoholic" beverages, and showed mildly reduced aggression (note: true alcohol actually tends to increase aggression) (Hull & Bond, 1986). Thinking they were drinking alcohol changed how participants behaved after drinking. Presumably, social beliefs that drinking alcohol disinhibits sexual behavior, makes it hard to stop drinking and makes people more relaxed and mellow made people more likely to act this way when they thought they were drinking. Peoples' expectations about how they would behave when they drank alcohol changed how they actually behaved after they drank a beverage. Presumably, people felt that it was more socially acceptable to act in these ways when they were drinking. By changing behavior to match preconceived beliefs about alcohol's effects, expectations not only increase the expected value of an opportunity but also alter one's experience to reinforce the original beliefs.

Advertising, observation and cultural mores can shape expectations about alcohol and other substances. Expectations about alcohol can have profound and prolonged effects upon health starting at an early age, as they predict how much, when and why one drinks both now and in the future. For example, it has been demonstrated that expectations about the effects of alcohol were associated with how teenagers drank alcohol (Christiansen et al., 1983). Teenagers who believed alcohol would make them more social tended to drink frequently with friends. Teenagers who believed alcohol would improve their cognitive and motor functioning were more likely to report having alcohol-related problems. To demonstrate that these beliefs also influenced future behavior, they asked seventh and eighth graders what they thought the effect of drinking alcohol would be on their feelings, behaviors and social interactions. When they assessed actual alcohol drinking behavior in these same children a year later, they found that their beliefs about the effects of drinking one year earlier predicted how much, how often and how problematically they were drinking now (Christiansen et al., 1989). Our beliefs about the effects of a behavior directly impact the decisions we make about when, where, and how often to do that behavior.

How to challenge alcohol-related expectancies

A few studies have tested interventions that challenge alcohol expectancies by having groups of people experience alcohol use in a situation where people do not know whether they or others are drinking alcoholic or non-alcoholic drinks. Following this experience, the group members discuss who they thought was drinking alcohol and how they came to that conclusion. They are then told who actually was or was not drinking alcohol. Inevitably, many of the guesses about whether or not individuals were drinking alcohol are wrong, thus providing a direct example and opportunity for discussion about the errors in their assumptions. This intervention has been tried with groups of college-age students in single or multiple sessions, and with content tailored towards typical male versus female expectations about the effects of alcohol. While the intervention is still in early stages of development and long-term testing, there is evidence that it can change expectations about the effects of alcohol in young adults and lead to reductions in alcohol use over the subsequent weeks to month (Darkes & Goldman, 1993; Darkes & Goldman, 1998; Lau-Barraco & Dunn, 2008). The intervention demonstrated to young adults that their beliefs about the effects of alcohol were not accurate and many of the effects of alcohol depended on what people thought they were drinking rather than what they actually were drinking. This simple demonstration produced changes in their beliefs about the effects of alcohol and the changes in beliefs were associated with reductions in actual drinking behavior in the next month. These studies provide experimental evidence that our beliefs about the effects of our behaviors, in this case alcohol use, have a direct impact on whether we choose to do the behavior. It also shows that changing our beliefs changes our behavior. When we have exaggerated expectations of the positive effects that an unhealthful behavior will produce or underestimate the immediate negative effects of an unhealthful behavior, we are apt to develop unhealthful patterns of behavior. However, it is possible to train ourselves to develop more realistic expectations of the effects of certain behaviors. To translate these findings into practical results, we urge parents and health professionals to avoid unwittingly promoting positive expectations related to alcohol or nicotine use or other unhealthful behaviors. It may be useful to ask a child or teenager what he or she thinks it would be like to smoke or drink and guide him or her to more accurate information about the objective effects of these substances.

Challenging our beliefs about the effects of our behaviors can help us develop more accurate expectations about the outcomes of our behaviors and potentially improve our health. We may challenge our beliefs by directly observing outcomes on ourselves, by asking other people to report their observations about the outcomes of a behavior, or even by learning more about the objective effects of a behavior, perhaps by reading medical reports or scientific studies. When our brains make decisions using more accurate information about the outcomes of our choices, we tend to make decisions that provide greater benefit for our health and happiness. We will discuss techniques and exercises to encourage this process at the end of this chapter.

How do advertisers seduce us into buying their products?

Random cues, items, behaviors or feeling states can become overvalued and overused when they become paired with unexpected rewards. Such pairings are created intentionally all the time by advertisers intent on training you to favor their product. By linking immediate gratification – a pretty face, the suggestion of sex, the promise of money or power – with a commercial product, advertisers create an association between their product and these unexpected rewards in your limbic system. Whether the product is a can of soda, a car, or a financial service, your brain will now relate that product with the opportunity for reward, most commonly in the form of approval from the opposite sex or a position of status among your peers. These associations, whether or not you are aware of them, can alter your estimates of the value of a behavior or thing, and thus bias your choices.

In an elegant study, researchers mimicked the advertising process by showing volunteers arbitrary cues (pictures of unrelated things) along with pictures of attractive female faces and measuring their brain activity using fMRI (Bray & O'Doherty, 2007). Viewing the attractive faces activated the reward circuits, indicated by an increase in blood flow to the nucleus accumbens. This suggests that seeing attractive faces is rewarding, and might train the volunteers' brains to seek out cues that were associated with the faces. As it turns out, the volunteers had developed behavioral preferences for the arbitrary cues, liking cues that had been linked with attractive faces more than cues that had not been linked with attractive faces. *In other words, they overvalued things that had been associated with people they found attractive.* The study showed that the amount of nucleus accumbens activity predicted how much the person learned to prefer the cue associated with the attractive face. This suggests that the more rewarding the dopamine neurons in the reward circuits found the attractive faces, the more the person learned to value the cue. In other words, the value that the pretty face added to the cue predicted how much the person would favor the cue in the future.

Another study demonstrated that activation of the nucleus accumbens was related to behavioral measures of preference for an attractive face (i.e. how much you would press a button to see the face), but not your stated assessment of how attractive the face appeared (Aharon et al., 2001). This suggests that learning directed by the reward circuits controls your tendency to do a behavior, but not necessarily your conscious assessment of the value of doing that behavior. Pairing rewards and cues might train you to actively seek a cue and do more work to get the cue, even if you were not aware that you liked or wanted the cue more. In other words, you may not even be aware that your brain values a behavior and causes you to repeat it. For example, a commercial that showed an attractive person drinking a specific soda might train you to actually drink more of that soda even if you still thought and told people that you did not really like that beverage.

This same reward learning process may also overvalue cues when they are paired with rewards by chance rather than capitalist intention. For example, your new jeans might become your favorite when the queen bee of your middle school compliments you on them; your smelly gym socks may become crucially important to your participation in future athletic competitions when you win the biggest competition of your life while wearing them; you may decide pears are the most amazing fruit in the world when the person you've had a crush on for the last two years bakes you pear tarts for your birthday. The cue takes on the value of the outcome with which it was associated, even if those associations were completely arbitrary or random. Regardless of whether these associations stem from advertising or coincidence, they can lead to irrational and sometimes impulsive behaviors.

Marketing your own expectations and rewards

In short, our beliefs about the effects of behaviors or things have an enormous impact on how we value opportunities to do these behaviors or gain these things. In addition, external advertising or coincidental associations may lead us to develop incorrect believes that inaccurately associate certain cues and behaviors with reward.

These beliefs can lead us to make choices that are bad for our health. We may ignore our doctors' warnings to cut back on cholesterol by substituting soy products for animal products because we think soy will taste bad or be disgusting. We may avoid getting screened for breast or colon cancer because we fear it will be a painful, terrible experience. We may drink large quantities of alcohol on the weekends because we think it will make us more attractive and social and will help us have more fun. Objectively, we may not even notice the difference in taste between soy and animal products, the injury and discomfort from the screening tests may be far less than that we experience playing our favorite sport, and alcohol may make us act in embarrassing ways, smell funny, and make us feel terrible the next day. But we may never experience or notice these realities while our beliefs contradict them. Changing your beliefs about the effects of behaviors can have a huge impact on your health choices. Correcting such beliefs is a large component of many psychosocial interventions that improve health behaviors.

Try to create your own "commercials" or associations between the behaviors you want to do and cues that attract you. For example, if I ruminate on how much I love getting together with family at Thanksgiving and how my aunt's green bean and pearl onion dish is so delicious, I may be able to trigger warm positive feelings and overeating responses to green beans. To help reinforce this more, I might post some pictures of my favorite people eating green beans on my refrigerator. If I gorge myself on green beans, I will likely eat less of other less healthful options. If I want to start running regularly, and I know I enjoy spending time with my friends, then I can plan an outing with a friend each time I complete a run. If I let my friends know this is my plan, they can also ask me about my running behavior when they are planning something with me. Some of my friends may want to start running with me to achieve similar goals, creating external reminders of the associated cue between running and time spent with friends. If I run regularly, I will be less likely to sit in front of the TV and stay inside all day. The best way to discourage or reduce a behavior with "commercials" and cues is to encourage another one, such as eating green beans to prevent yourself from eating three servings of pie and running to avoid spending the entire day on the couch.

To help identify cues that trigger your healthful or unhealthful behaviors, see Exercise 1B (page 63). To practice creating "cues you can use" to encourage healthful behaviors, see Exercise 1C (page 64).

Chapter 1.3: Social Factors that Can Overvalue Habits and Sabotage Our Health

Our beliefs about what other people do and consider normal will also shape our evaluation of an opportunity and change our behavior. People are socially influenced and do not like to do behaviors that are different from their peers. Moreover, people tend to surround themselves with people who act like they do. For example, a person who smokes is much more likely to know other smokers than is a non-smoker (Christakis & Fowler, 2008). Smokers will spend more time in places with high numbers of smokers; smokers necessarily cluster in smoking areas and frequent places where cigarettes are purchased. While they are smoking, smokers will tend to receive more positive feedback from other smokers, and thus may prefer to be around them. Thus, people tend to create social networks where the people they see act like they do. Based on their experience, they tend to overestimate how common or normal it is to do a behavior. Because of their desire to act like others, they will favor doing behaviors that are similar to those around them, overvaluing reward opportunities that make them seem more like their peers.

Habits are contagious

Interestingly, this tendency to overvalue conformity can lead to the spread of behaviors in patterns similar to the spread of a disease. Behaviors and thus their health consequences appear to be contagious. For example, obesity appears to spread through social ties. Drs. Christakis and Fowler (2007) examined how weight gain spread through a social network of over 12,000 people during a 32-year period. People with close social ties were more likely to have a similar body mass index, showing that obesity tended to cluster in social networks. Moreover, when one person gained weight the chance that their friends and relatives gained weight in the near future increased substantially. If a friend became obese, a person's risk of becoming obese subsequently increased 57%. If a sibling or spouse became obese, their risk increased 40% and 37% respectively. Weight gain in neighbors did not increase risk of obesity. Thus, spread of obesity was not due to location, but to social interactions. A very similar pattern was observed for spread of smoking and smoking cessation behaviors in these same networks (Christakis & Fowler, 2008). Our desire to be like those around us even shapes the emotions we feel from day to day. Examination of these networks showed that even emotional responses, specifically feeling happy, spread socially through groups based upon the closeness of their ties (Fowler & Christakis, 2008). People who reported being happy tended to have close relationships with other people who reported being happy. These studies highlight the importance of social norms and reinforcement of behaviors in close networks of family and friends in modifying health risk. We tend to mimic the behaviors of people close to us. If friends and family behave in ways that increase health risk, we are at risk of sharing their illnesses. But if family and friends make healthful choices, we may just "catch" their health.

Why do those we love sabotage our attempts at self-improvement?

Notably, part of the reason that social norms are so contagious is that people regularly punish others for violating social norms. People express satisfaction with and are willing to continue punishing others for breaking social norms even when it costs them substantially to carry out the punishment. In an elegant study, researchers demonstrated that punishing others for purposely not following expected social behavior activates brain reward circuits (de Quervain et al., 2004). *In other words, punishing others for breaking social norms is personally rewarding.* This particular study involved a game in which two players were given money. If the first player chose to give some of that money to the second player, the money that was shared would be quadrupled. The second player was then given the opportunity to give some of that money back to the first player. Thus, the expected best strategy would be for the first to give all of money to the second, and the second to give half of the quadrupled money back. But if the second chose to not follow expected social norms and kept all the money, the first would lose all the money from that round. Following such an unfair interaction, the first player was given the option of punishing the second player. In the real punishment condition, the first player could pay \$1 for every \$2 that would be taken away from the second player. In the symbolic punishment condition, the first player could assign as many "punishment units" as they desired to the second player, but it had no effect on either player's money.

To compare the effects of the second player's intentional desire to keep the money versus simply being a passive recipient of it, the researchers looked at a few scenarios while the first player was in a positron emission tomography (PET) scanner. Sometimes, a study team member played the second player and purposely kept the money. At other times, the first player was told that a computer would decide how much money the second player kept, so that he or she was not really responsible if any money was kept. The researchers were interested in the brain activity during the time when the first player was deciding whether or not to punish the second player's decision.

The researchers discovered that real punishment but not symbolic punishment activated the reward circuits of the first player. In other words, the first player's reward circuits were activated when the second player experienced real punishment for his or her decision not to return half of the money to the first player. The greater the activation of the reward circuits while deciding whether to punish, the more a person was willing to spend to punish second player for breaking expectations. Additionally, the first player chose to punish the second player more and their reward circuits were activated more when they believed the second player made the decision to keep the money than when the computer made the decision to keep the money. In other words, the participants only found it rewarding to punish people who had purposely treated them unfairly even though they were just as hurt by the response in both cases. Human brains are wired to encourage us to punish others for breaking social norms, even if it costs us to enforce the punishment. However, if the person who treated us unfairly had done so accidentally, then we do not find it rewarding to punish them. *These studies tell us that revenge for being intentionally hurt by another person is rewarding, and likely an automatic response in our brains.*

This tendency to punish intentional norm breaking can make it difficult to change our unhealthful habits if those around us share our unhealthful behaviors. Refusing to do something that everyone else in the group is doing, even if it is harmful or unhealthy, is breaking the social norms of the group. Group members are apt to go out of their way to punish you for your attempts at new healthful behavior. Tell your drinking buddies that you have decided not to drink any more and, at a minimum, it is unlikely that they will be particularly helpful and supportive of your new habit. It is much more likely that you get mocked and insulted. Likewise, tell your friends with whom you used to discuss your favorite TV show that you have decided to take a yoga class at that time instead, and they probably will not congratulate you on your healthy decision and encourage you to keep going. This is one of the reasons why mutual help groups consisting of those dedicated to meeting a shared health goal, such as Alcoholic Anonymous for those attempting to remaining sober, can be especially helpful by creating a supportive peer group that encourages change.

This helps to explain why people who associate with groups with extreme behaviors tend to follow those behaviors despite the potential harms from conforming. Not only do people receive social approval for acting like those around them, they are also likely to be punished by their peers when they act differently. Thus, it can be very helpful for people in social groups with extreme behaviors to begin associating with people from social groups with different norms. Making people in these extreme social groups aware that other peers outside the social group do not follow these norms can be a substantial step in that direction. Thus, a number of effective interventions focus on making people aware of more healthful social norms in the broader population or encourage people to associate more with people with more healthful social norms. Without changing these social influences, it can be extremely difficult for a person to stop engaging in the dangerous behaviors of their friends and family. Why would you continue to do a new healthful behavior when those around you punish you every time you try to do it?

To research ways to become more aware of the norms surrounding your target health behavior, see Exercise 1D (page 66).

When helping is hurtful: Rescuing, doting and enabling

From the time we are toddlers, we are taught the importance of being nice to other people. It seems like a simple concept. Anything we do to help people and make them feel better is a good thing, right? If someone were having a hard time with something, then presumably helping him or her would be a particularly nice thing to do. But unfortunately, behavior is not that simple. In certain situations, helping people can make them worse and even train them to be chronically sick or miserable.

Being too nice to someone when they feel bad, are anxious, do something wrong, or are hesitant to try something can reinforce unpleasant feelings or bad behaviors. While these responses to other people's distress or discomfort are generally well intentioned, they can have extremely negative effects on others health, mood, and life functioning. If unpleasant feelings, thoughts or behaviors are rewarded, the brain will encourage them to be repeated, attracting people to situations and encouraging responses that recreate the unpleasant experience. Over time, having their bad feelings, thoughts or behaviors rewarded can lead people to chronically feel bad, think bad things, or misbehave. *Thus, for a number of chronic behavioral and mood disorders, such as chronic pain, substance use disorders, and conduct disorders, having an important person in your life who rescues you, dotes upon you, or enables your misbehavior when you feel bad has been shown to be a major risk factor for development of or poor recovery from these disorders.*

To demonstrate how this process occurs, we present an example of how children can be trained to misbehave and not pay attention at school. In the extreme, such training could potentially win them a diagnosis of conduct disorder or ADHD. More commonly, it may lead to isolated problems with classroom discipline and learning.

As we can likely remember from our own childhood experiences, everyone feels bored or restless every now and again at school. Moreover, most children crave attention and acknowledgement. Some children may feel bored and restless more often than others to start, and some children may be more starved for attention then others. Such variation may make some children more vulnerable to learning bad behavior. But what provides the training? Consider (1) an over-crowded classroom where the teacher has no hope of providing regular individual attention to each student, and (2) a teacher with a low tolerance for disorganization or a strong need to feel her students are focused directly on her. In an attempt to keep her classroom in line, the teacher quickly responds to any perceived misbehavior. "Johnny, stop fiddling with your pencil." "Sue, stop whispering to your friend." "Aiden, don't call out answers without raising your hand." The problem with this technique is that it assumes that because the teacher's attention is negative and critical, it is a punishment and not a reward. This may be true for some of the children, particularly those who are shy, get plenty of positive attention and are very sensitive to criticism. But for other children, any attention from adults is rewarding. First, the child got a busy teacher to focus on them. Second, they just figured out a way to get a reaction out of an authority figure. They managed to gain at least temporary control over a big powerful person, which is surely some sign of power and status. If the child finds this response from the teacher rewarding, even if it only remains rewarding briefly before becoming a hassle, the behavior *and the feeling that preceded it will be reinforced.* Thus, the child will be more likely to misbehave again and feel bored and restless more often.

As evidence that this technique does contribute to conduct problems in children, there are a number of programs that effectively reduce conduct problems in children by teaching parents and teachers to avoid unintentionally rewarding bad behaviors, thoughts and feelings. These programs focus primarily on getting teachers or parents to stop attending to bad behavior, and start explicitly rewarding good behavior instead. For example, a program called "Peace Builders" has been shown to reduce conduct problems in schools where bad and even violent behavior had become a problem (Flannery et al., 2003; Krug et al., 1997; Embry et al., 1996). This program uses mediation to resolve disputes and trains teachers to ignore non-dangerous misbehavior and provide praise to children they catch acting appropriately. Thus, this program helps teachers stop reinforcing bad behaviors with attention. In parallel, it encourages teachers to reinforce good behavior with attention. This concept is also a primary focus of other evidence-based treatments for conduct disorder and ADHD, including "The Incredible Years Program" (Larsson et al., 2009; Jones et al., 2008; Webster-Stratton et al., 2008; Jones et al., 2007), "Parent-Child Interaction Therapy" (Thomas & Zimmer-Gembeck, 2007; Nixon et al., 2004;

Nixon et al., 2003; Eyberg et al., 1995), and "Problem-solving skills training with parent management training" (Kazdin et al., 1992). *When bad behaviors and the feelings that lead to them are ignored and not rewarded, they lose their value and are no longer worth doing.*

WARNING: Extinction bursts

Ending rewards for a bad behavior, whether or not those rewards were intentionally provided, is crucial to getting rid of the bad behavior. However, the bad behavior will not disappear immediately when the rewards are stopped. In fact, the *bad behavior will tend to escalate the first few times the reward is not received, even in adults.* Behavioral scientists refer to this increase in the behavior when the reward is withheld as an "extinction burst". Only later, after the behavior has consistently stopped eliciting a reward, will the behavior go away. When you are trying to get rid of bad behaviors by eliminating rewards, the behavior will temporarily get worse before it gets better.

To understand "extinction bursts" without straying too far from the rat models where it was first described, think of a soda machine. Most of us have been trained that when we put money in the machine and press the button of our choice, a soda will fall out of the slot in the bottom. Think of a time when a soda machine did not work when someone put money in and pressed the button. Did the person immediately decide that the machine did not work or was empty and walk away? Probably not. Chances are they pressed the button repeatedly, perhaps pushing harder and more angrily with each try. Maybe they pressed all the other buttons including the change return, shook the machine, yelled at the machine, tried reaching up the soda delivery slot, or went looking for the machine's owner to complain. Maybe they tried adding more money and pressing the button again. In other words, they escalated the behavior that normally provides the soda reward, making it bigger and more dramatic. The first response to a missing reward is to make the typically rewarded behavior more extreme, perhaps just to make sure that the lack of a reward was not because the behavior was not noticed.

One broken soda machine is probably not enough to lead someone to give up on soda machines and never use them again. However, if someone put money in ten soda machines in a row and none of them delivered a soda when a button was pressed, then they might give up on soda machines, stop noticing them, and stop trying to make them work. But, when you are trying to get someone to stop a behavior, you should expect to go through a period of time when that person throws temper tantrums before you achieve your goal.

The problem with extinction bursts is that they can be extremely unpleasant to endure, and very discouraging to the person withholding the reward. Withholding a reward may cause screaming, crying, begging, anger, frustration, sadness, and other unpleasant reactions from the person used to getting the reward. It will almost certainly be easier for the person withholding the reward to give in and provide the reward than it will be to bear witnessing the person's response. It may also be difficult to realize that the process may eventually achieve your goal of eliminating the undesirable behavior. This fact has resulted in hoards of toddlers getting cookies that surely ruined their appetite for dinner, young children staying up past their bedtime, and adults being given just one more drink even though everyone else knows they have had too much already. Extinction bursts are extremely effective for ending people's well-intentioned attempts to stop enabling bad behaviors in those close to them.

Understanding and expecting extinction bursts can make it a bit easier to stop rewarding bad behaviors in others. If you are expecting and are prepared for an outburst, you have a better chance of persevering through the reaction. When the person withholding the reward knows the reaction is only temporary and will eventually go away after the reward is withheld consistently, they may be better able to stick to their intentions. For example, providing warnings before encouraging parents to stop rewarding a bad behavior in their children may greatly increase the chance that they successfully eliminate the reward because they will know that a previously rewarded bad behavior will get worse before it is eliminated.

Behavioral training not only encourages behavioral problems in children, but also can lead to chronic emotional problems in adults. For example, studies of the mechanisms that encourage development of chronic pain problems and factors associated with poor recovery have identified "solicitous spouses" as a contributor to long-term experience of pain following an injury (e.g. see Romano et al., 1995; Sorbi et al., 2006). A "solicitous spouse" refers to someone close to a person with an injury or pain problem who immediately pampers or rescues their loved one whenever they experience or complain of pain. A "solicitous spouse" could be the wife who encourages her husband to rest whenever his back hurts, gets him his pain meds, and then fluffs his pillows before making him dinner. Alternatively, it could be the father who lets his son who hates school stay home, watch movies and eat ice cream whenever his stomach hurts. In these cases, the "solicitous" family member rewards their loved one every time they feel bad. While this may help a genuinely hurting person feel better, because reward encourages your brain to repeat the state that preceded getting the reward, this reward will train the loved one to feel bad more often. The husband's back will start hurting more and more often. The son may develop chronic stomachaches. Typically, the best way to get rid of such pain is to have the solicitous family member stop being so nice when their loved one feels sick.

How verbal reinforcement can alter sensory and emotional experience

Positive reinforcement can rapidly alter perceived pain. Jolliffe and Nicholas (2004) provided simple verbal reinforcement, saying things like "that's right," or "very good," when volunteers reported that having their arm squeezed with a blood pressure cuff was marginally more painful than they did the time before. This verbal reinforcement lead volunteers to report an increase in the amount of pain produced by the blood pressure cuff stimulus an hour later. The increase in pain associated with just one hour of verbal encouragement was more than 1 point on a 0-10 pain scale from "no pain" to "worst pain imaginable." To put the magnitude of this change in pain in context, this one point change in pain produced solely by an hour of verbal encouragement is greater than that produced by medical marijuana or opioid analgesics (i.e. narcotic painkillers) in trials in chronic pain clients (Martín-Sánchez et al., 2009; Martell et al., 2007). When volunteers were encouraged to experience more pain when their arm was squeezed, they reported more pain in response to the same amount of squeezing. A group of volunteers who experienced the same pressure stimuli without the verbal reinforcement did not show this increase in pain level. Hölzl and colleagues (2005) did a similar study but actually changed the intensity of the pain stimulus in response to pain perception. Specifically, they rewarded increases in perceived temperature from a painful heat stimulus with reductions in the temperature of the heat stimulus. In other words, when participants reported that a stimulus was hotter, they were rewarded by having the painful heat reduced on the next exposure. They found that rewarding participants with this reduction in heat intensity lead to changes in heat perception within an hour of testing. By the end of the hour, rewarded participants reported thinking that a given temperature stimulus was hotter than they did at the start of the study. They had also changed their perception of temperature compared to non-rewarded participants. The reward provided by the reduction in heat made them more sensitive to potentially painful heat.

Flor and colleagues (2002) directly studied the impact of a solicitous spouse on pain experience and brain activation in clients with chronic back pain. They brought in participants with chronic lower back pain who had a solicitous spouse. These spouses were known to pamper and attend to the client whenever they experienced or complained about back pain. They exposed these participants to a painful shock to their lower back or finger (i.e. a site where they had not been rewarded for experiencing pain) while recording brain activity in the limbic cortex by EEG. They repeated this process in two different ways: 1) when the spouse was not present, and 2) when the spouse was present. They found that while the solicitous spouses were out of the room, the back pain clients reported similar moderate levels of pain and had similar brain activity in response to the painful shock whether it was applied to the back or the finger. However, when the spouses were in the room, the clients reported a near doubling of the amount of pain that the shock to their back elicited, and activity in their limbic cortex was similarly elevated. There was no change in response to the stimulus to the finger. This suggests that the solicitous spouses had trained an increase in back pain experience in their loved ones. A stimulus to the back now caused more pain when the spouse was present. The spouses well-meaning attempts to save their loved one from feeling pain had trained the loved one to experience more intense back pain when the spouses were around.

In essence, when someone receives rewards when he feels or acts badly, he will be encouraged to feel or act badly again, even if those feelings or behaviors hurt him severely over the longer-term. The rewards may be simple and unintended: attention from others, the power to change a situation or get a reaction out of someone, sympathetic comments or responses, encouragement, special treats, favors or expressions of love or affection. It can be very difficult to stop others from providing maladaptive rewards, and sometimes the best or only solution is to remove oneself from those interactions. These social rewards can greatly inflate estimates of the value of an unhealthful behavior, even so far as to take an experience that would normally be punishing (e.g. criticism or pain) and make it reinforcing.

TIPS FOR HEALTH PROFESSIONALS: What helps, what hurts

The above sections have described how oversolicitous spouses or health professionals can increase the perception of pain. In addition, pain reduction provided by an hour of verbal encouragement is greater than that provided by medical marijuana or opioid analgesics. As the "Tips for Health Professionals" on page 33 recommend: 1. Talk about wellness, not pain, 2. Model positive outcomes, and 3. Provide hope.

One elaboration of these recommendations is to monitor functional or recovery outcomes (e.g. whether the client is doing things in life that matter to them, like work, interacting with family, engaging in valued activities) rather than monitoring pain level. Using these outcomes to gauge treatment success and guide pain treatment planning can improve outcomes and is a major recommendation of recent pain management guidelines. Family members could benefit from shifting their focus here as well – help the client by facilitating their engagement in life rather than trying to ease their pain.

To assess social influences that may hurt or help your efforts to improve a health behavior, see Exercise 1E (page 67) and Exercise 1F (page 69).

Chapter 1.4: Hijacking The Brain's Reward System: The Attraction of Addictive Substances

Drugs of abuse, specifically alcohol, tobacco, cannabis (i.e. marijuana), opioids (e.g. heroin, narcotic pain-killers), stimulants (e.g. cocaine, amphetamines (meth)), benzodiazepines, barbiturates, and even caffeine, have special effects on our dopamine neurons. Drugs of abuse differ from other drugs specifically in their ability to trick the brain into over-valuing them over other opportunities. This ability to trick the brain into over-valuing them has something to do with the fact that these substances increase firing from the dopamine neurons that code reward value.

These addictive substances cause many different effects on the brain and body, but they all share one common effect: they all pharmacologically cause the dopamine neurons to fire and induce release of dopamine in the nucleus accumbens (Wise and Bozarth, 1985; Bardo, 1998). Because of the direct actions of these drugs, these dopamine neurons will fire even if the signals they receive from other neurons would not normally encourage dopamine neuron firing. *In other words, drugs of abuse hijack the reward system, making the brain think they are highly rewarding and valuable, even when the drugs are objectively causing harm or worsening well-being.*

Dopamine neuron firing after taking drugs of abuse depends on the properties of the drug rather than the social, environmental or physiological effects of taking the drug. Regardless of what you have previously learned, your expectations, or what you actually experience when you take the drug, these chemicals will make your dopamine neurons release dopamine into your nucleus accumbens. This pharmacological property disrupts and confuses your brain's natural system for judging the value of various opportunities.

Spiraling out of control: The stepwise increase in overvaluation of drug reward

The first time a person uses drugs of abuse, the effect on the user's dopamine neurons are about the same as the effects of any other unexpected reward. Dopamine neurons fire at their normal (tonic) baseline rate until the drug is taken. Then the drug causes those neurons to increase their firing and release dopamine. Thus, the drug produces a signal that a new unexpected opportunity for life improvement has been identified and the brain should do its best to learn to repeat this opportunity.

The next time there is an opportunity to use drugs, our dopamine neurons recognize this, and increase their firing to indicate the expected value of this opportunity based upon the amount of dopamine released last time when you used the substance. If this were a normal reward, there would be no further increase in dopamine neuron firing when you actually took the drug because your brain had already perfectly predicted the effect of the drug. If this were a normal reward, it would produce changes in the environment or your physiology that are detected by your sensory systems and then interpreted by your reward system to trigger dopamine release. However, because these drugs act directly on receptors or proteins on reward system neurons to pharmacologically increase dopamine release, your dopamine neurons will fire again when you take the drug regardless of what you experience or sense through other brain systems. This indicates to your brain that this time the drug reward was even better than predicted. Thus, your brain looks for more cues to predict the availability of drug reward and increases its estimation of how good taking drugs will be. This process will continue each and every time you use a drug of abuse until eventually your reward circuitry has so greatly overvalued drug reward that your dopamine neurons cannot fire any faster. In order to kept comparisons between natural rewards and drug rewards to scale, your brain is forced to start reducing dopamine neuron firing in response to natural rewards.

FIGURE: Dopamine neuron firing rate in addiction

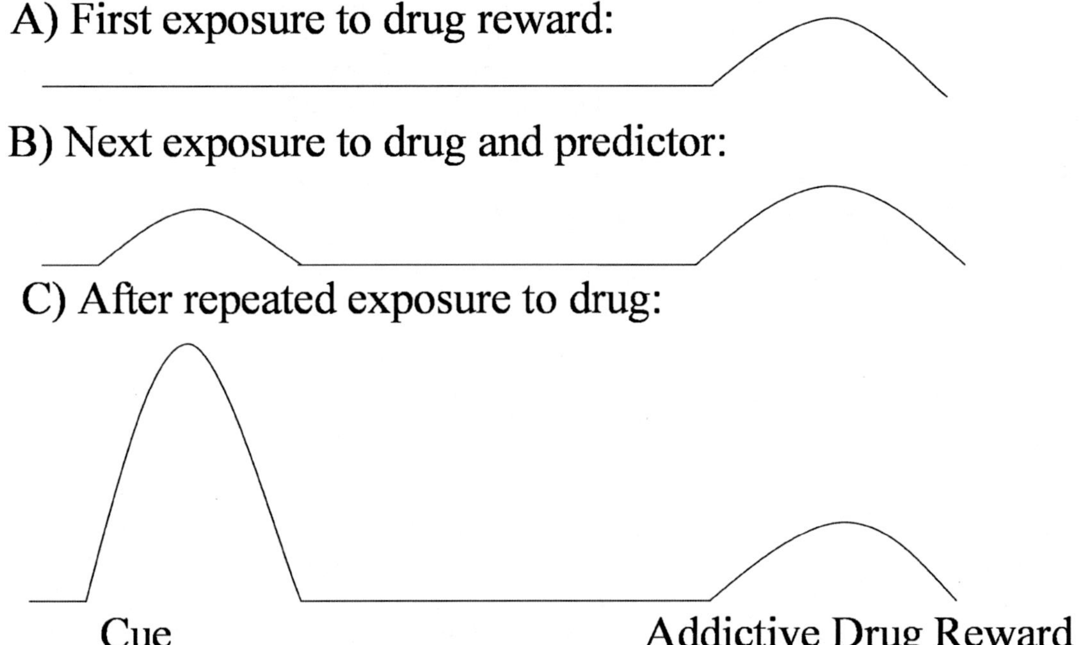

Legend: A) The rate of dopamine neuron firing following the first use of the drug (the same as unexpected cookies at a seminar), B) The next exposure to the drug leads to an increase in dopamine neuron firing in anticipation of the reward (just like the expectation of cookies at a seminar) but then the neurons fire again when the drug is used (unlike when the expected cookies are received, and because of the direct pharmacological effects of the drug on dopamine neurons rather than the brain's perception of rewarding effects of drug use), C) After repeated exposure to the drug, the anticipation of the drug leads to a high rate of dopamine firing that continually increases with each exposure because the firing when drug itself is used causes the neurons to recalculate their expectation of the reward (even though the benefits from the drug remain unchanged, and may be low or non-existent).

Therefore, as you continue to take drugs of abuse three things happen: First, your limbic reward circuit predicts enormous rewards for taking drugs. Objectively, the drug does not improve well-being much if at all, but your limbic reward circuit will always think that you lucked out and got even more than the jackpot you expected. Second, because the drug causes additional dopamine release every time it is taken, your limbic reward circuit will start to learn that every possible feeling, object, person or place that is around while they use drugs indicates an opportunity to use drugs. Drug cues will become ubiquitous—they will be everywhere. Every liquor store, every association with a person with whom you have been drinking, every mood and thought that preceded the drinking, will remind you of the drug reward. And these cues will induce cravings to take drugs when they are around. You will start craving drugs more and more frequently. Lastly, at least to your limbic reward circuit, everyday rewards will seem miniscule and worthless in comparison to the opportunities provided by drugs. Gaining social approval will not seem very important. Doing well in school or work will become much less important than using drugs. Taking good care of yourself will get moved down the list of priorities. Drugs become so overvalued that the things that actually improve well-being become ignored. Natural true rewards will no longer drive automatic behaviors, and your body will lose part of its ability to maintain its well-being.

Typically, when this process is explained to health professionals there are several reactions. First, people say, "Well that sounds grim. Does that mean drug-users are doomed to slowly die as their lives are taken over by drug use?" Second, they say, "Wait a minute. That doesn't make sense. I know lots of people who drink a little bit of alcohol every night or take drugs occasionally, and they still prioritize other things in their lives." Luckily, that second viewpoint is right and this is not just a doom and gloom story. Happily, we do have other parts of our brain, particularly our prefrontal cortex, that can over-ride the suggestions and estimates of our limbic reward circuit. We will discuss this in detail in Brain Challenge #5.

Speed and intensity of drug absorption separate addiction from recreation

It is also important to consider what pharmacologists call the "pharmacokinetics" of a drug of abuse. The limbic response to drugs of abuse depends not only on what chemical is ingested, but also how much hits the brain and how fast the drug is absorbed. Remember that your limbic brain only pays attention to immediate effects, say ten minutes into the future. It learns best when a drug of abuse hits the brain quickly and all at once – when blood concentrations go from low to high almost immediately. The slower and more gradually the drug concentrations in your blood change, the less dramatic is the learning, and the less your limbic brain will overvalue the drug.

Thus, how someone takes a drug of abuse will have a big effect on whether or not the drug becomes overvalued and starts to take over his or her life. Directly injecting a drug of abuse into one's blood stream will almost instantaneously increase drug concentrations in the brain and thus dopamine release in the nucleus accumbens. This intravenous use will rapidly lead to over-valuation of drug reward and its associated consequences. Smoking a drug of abuse delivers the drug to the brain nearly as rapidly. One's lungs take up the drug rapidly from the air and deliver it straight to the brain. Thus this method of use is also extremely addictive. Snorting a drug of abuse is a bit slower, but still a pretty quick way of increasing drug concentrations in the brain. Swallowing a drug of abuse takes longer to increase drug concentrations in the brain than these other methods. It may or may not deliver the drug to the brain quickly enough to powerfully and swiftly release dopamine in the nucleus accumbens.

Filling an empty stomach with a ready-to-absorb drug will still increase blood levels of drug rapidly. However, slowly consuming a drug over an hour or two in combination with a large, high-fiber meal will increase drug concentrations in the blood more slowly; perhaps slowly enough that the nucleus accumbens barely notices. For example, downing two glasses of wine in two minutes on an empty stomach will lead to greater over-valuation of alcohol reward than will drinking the same two glasses of wine over the course of a three-hour five-course meal. From the perspective of your nucleus accumbens, the first case would cause a clear spike in dopamine neuron firing after chugging the wine so it would not be too hard for your brain to guess that this big increase is related to the drinking and to attribute that bump in dopamine to the alcohol. In the second case, there would be a long, slow drift towards increased dopamine neuron firing over the course of dinner. Not only does this make it less likely that the dopamine neurons notice the increase, but it also decreases the chance that the nucleus accumbens correctly attributes the increase in dopamine neuron firing to the wine. Maybe it is the restaurant that is slowly making your life seem better. Maybe it is the wonderful food. Maybe it is the charming person with whom you are dining, the way she is looking at you, or the fascinating conversation in which you are engaged. The slow uptake of the alcohol makes it both less likely that your nucleus accumbens notices the increase in dopamine release and more likely that it associates the increase with something other than alcohol use. Thus, chugging wine is likely to lead you to overvalue wine and encourage you to drink more. Slowly drinking wine with fine dinners is likely to lead you to overvalue fine-dining or your dinner companion, and encourage you to spend a disproportionate amount of money on fancy meals and your dinner date.

Chapter 1.5: Getting What You Pay For: How to Assess the True Value of a Reward

As we have reviewed in the last chapters, there are many different ways in which our brains can be tricked to over value specific rewards. When this happens we will tend to work hard to get these rewards, even though the benefits we obtain from them may be low or the harms may be great. In essence, we are being bamboozled by our culture and experience. We've been trained to pay more, in effort, for rewards that simply are not as good as we expect. How can we fix this training, so that we only pay for what we truly get?

How can we correct our value estimates?
A number of effective therapies have been developed which include a focus on changing expectations about the relative value of healthful or unhealthful behaviors. Cognitive Behavioral Therapies and Motivational Interviewing are two effective treatments for treating addictive and mood disorders, and encouraging more healthful habits.

Part of generating accurate value estimates is identifying what already has value estimates associated with them. In addition to requiring knowledge about the consequences of thoughts and behaviors, we also need to be aware of our own habits. Often, we do things so automatically that we do not even know we are doing them. People close to us may be more aware of our tendencies and behaviors. Thus, it can be helpful to ask others to point out things that we do or think that are getting in the way of reaching our goals. It can be much easier for someone on the outside to objectively see the patterns in our thoughts and behaviors. The more habitual our behaviors, the less likely it is that we notice ourselves doing them.

Cognitive behavioral therapy teaches that, with practice, we are able to revise the mistaken assumptions we tend to habitually make in our thinking. Correcting these assumptions helps us make more objectively accurate health-related decisions. Cognitive behavioral therapy is designed to change thoughts and behaviors that are important to health. It has an enduring effect in the treatment of major depression and anxiety disorders and reduces the risk of relapse (Hollon et al., 2006). This enduring effect is particularly evident in comparison to treatment with drugs for anxiety and depression (anxiolytics and antidepressants). Cognitive behavioral therapy is also an effective treatment for chronic pain, insomnia, substance use disorders, eating disorders, and other health problems with a behavioral component. To get started, let's consider some of the most common methods used to change inaccurate expectations.

Reframing: Adopting a new perspective
Our psychological responses and emotions depend not so much as what happens to us as the way we think about things. Our thoughts about health behaviors and situations tend to become patterned and habitual over time. The habits we acquire that involve relatively automatic actions, tying one's shoes, brushing one's teeth, shaving, or preparing the morning coffee, are paralleled by mental habits we acquire. These habits, both physical and mental, can be redirected by the prefrontal cortex. In the language of contemporary

psychology, in particular cognitive-behavioral therapy, the term "reframe" is used to describe a process of rethinking our assumptions, generally for the purpose of modifying all forms of habits. Reframing involves the practice of reconsidering your initial reaction to a situation or behavioral choice to broaden your perspective. By reframing your beliefs about an opportunity, you may discover new reasons or motivations for not doing unhealthful or doing healthful things. This concept and practice is at the core of highly effective cognitive therapies that have been developed and tested for a wide variety of health problems (Beck, 1976).

Rather than thinking about the effects of a behavior or situation as a whole, we often focus on only one aspect of the situation, and ignore the other effects. When we habitually think of only the good aspects of an unhealthful behavior or only the bad aspects of a healthful behavior, these thought patterns can encourage us to act in ways that harm our health. Stepping back from our initial thoughts and reactions and considering other aspects of the situation can help us make a more objective and balanced assessment of the costs and benefits of doing a behavior. Simply taking another perspective can help fix the errors we make when we determine the value of a given opportunity.

For example, someone's first thoughts about going to the gym might be habitually negative. "I'm already busy and it is going to take time that I don't have to work out." "I'm going to get all sweaty and soggy and I hate that feeling." "All the really in shape people at the gym will make me feel bad about myself." "Exercising makes my muscles hurt and takes effort." If these thoughts are the only ones you have when you consider going to the gym, then chances are you won't go. Why would you go if it is going to be a miserable and negative experience? If you catch yourself having negative thoughts about a good behavior, pausing and trying to reframe can both encourage you to go to the gym and help break these unhelpful thought patterns. Reframing is in many ways simple. All you need to do is ask yourself "Why would I want to go to the gym?" "What good things are there about exercising?" Then brainstorm answers and see if they make sense to you. How might I reframe my thoughts about going to the gym? "Exercise will help energize me and help me think more clearly, so even though it takes time, I may be more efficient in getting things done." "Sweating will clean out my pores and make me feel really clean and fresh after I shower and change." "There are a lot of nice people at the gym and it can be fun to talk with them or make new friends as we exercise together." "Exercise makes me stronger and will keep me from getting tired and sore from my everyday activities." You may not only find that you can counter all your own arguments against going to the gym, but also come up with additional reasons to go. "If I work out for an hour, I can have that slice of cake I've been dying for without gaining weight." "I've always wanted to learn a headstand, and the yoga instructor says I'm only about a month of practice away from succeeding." "I've been having back pain lately, and my doctor says that building core strength and losing some weight is my best bet for preventing it from becoming chronic." Bringing positive thoughts about a healthful behavior to the forefront will encourage you to make a healthful decision. In this case, reframing may increase the chances you decide to go to the gym. It will also shape your experience at the gym. If you are thinking about the positive aspects of going to the gym, you will notice the positive aspects of going to the gym. Chances are you will have a much better experience when you are there.

While in principle the concept of reframing is simple, becoming good at it requires practice. For people who are really stuck in unhelpful thought patterns, it may be really difficult to even come up with other ways of thinking about things. For this reason, it can be helpful get others involved in your early attempts to reframe. You could ask a friend, therapist, or members of a support group to point out when you are being overly negative or positive about a situation to help you learn to recognize when your biased thoughts are favoring bad choices. When you or your friend identifies such a situation, you can brainstorm together to come up with other ways of looking at the situation. This may generate a lot more ideas and thoughts than if you tried alone. If you take the time to think about your friends' ideas of other way of thinking about the choice, you may find that some of their thoughts ring true for you, even if you never would have thought of them yourself. I note that picking a friend that already does the behavior that you want to adopt can be particularly helpful. They obviously have some reason and motivation that keeps them doing that behavior. Someone who has the same behavior and thought patterns as you could wind up just reinforcing your current skewed perspectives. So, if you want to get fit but just can't think nice things about the gym, get a friend who does go to the gym to help you reframe. If you want to quit smoking, but all you can think about is how much better it will make you feel in this anxious moment, get a friend who has quit smoking to help you rethink that decision. Over time, as you practice reframing with a friend, you will find that you get better at both noticing when you are having unhelpful thoughts and coming up with alternate ways of thinking about things.

If you want to read more about how to reframe, we recommend the following online resources: http://www.mentalhelp.net/poc/view_doc.php?type=doc&id=9749&cn=353 and http://www.mindtools.com/stress/rt/CognitiveRestructuring.htm.

To practice in cognitive restructuring or reframing, see Exercise 1G (page 73).

Challenging expectations: Tackling irrational fears through graded exposure

Many of us have morbid fears; spiders, snakes, needles and pain are common fears. Whether innate or resulting from experience, the amygdala and other centers of the brain make avoidance a natural consequence. Avoidance works in the short-term, but long-term avoidance of some fears, such as needles or dental drills, for example, can have long-term negative effects on obtaining medical and dental care. For phobic disorders in which one or more irrational fears interfere with a person's life, graded exposure can be a remarkably effective treatment.

Graded exposure is not to be confused with being called out in class for getting a poor grade. It is a clinical procedure in which a client is guided through the experience the behavior and its consequences intentionally in a safe and reflective manner, typically starting with something totally unthreatening, for example, the word "spider," followed by something a little more threatening, for example, a picture of a spider. With each approximation toward the heart of the phobic disorder, the client is gradually able to extinguish this fear. Virtual reality systems that simulate contact with spiders have even been developed, tested and shown to effectively reduce fear and avoidance of spiders in people with arachnophobia or extreme fear of spiders (Cote & Bouchard, 2005). Thus, guided exposure can be effectively applied to many different behavioral problems that stem from inaccurate beliefs or expectations about a situation or behavior.

Graded exposure is a particularly useful technique when a person has inaccurate or exaggerated fears or negative expectations about a healthful behavior. Having a friendly and more experienced person walk them through the healthful behavior (or do it with them) and encourage them to reflect on what they are actually experiencing on a moment by moment basis can be a powerful method for changing expectations.

This strategy can be used formally or informally. Something as simple as inviting your junk food-eating friend to try some of the more healthful, but unfamiliar food you brought for lunch (e.g. try a piece of my persimmon or my tofurkey sandwich) could change their expectations through exposure and might increase the chance that they at least contemplate these products the next time they go to the grocery store. An office lunch workshop where a nutritionist brings in healthful lunch options that are available in the cafeteria or in nearby restaurants, explains their nutritional value in comparison to other choices, and then encourages people to sample each one and comment on their tastiness, would be a more formal version of the same strategy. Exposure interventions change expectations through experience and make people aware of choices that they could make or things that they could do that they may not have even considered before. In many cases, simply having a friendly and trustworthy face help us navigate the fear of the unknown is enough to change expectations and subsequently behavior through experience. Most people tend to think that anything they haven't done or tried already is bad, unpleasant or at least at little scary. Improving their expectations about healthful behaviors makes them at least a bit more likely to do the behaviors in the future.

EXAMPLE: Applications for phobic or catastrophic responses to injury or pain

Notably, exposure is helpful for more than encouraging people to try something new. Exposure can also be extremely helpful in retraining or rehabilitating people who had a bad experience with something and now fear or avoid it unreasonably. For example, graded exposure has been used to great effect with chronic pain clients who have learned to fear movement. When someone is injured, he or she inevitably experiences pain and some loss of function around the injury. For example, if I sprain my ankle, it will hurt if I try to walk on it, and until my ankle completes the initial healing process, I will risk injuring it more if I try to walk. However, even after my ankle has healed enough for me to start moving it normally and walking again, my ankle will hurt when I move and walk on it until I strengthen the surrounding muscles and ligaments and work out remaining inflammation and scar tissue that built up when I was immobile. But, I need to move my ankle despite the discomfort to get it back to its normal, functioning, pain-free state. Some people become so fearful about experiencing pain or reinjuring themselves that they never try to move during this later recovery period. This can lead to chronic disability and pain. Coaching people through the movements they fear and breaking expectations that movement will lead to excruciating pain or injury can be both highly effective and necessary to get chronic pain clients to recover.

This general strategy has been developed into a structured treatment plan for people with chronic pain and fear of movement (Vlaeyen et al., 2001). In short, chronic pain clients with fear of movement are helped to generate a list of movements that they are afraid to do or that they think might cause extreme pain or injury. The clients then rank these movements from lowest to highest in terms of fear and perceived danger. Treatment consists of the therapist working with the client to do the behaviors on the list. The therapist encourages the client to reflect on their pain and their ability to do the movements safely as they complete them. The treatment starts with the least scary movements and progresses as the client experiences success with completing less feared tasks. This treatment has been shown to be highly effective for reducing fear of movement and catastrophizing about pain in clients with chronic back pain in case-studies and trials (Woods & Asmundson, 2008; George et al., 2008; Leeuw et al., 2008). The treatment also tends to improve pain-related disability, although perhaps not any more so than other effective physical and behavioral therapies. The treatment changes clients' expectations about the danger and negative consequences of doing the movements and other activities required to recover. These changes in thoughts and beliefs tend to lead to healthful changes in behavior, even in people whose beliefs may be based on negative experiences in the past.

Comparing against others: Correcting perceptions through normative feedback

Correcting biased perceptions of what other people do can help encourage behavior change. Interventions may help people understand that (1) the unhealthful behavior that they do is not common in the broader population of their peers or (2) a healthful behavior is common among the broader population of their peers. These interventions are referred to as *normative comparisons.* They typically consist of:

1) Assessment: asking people about the details of their current behavior, and
2) Feedback: providing them factual information about how their behavior compares to that of other people like them in the general population.

For example, you might ask a person how much he or she drinks, and then provide him or her with information on the percentage of people of their age and gender that drink more or less than they do. Interventions using normative comparisons have been shown to be effective for preventing or reducing alcohol use and risky sexual behaviors in college-age populations, and dietary fat intake in adults (Moreira et al, 2009; Chernoff & Davison, 2005; Kroeze et al., 2008).

To use this strategy, you need factual information on how people behave in the general population. Epidemiologists have collected this information for some behaviors. Tools to help people use such information have been made to help change specific behaviors. For example, a web-based computer program is available that will provide feedback comparing individual student use of alcohol and marijuana to rates of use in the U.S. student population overall (i.e. www.e-CHUG.com, www.e-TOKE.com). However, it can be hard to find epidemiological data for some behaviors. Lack of information to provide accurate feedback can be a barrier to using this type of intervention.

Notably, this strategy has the potential to change behavior in undesirable directions. Normative comparisons can also make unhealthful behaviors appear normal. Feedback about norms in the general population may increase unhealthful behaviors in people in particularly healthful social groups. For example, a teenager who does not drink alcohol and has no friends that do, might be more likely drink alcohol after finding out that she drinks less than many other people her age. Thus, it can be important to target these interventions to people with relatively uncommon, unhealthful behaviors. Americans on average do some pretty unhealthful behaviors, and generally our goal is not to get all people to this mediocre state. Interventions that teach people with extremely unhealthful behaviors that most people act differently from them can be very effective for encouraging them to drift towards the more healthful norm. If these same interventions teach people with extremely healthful behaviors that most people act differently from them or stigmatize their exceptional behaviors in some way, then we are doing them a disservice. It is hard enough to keep up healthful behaviors without professionals pointing out how rare it is to do so. Thus, these interventions should be saved and used selectively for people identified as being on the extremely unhealthful end of the bell curve.

Revealing internal contradictions between our behavior and our values and goals
Thoughts about a given situation or behavior, for example, overeating, can be particularly powerful motivators when one can identify a contradiction between the behavior and personal values or goals. We all have images of how we ideally would like to be and how we would like to act. But our behaviors frequently do not match up with our ideals. In many cases, we are not aware of the disconnect between how we actually behave and how we want to behave, or what we do and what we are trying to achieve. We may be doing things that prevent us from reaching our goals or from being the person we want to be. When we consider our individual behaviors in the context of our personal values and goals, we may find that we would like to make different choices. This may increase our motivation to alter our habits. When we recognize the connection between our behavioral choices and our values and goals, we may change our assessments of our opportunities and start acting in ways that are consistent with our long-term goals and personal ideals. By relating our current choices to our longer-term goals for ourselves, we may drastically change our estimation of the value of a short-term reward opportunity. We may not find feeling better in the moment as appealing if we are clearly aware and consider the fact that it will cause us problems and prevent us from reaching goals that are really important to us. Helping people to recognize when their behaviors are in conflict with their values and goals and using this to motivate behavior change is an explicit component of several highly effective therapies for promoting behavior change, specifically *Motivational Interviewing* (Miller & Rollnick, 2002) and *Acceptance and Commitment Therapy* (Hayes et al., 1999*)*.

Motivational interviewing, for example, highlights the disagreement between a client's actual behaviors and their stated goals to help motivate change. In this therapy, the provider is taught to provide simple, objective feedback to the client about how their choices or behaviors may be opposed to their stated goals. The provider encourages the client to explore these discrepancies so that association between the client's unhealthful behaviors and his goals become explicit and clear to the client. By asking the right questions, the provider can let the client give the reasons for doing the behavior then arguments against doing the behavior. The client's own reasons are likely to be the most persuasive—they are the ones the provider can effectively repeat to the client. The provider does not tell the client that the unhealthful behaviors are a problem that they must change, but instead gives the client enough objective information about the behavior and its typical consequences to allow the client to reevaluate whether the unhealthful behavior is worth doing. In essence, the provider simply provides missing or ignored information that may change the client's judgment of the value of an opportunity and allows the client to readjust their ideas about the value of the behavior themselves. Because our decision of whether or not to do a behavior depends strongly on our estimation of the value of making that effort, new information that greatly increases or decreases our estimates about the value of anticipated rewards can have a dramatic impact on our subsequent choices. Overall, motivational interviewing enhances drive to change behavior. *This increased drive may be particularly powerful and sustained because it stems from personal, internally generated reasons for change rather than the encouragement of a health professional.*

Notably, motivational interviewing also avoids arguments between the client and provider by acknowledging that there is a choice involved in doing or withholding a behavior. This choice involves benefits and risks on either end; only the individual making the choice can decide which outcomes are more valuable to them. Doing a behavior may solve a short-term problem (e.g. help you deal with anxiety) but stop you from reaching your long-term goals (e.g. to stay healthy and active). For example, smoking might help you relax when you are immediately stressed, but cause a myriad of health problems that will cause much greater stress in the coming years. Similarly, doing a behavior may cause a short-term problem (e.g. disappoint or start and argument with a friend) but help you reach your long-term goals. For example, I (J.T.) might have to turn down the homemade cookies my friend baked last night in order to keep my gestational diabetes under control and reach my longer-term goal of having a safe delivery of a healthy baby. Since the longer-term consequences are both probabilistic and potentially far into the future, choosing the behavior that helps in the short-term could wind up being the better choice. If I am hit by a bus on the way to work today, I might as well have had that cookie. By respecting the difficult decisions made by our dopamine system, motivational interviewing helps promote more trusting, less confrontational and more collaborative relationships between a provider and client.

EXAMPLE: Using motivational interviewing to encourage undervalued health behaviors

To illustrate, let's consider how motivational interviewing might be used by a health professional to encourage a client to make an effort to change a behavior. Let us imagine an overweight client with diabetes and back pain who has repeatedly failed to make dietary changes despite poor diabetes control and dire warnings from their doctor about their need to manage their diet and lose weight to prevent diabetes complications. The client has come to the clinic complaining of worsening back pain, despite the pain medications that were prescribed at the last visit.

Health Professional: *So Mr. X, what brings you here today?*

Client: *My back is killing me. I can't concentrate. I'm angry and tired all the time, and it is hard to work. Those pills that you gave me last time barely helped at all.*

Health Professional: *I'm happy to try to come up with a pain management plan that will work better for you. Could you tell me a bit more about your goals? Knowing that all pain treatments have their strengths and weaknesses, what are your priorities? What would you consider a success?*

Client: *I just want the pain to stop interfering with my life. I want to be happy and able to focus on my family and job instead of the pain in my back.*

Health Professional: *That seems like a very good goal. There are a number of things that we could try that might help in that regard. Most simply, I could increase the dosage of your medication. But, that will also increase the side effects and may make you more tired and make it even harder to concentrate. It may also not be effective. Roughly one-third of people who try these medications don't find them effective at tolerable doses. Alternatively, one of the most common contributors to back pain is being overweight, and losing weight and exercising can substantially reduce back pain while also increasing energy, improving mood, and helping with your other health conditions, like your diabetes. A better, but more challenging solution, would be to try to start a diet and exercise plan to lose the weight that may be maintaining your back problems. Of course, this will take longer and require more effort, but this eventually should make it more likely that you will be able to keep up an active, social lifestyle. Alternatively, we could try a mix of the two. You could start a diet and exercise plan, and I could give you more powerful pain medication that you could use before you exercise, so that your back pain doesn't prevent you from doing the things that should eventually make it strong and pain free. It's your choice. I can play around with the medications and dosing and I can connect you with programs and support people who can help you with the diet and exercise, but the choice is ultimately yours and you are the one who will have to do the work. Does any of this sound helpful?*

Client: *The medication really didn't help that much with the pain and in other ways made me feel worse. I'm not so sure I'll be able to lose weight, but I suppose it wouldn't hurt to try the program you mentioned. How about we try the both option? Could you give me some more powerful medication and sign me up for the diet and exercise program?*

Health Professional: *Of course. Let's do that now, and plan to check back in a couple of weeks to see how this new plan is working for you...*

Note, the clinician focuses on getting the client to clarify his goals, and then presents factual information and choices that the client might consider as they relate to the client's own goals. The clinician highlights that the choice and responsibility to change behavior are the clients alone. The clinician can help, but can't do it for them. Then the clinician lets the client make his decision. Because the clinician hasn't pushed any particular choice on the client, there is nothing for the client to argue or push back about. This prevents him from becoming defensive. While there is obviously lots of additional work to do to help the client change behavior in a lasting way, the health professional has now linked weight loss with something that the client cares about, specifically stopping back pain from interfering in his life, thus increasing the expected value of a diet and exercise program. By focusing on the client's goal, rather than the provider's priority, which might be to get his client's diabetes controlled, he has helped the client to prioritize weight loss.

Motivational interviewing has been used to effectively manage diabetes, alcohol, nutrition and obesity, physical activity, and smoking. For example, motivational interviewing improves weight loss in women with type 2 diabetes (West et al., 2007) as long as the therapy is an adjunct to regular medical care. It outperforms traditional advice-giving in the treatment of a broad range of behavioral problems and diseases (Rubak et al., 2005). Motivational interviewing need not involve an actual interviewer; online motivational interviewing, in the form of assessment and individualized feedback, is also effective (Webber et al., 2008).

To practice in identifying values and goals and using these to foster behavior change, see Exercise 1H (page 81).

Brain Challenge #1 Exercises

Exercise 1A: Practice Creating Positive Expectations

From a practical point of view, health professionals can reduce the degree to which their clients experience pain or increase the benefits of a treatment by creating positive expectations. There are different ways the same treatment can be framed by a health professional to a client that may produce very different reactions and health behaviors.

Part 1: Helping To Reducing Pain

A child is being given a potentially painful vaccination. What do you say to him or her?

____

____

____

Example 1: "This is going to hurt, so hold still or I'll have to get someone to pin you down."

Example 2: "Remember how yucky it is to be sick and tired? The medicine I have here will prevent you from catching a type of bug that makes you really sick. You are really lucky to be able to get this medicine. Could I have your arm to give it to you?"

Example 1 is paraphrased from a truly terrible MD I (J.T.) visited as a child, who did pin me down and give me the injection. Since that visit, it has taken substantial cognitive effort for me to overcome my emotional aversion to doctors and needles. My lack of control over this minor pain turned a simple injection into a traumatic experience that continues to influence my thoughts and behaviors 30 years later.

Example 2 is roughly what I told my now 3-year old son before his last round of vaccinations. We practiced giving shots to a stuffed animal, and then he willingly and happily got his vaccinations and proudly told us all that evening that he had got the medicine that would make him healthy.

Review the statement you generated at the beginning of this section. Do you focus on the negative consequences or the positive outcomes? How can you re-word it so that the client feels informed and in control of what is going to happen to them?

____

____

____

Part 2: Helping To Quit Smoking

Your client continues to smoke despite five previous quit attempts including liberal use of nicotine replacement therapy. They are discouraged and feel like there is no point in trying again. You decide to suggest a newly approved medication for nicotine dependence. What do you say to the client?

____

____

____

Example 1: "I know quitting smoking is hard work, so I'm really impressed with all the effort you have been devoting toward this important health behavior. The average person requires 7 quit attempts to learn all the skills they need to be able to stop smoking, so you are well on your way. I'd like to be able to help you. There is a new medication that was just approved to help people quit smoking. It is a pharmacologically sophisticated drug that specifically targets the brain circuits that drive you to smoke. In trials, people receiving this medication quit smoking at higher rates than those receiving all existing treatments for smoking cessation. Would you like to try it?"

Example 2: "Quitting smoking requires a lot of effort. Maybe you just aren't ready to quit yet. There is a new medication I could prescribe to help you quit smoking, but it works similarly to nicotine replacement therapy and that didn't work well for you. Would you like to try it?"

While the content of both examples are true, Example 1 helps create an expectation that a quit attempt will eventually be successful and more likely if the client keeps trying and uses a fancy new drug. Example 2 echoes the client's belief that even with a new medication the outcome of another quit attempt will be another failure.

Review the statement you generated at the beginning of this section. Do you focus on the negative consequences or the positive outcomes? How can you re-word it so that the client feels informed and in control of their efforts toward behavior change?

____

____

____

Part 3: Other Medical and Surgical Examples

Below are a few more examples of situations where you may be able to increase treatment success or decrease pain by fostering the client's expectation of benefit. Brainstorm different ways of discussing these treatments, focusing on creating positive expectations about treatment effects and making the client feel in control of their own behavior and mood.

You believe a combination of a selective serotonin reuptake inhibitor plus 12 weeks of cognitive behavior therapy would benefit your depressed client. What do you say to her?

Response 1: ____

____

____

Response 2: ____

____

____

Response 3: ____

____

____

A client presents with low back pain that began three days ago. They want an MRI and think they need surgery. You think that they are likely to get better with some anti-inflammatory medications and healing time. What do you say to them?

Response 1: ____

____

____

Response 2: ____

____

____

Response 3: ____

____

____

A client is about to go into surgery and is very scared about being in pain afterwards. What do you say to them?

Response 1: ____

____

____

Response 2: ____

____

____

Response 3: ____

____

____

Review the different responses for each of the examples above. Which ones focus on the negative consequences or the positive outcomes? Do you talk about wellness, model positive outcomes, and provide hope? How can you re-word it so that the client feels informed and in control of their efforts toward behavior change?

Exercise 1B: Identify Positive Associations for Behavior Change

Associations between rewards in your life and people, settings, things, thoughts or situations can develop that encourage or discourage unhealthful behavior, thoughts or moods. If you can identify these associations and become aware of them, you can take advantage of them to alter your exposure or response to these situations.

Part I: Identify Positive Associations

Try to keep a behavior or mood diary for at least a few days. Design your own method for recording this information easily and conveniently (e.g. in a small notebook or on an electronic device). Below is a list of what you should record, as well as a table you can modify to best record your own goals and associations:

1. Write down the mood, thought or behavior that you want to change.
2. Record the date and day of the week.
3. Regularly throughout the day, record the following:
    a. The intensity of the feeling or the drive to do the behavior you want to change.
    b. Things you notice in the environment/situation and people that are present.
    c. How you respond to the environment/situation and people that are present.
    d. Anything else you observe or think of at that time.

Target Feeling/Behavior:

Date: ______________________________				
Time	**Intensity**	**Surroundings**	**Response**	**Other**
Date: ______________________________				

Part 2: Minimize Negative Associations

Review the diary to look for patterns or situations in which the feeling or desire to do the behavior is more or less intense. This will provide clues to help you identify associations that encourage that feeling or behavior. You may find it helpful to have someone else look at the diary with you. They may be more open to noticing patterns that you do not see. Once you have found things that tend to make you feel or behave in ways that you are trying to change, you can work to alter your exposure to those cues.

Exercise 1C: Cues You Can Use

Consider one or two of your health-oriented goals. Think carefully about the cues that encourage your healthful activities. What reminds you to eat wisely, get regular physical activity or relax to manage your emotions during emotionally distressing events? Fill your everyday environments with cues that you associate with healthful actions and you will find you do them more often. Think like an advertising executive and expose yourself to sites, sounds, phrases, memories and other reminders of your wellness goals to trigger healthful practices throughout the day

To get you started, we provide some ideas that we have found helpful:

1. **Written Cues:** A notebook where weight, body fat, physical activity and other health data are recorded once a day, reminds me (W.G.) to stick to a diet and exercise plan.
2. **Visual Cues:** It is easier to take pills if they are in plain sight than if they are hidden in a medicine cabinet. My (W.G.) 90-year-old mother keeps her pills on the kitchen table so she unfailingly takes them at breakfast. In particular, photographs can be powerful visual cues. Pictures of places where you have hiked or pictures of yourself in optimal states can serve as daily reminders to emulate or recreate those states.
3. **Verbal Cues:** Asking a close friend or family member to remind you of your goals, particularly during times of weakness, can be helpful. Having my spouse remind me of the dessert I (J.T.) had at lunch when I am contemplating ice cream after dinner can help me moderate my diet.
4. **Musical Cues:** If you workout with an MP3 player, you can download music that you associate with previous exercise highs to help keep you going. I (J.T.) successfully used my favorite dance music first to stay positive and productive at work during extreme pregnancy-induced nausea that otherwise had me vomiting 4+ times/day, and then later to keep me going through 42 hours of labor with my first child.
5. **Tactile Cues:** Put aside the clothes in which you would like to be able to fit, or the clothes you plan to use to take an exercise break, or wear the kind of shoes you would like to use for walking at a time when you are able to "get away from it all". You can also remove negative cues; for example, donate clothing that is now too large.
6. **Social Cues:** Find others who enjoy the activities you do and surround yourself with them as often as possible. Spend time with those with whom you can walk, cycle, play or cook healthfully, and you will be more likely to do these things regularly.
7. **Digital Cues:** Schedule your computer, cell phone or other digital devices to send you reminders of what you wish to accomplish on a daily or weekly basis. Numerous programs exist to remind and also to help you monitor what you eat, how much and in what kind of physical activity you engage, and how you feel after doing these.
8. **Scheduling Cues:** The paradox is that many of us take better care of cars than ourselves. Treat your daily health-related decisions like necessary maintenance rather than choices and put them in your appointment book or computer datebook to provide automatic reminders.

What works for you is likely to be different than what works for another person. Use the worksheet on the next page to help brainstorm cues you can use and come up with plans to incorporate them into your daily life.

WORKSHEET: Your Healthful Behavior Cues

Review the list on the previous page and then use the chart below to brainstorm cues you can use to promote your health goals and develop actionable plans to incorporate these cues into your life. How can you place these cues to create cravings for wellness activities? Bombard yourself with advertising for activities for a healthier you.

Type of cue	What are the desired cue(s)?	Where will the cue(s) be?	What will the cue(s) trigger?

Exercise 1D: Researching Your Own Personalized Normative Feedback

A common intervention technique used to target both individuals and populations is to provide normative feedback; in other words, to look up facts and statistics for what is actually "normal" for similar individuals or in your community. One of the ways in which this method has been used is to decrease alcohol consumption on university and college campuses by providing data on the drinking rates for the "typical college student". The goal is to correct over- or underestimated social norms by demonstrating that unhealthful behaviors are not as common or healthful behaviors are more common than may have been believed. Of course, this plan can backfire and reinforce unhealthful behaviors if it turns out unhealthful behaviors are more common or healthful behaviors are less common than expected.

For this exercise, we cannot provide you with normative feedback without knowing your target behavior or the social norms of the communities in which you live. However, with the Internet at your fingertips, it should be easy to find some hard facts from respectable websites such as the Centers for Disease Control and Prevention (e.g. http://www.cdc.gov/HealthyLiving/) and the U.S. Department of Health and Human Services (e.g. http://www.hhs.gov/safety/index.html). You may be able to look up more local data for you state, county or city as well. You can either look up the unhealthful behavior you wish to decrease (e.g., smoking) to show it is less common than you or your client think or look up the healthful behavior you wish to increase (e.g., exercise) to show it is more common than you or your client think.

Here are some questions to consider when researching normative habits:

- What percentage of people engages in this behavior?
- How often do people typically engage in the behavior?
- How much do to people typically engage in the behavior (e.g., number of cigarettes)?
- What are the success rates of quitting (or starting) this behavior?
- What are the health consequences (or the health benefits) of this behavior?
- What is the average life expectancy of people who do (or do not) engage in this behavior?

Feel free to add to the list. What would change your mind about a health behavior? When considering the questions above and any others you may generate, we encourage you to jot down your own guesses about the correct answers before looking up the actual data. You may be surprised to see how much your social norms have biased your perceptions of certain behaviors.

Exercise 1E: Identifying Social Enablers versus Disablers

It is not uncommon for people in close relationships to discover that their spouse or partner is unwittingly sabotaging efforts to help achieve a health-related goal. That social influence may be even greater when it comes in social situations. For example, the social norm of finishing one's plate, of eating more when in groups, of eating more when in restaurants and of eating all of what is served, pits social norms against individual healthy choices. However, social pressure can also support healthy choices. Working out with others who support and enjoy similar healthful activities promotes greater physical activity, more opportunities to work out, longer participation and greater enjoyment.

Consider a health behavior you want to change, and then think about times that you feel pressured or tend to do the behavior in social situations. Are there specific social situations where you do or do not feel pressure to do the behavior? If so, what? Are there specific people that encourage or discourage you to do the behavior? If so, who? Brainstorm situations and people that encourage you to continue your bad habit.

Part 1: Situations That Encourage Bad Behaviors

To get you thinking, here are some social situations that tend to encourage bad behaviors in some people:

1) When I'm around someone I want to impress who does the bad habit.
2) When I'm around family or old friends who expect me to act like my old self.
3) When I'm celebrating.
4) When I'm around someone who is really nice to me when I make mistakes or feel bad.
5) When I'm around someone who benefits when I do bad behaviors.
6) When everyone else is doing the bad habit.

Now write some social situations in which you have trouble with a health behavior here:

____

____

____

____

Pick one of the social situations when you have trouble acting healthfully. Consider ways in which you can either avoid being in the situation or, more likely, act differently in the situation. Think of new things you could say or do when you feel pressured to do your bad habit. Find a supportive friend and role-play the situation. Practice these new responses so they seem easy and natural when you are in the real situation.

Part 2: People That Encourage Good Behaviors

Consider ways in which you might be able use social support to improve health-related activities. Are there people who encourage your healthful behaviors? What could loved ones, friends or colleagues do to support your healthful behavior? How might you encourage your social contacts to support you? To get you thinking, here are some ways you may increase support from existing social contacts:

1) Include friends in your attempt to change behavior (e.g. quitting smoking or going to the gym together).
2) Express your appreciation for their support, letting them know how important this change is for your health and well-being.
3) Encourage them to reward your good behavior.
4) Find new contacts that already do or encourage your new healthful behavior.

Now brainstorm some ways you can deploy social support to enhance your goals to change your health behavior:

____

____

____

____

Exercise 1F: Visualizing Social Networks that Enable and Disable Health-Related Habits

It is far easier to attain goals of fitness, weight, and managing difficult emotions when you have others who support you and who actively participate with you; for example, exercising together, eating the same healthful diet, or having emotionally intelligent discussions about feelings of anger, anxiety or sadness.

As we have discussed, social interactions can contribute substantially to overvaluation of unhealthful behavior or undervaluation of healthful behavior. Identifying unhealthful behavior patterns in your family or social network can help you modify or reframe social interactions to make it easier for you to keep up more healthful behaviors.

For many people, it is easier to recognize patterns of social interaction and behavior when they are described visually. Drawing out connections between people that include their nature and quality can help describe a family or social network. You can then add symbols or codes to represent whether each person has a given behavior or health concern, and how they react to your behavior. The resulting pictures may give you a sense of the networks that do and do not support a given behavior pattern. This can help you identify existing social support for your healthful behavior. It can also warn you of groups or situations where it is likely that you will be encouraged to act unhealthfully.

Part 1: Informal Visualization

Draw an informal visualization using a simple set of symbols that you make up. For example, if I (J.T.) wanted to identify support for a vegetarian diet in my family, I could draw a family tree to 1) color code the symbols to indicate each person's behavior and 2) draw lines to indicate their support for my diet. In the box on the next page, I go through this exercise to create a visual representation of the familial support I do or do not receive for my vegetarian diet. Each square represents a male family member, each circle a female family member. The colors inside the symbols indicate what each family member eats. The black lines indicate family relationships as done in a standard family tree. The colored, dashed lines indicate the reactions I tend to get from family members regarding the lack of meat in my diet. I am the green circle at the bottom right.

As you can see, my husband, my son, one of my sisters, and one of my first cousins are vegetarian. Another first cousin is pescaterian, vegetarian plus fish. We are all very supportive of each others' diets and work together to ensure family dinners include vegetarian options. My other sister and first cousin both eat standard meat-heavy diets, but are supportive of other diets and consider others' food needs when we get together. My parents, grandparents, aunt and uncle all eat meat-heavy diets but vary in their reactions. My father and grandparents seem somewhat incapable of even acknowledging that we do not eat meat. They regularly try to put meat on our plates, include meat in vegetable dishes, and make comments indicating distaste for our diets. My mother and uncle are verbally supportive as long as we do not try to make them eat what we are eating. My aunt is mostly supportive, but sometimes expresses concern that we might be damaging our health.

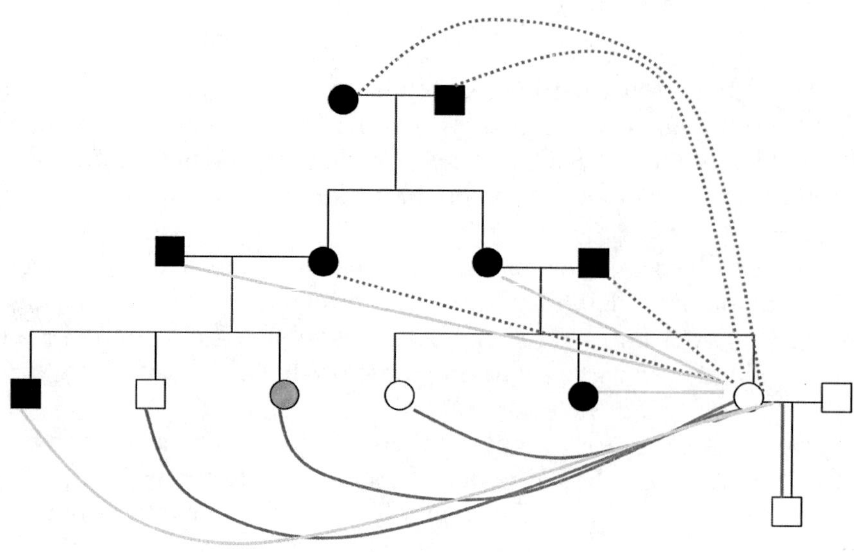

<u>Shape Codes (Gender)</u>
Circle – Female
Square – Male

<u>Shape Color Codes (Diet)</u>
White– Vegetarian
Gray – Pescaterian (i.e. vegetarian plus fish consumption)
Black – Omnivore

<u>Line Color Codes (Support Level)</u>
Solid – supportive – only eat vegetarian or express support for diet
Dashed – not supportive – express concerns about or distain for vegetarian diet

This diagram clearly indicates social support within my family that helps me eat vegetarian, and warns about potential pressure from older generations that may make it more difficult to follow my health choices.

In making such informal visualizations, you should feel free to describe connections between people in whatever way you think makes most sense. If you were interested in relationships at your work, you could start by using the floor plan of your office to describe how people in your building interact. Alternatively, you could draw out supervisory hierarchies to initially describe relationships (like the black lines on the family tree) and then indicate less formal relationships or behavioral interactions between individuals (like the colored lines on the family tree). Another possibility would be to simply draw connections between each person that talks to each other. These lines could be color coded to show the type of interaction (e.g. friendship, supervisor, job partnership). You should feel free to be creative in drawing up maps of social connections and their relationship to health behavior. Follow your instinct in choosing what you think is important to include.

Try drawing a picture of social interactions around a target behavior of your choice. On the next page, first brainstorm your coding system then sketch your visualization using that coding system. Which people do you want to include and on what dimensions do they vary (e.g., how they are connected, whether they do the behavior, level of support)?

Coding System:

____

____

____

____

____

Visualization:

Look at your visualization. Are there parts of your network that appear more supportive of healthful behavior? Are their groups of people you may need to be very careful around? Do you need to reach out and seek additional support?

Part 2: Formal Visualization

There are several more formal techniques for assessing interconnections between people and their relationship to health or behavior. These techniques are used by scientists and health professionals to depict and study interpersonal relationships and their impact. There are software programs to help draw and analyze these relationships, and they use relatively standard symbols and structures to indicate relationships and behavior. If you are interested in using these more formal techniques, below are some links that describe these techniques (specifically, genograms and social network), and examples of software programs available to help draw, build and analyze these social interconnections.

Genograms
http://www.genopro.com/genogram/
GenoPro is a software program for drawing family trees and genograms. Genograms are family trees with additional information about relationships, behaviors or diseases included. This website does a good job of describing and showing examples of genograms and links directly to their software product if you are interested in using it.

Social Network Analysis
http://en.wikipedia.org/wiki/Social_network
Wikipedia provides a nice overview of social network analysis to get you oriented to its use, techniques and tools.

http://www.analytictech.com/networks
This website includes a description of various types of social network analysis, history of social network analysis, and detailed information on how to collect data, depict it, and analyze it. There are links to software programs to help if you are interested.

Exercise 1G: Modifying the Thoughts that Undermine Our Goals: The Power of Cognitive Restructuring or Reframing

How much we value healthful versus unhealthful behaviors is greatly influenced by our thoughts and expectations about the situation and our behavior. Psychologists have developed exercises to help people recognize when they are having thoughts that encourage or overvalue unhealthful behaviors or discourage or undervalue healthful behaviors. Once you recognize these thoughts, then you can evaluate them to determine whether or not they are accurate and helpful. When you identify unhelpful thought patterns, you can develop and practice alternative thoughts that lead to more balanced, healthful decisions.

Practices that help you identify unhelpful thought patterns and develop new helpful patterns are typically called cognitive restructuring or reframing. You can find many examples of these exercises in self-help or therapy manuals that use a cognitive-behavioral perspective. In this exercise, we will provide a general example of cognitive restructuring for changing health behavior. If you are have trouble relating this exercise to your own problem, you may find it helpful to look at exercises in a self-help or therapy manual written specifically for the health problem you are experiencing. These manuals will include specific examples of thoughts and expectations that are commonly held by people with that health problem (e.g. Burns, 1989; Antony & Swinson, 2008).

To begin, we will walk you through three steps of the restructuring or reframing process. During the exercise, we provide two different worksheets to assist you in the process. We use examples throughout so that you will have a sense of how to tackle your own health behavior goal.

Step 1: Identify Unhelpful Thoughts

In order to change thoughts that overvalue unhealthful or undervalue healthful behaviors, you first need to be aware of your own unhelpful thought patterns. It is essential to know precisely what thoughts you return to in given situations and how they influence your feelings and behavior. Often thoughts occur automatically and go by without notice. By monitoring your thoughts, feelings, and behavior in various circumstances, you can identify thoughts that encourage bad behaviors.

It can be difficult to accurately remember thoughts even immediately after you have them, let alone specific thoughts you had days or weeks ago. Thus, the first step is to develop an accurate and consistent method of monitoring your thoughts around your target health behavior. We provide you with a Thought Monitoring Form that you can use to record the thoughts you have about your target health problem, along with information about (1) when or in what situation you had the thoughts, (2) what your behavioral response was in that situation, (3) what happened when you did that behavior, and (4) the thoughts you had about the outcome of your behavior. Once you have a record of the thoughts you have habitually, the contexts in which you have them, and their impact on your health behaviors, then it will be possible to begin to evaluate their accuracy and change them if they are unhelpful.

Spend the next several days to weeks monitoring thoughts you have associated with your target health behavior in various situations. Record your observations in the Thought Monitoring Form, and take special care to record thoughts that you have repeatedly. We will come back to evaluate your records in Step 2.

Example: J.T.'s thought monitoring about sticking to her low-carbohydrate gestational diabetes diet.

Situation	Thoughts	Behavior	Consequences	Thoughts
I really want dessert and my husband and son are eating ice cream.	"I already had to skip the pasta and bread at dinner and now I can't have any ice cream either. It isn't fair. Pregnancy is miserable. I hate being a woman. Everyone around me is completely inconsiderate for eating carbohydrates all the time."	Feel bad for myself. Complain to my family about being pregnant. Notice all of the other unpleasant pregnancy sensations I am having.	Upset my husband and son by making them feel guilty about my being pregnant and anxious about my complaints. Make all my pregnancy symptoms seem more severe.	"I'm a terrible wife and mother. I wish I could go into hibernation until this pregnancy is over. I never want to be pregnant again."

WORKSHEET: Thought Monitoring Form

<u>Directions:</u> What were the automatic thoughts that occurred when you were considering your target health behavior? What did you do in response to your thoughts? What was the consequence of your action? And finally, what were your thoughts after the consequence of your action?

Date:

Situation	Thoughts	Behavior	Consequences	Thoughts

Date:

Situation	Thoughts	Behavior	Consequences	Thoughts

Date:

Situation	Thoughts	Behavior	Consequences	Thoughts

Date:

Situation	Thoughts	Behavior	Consequences	Thoughts

Notes & Observations:

Step 2: Identify Cognitive Errors

David Burns, MD (1989) devised a chart of common cognitive errors that he observed in his clients. W.G. adds a parallel set of cognitive errors that may be found in individuals who fail to take action to address a health risk. Below are two tables with these errors. People tend to make these thinking mistakes in general and sometimes being stressed and tired can make people more prone to them. I (J.T.) have included examples to go along with my low-carbohydrate gestational diabetes diet example from above. After reviewing the two tables of common cognitive errors, consider your Thought Monitoring Form. Are they biased by these thinking errors? Note thoughts and situations on your Thought Monitoring Form where you think you may be making these thinking errors.

Common Cognitive Errors (after Burns, 1989) and Examples During Attempts at Behavior Change (i.e. J.T.)

Thinking Error	Description	Example
Overgeneralization	Assuming that the outcome from a specific event or situation will occur in a large range of situations.	"Everyone else gets to eat whatever they want during pregnancy. I fail every medical screening test I'm given. I must be some sort of freak."
Catastrophizing	Focusing only on the worst, most extreme possibility regardless of how likely it is to occur.	"If my blood glucose levels are a little over target, I'll set my daughter up for a dangerous birth and a life of fighting obesity, diabetes and cardiovascular risk."
All-or-None Thinking	Focusing on only the extreme "best" or "worst" of a situation without regard to the full range of alternatives.	"If I can't eat exactly what I'm craving, I cannot enjoy anything I eat."
Jumping to Conclusions	Interpreting a situation with limited information and without a rational evaluation of its likelihood.	"Since he hasn't called back, my doctor must be avoiding me because he thinks I'm a hopeless case."
Selective Attention	Selectively attending to negative aspects of a situation while ignoring any positive aspects.	"Pregnancy messes up my normal diet, makes me tired, unable to do my normal exercise, gives me back aches, and generally ruins my body."
Negative Predictions	Assuming the worst will happen in a situation.	"If I don't perfectly follow health recommendations, my baby will die, be really sick, or hate me for the rest of my life."
Mind Reading	Assuming what people are thinking instead of finding out what they are really thinking.	"My husband wants to get away from me when I'm complaining about my pregnancy because he doesn't love me anymore and doesn't want the baby."

There are other categories of maladaptive thinking that occur in those reluctant to change behaviors that are also worth exploring. In this case, let us consider cognitive errors that might have stopped me from managing my gestational diabetes.

Additional Cognitive Errors (proposed by W.G.) and Examples That May Prevent Attempts to Modify Health Behavior (i.e. J.T.)

Thinking Error	Description	Example
Denial	Assuming that the outcome from a past set of events will not occur in the future.	"Just because my body couldn't process the glucose in the lab test doesn't mean I have a problem. The lab test is totally artificial. I'm healthy, I'm sure my body will handle sugar fine when I eat normal meals."
Positive Illusions	Assuming that things are fine in spite of significant evidence to the contrary.	"Although my doctors say I'm at high risk of pregnancy complications and I've screened positive for gestational diabetes on two lab tests, I don't need to change my eating patterns. I've never had health problems before."
Indecisiveness	Concluding that there are too many possible scenarios to make a decision or take action.	"There are so many different foods, I couldn't possibly keep track of how much sugar there is in each. Why even try to make low-carbohydrate meals when I'm sure to make mistakes?"
Rumination	Continuing to gather information or recycle one's thoughts without being able to determine when enough has been gathered to make a decision.	"Maybe I should get back on the internet and read more about this disorder. Each clinician told me slightly different ways of managing my diabetes. I clearly need more information to determine which is really the perfect strategy."
Helplessness	Assuming that you have no control over the problem and thus there is no point in trying to fix it.	"This is just one more example of my miserable genetic inheritance. You can't change what you were born with, so why bother to fight my biology?"

Step 3: Generating New and More Helpful Thoughts

After you have identified mistakes in your thought patterns, the next step is to come up with new more helpful thoughts to correct them and support more healthful behaviors.

To generate these new thoughts, it can help to look at your specific thoughts more closely and challenge the logic behind each one. Is the thought based on facts or assumptions? It can be helpful to check the accuracy of the facts and assumptions included in your thoughts. Oftentimes a quick Internet search of good medical websites can help correct false beliefs that can lead to inaccurate thoughts and thinking errors. Below is a table with example questions to help you challenge your thought patterns. Challenge the thoughts in your Thought Monitoring Form with these questions and note places where they might be wrong and ideas for other ways of thinking about the situation.

Challenge	Specific Questions
What is the evidence?	What is the evidence to support these thoughts, assumptions, or conclusions?
What are the alternative views?	Are there other ways to think about the situation? How might someone else view this situation? If this were happening to someone else, how would you view it?
Is the thinking narrow?	Are there other aspects of the situation that you are ignoring? If you pay attention to other things going on at the same time would you think about it differently or see different ways of responding?
Is the thinking distorted?	Are you only attending to the dark side of things? Are you assuming that you can do absolutely nothing to change things?
What action can you take?	Where does thinking like this get you? If you thought something different or had a different response, how would that change the situation? What can you do to change the situation or how you feel?

Lastly, you can use the Cognitive Restructuring Form to systematically respond to your unhelpful thoughts by first identifying the specific situation, then tracking your immediate thoughts, identify the cognitive errors involved, imagining the outcome that will ensue if you engage in those thoughts, and then generating alternate coping thoughts that will help you avoid the undesirable outcome and engage in the healthful one. On the next page, we provide a sample of the worksheet that continues with J.T.'s low-carbohydrate gestational diabetes diet. On the page following that, we provide the blank worksheet for your use.

Example of the Cognitive Restructuring Form

Situation: I am pregnant, have been diagnosed with gestational diabetes, and have been put on a very low carbohydrate diet and strict blood glucose monitoring schedule to prevent birth complications and reduce health risks for my baby. I know the diet is important and that even little indulgences will throw my blood glucose off substantially. However, I really want dessert and my husband and son are eating ice cream in front of me.

Immediate Thoughts:

1) "If my husband and son really cared about me, they wouldn't eat anything that I'm supposed to avoid."

Type of Thinking Error: Mind Reading

Outcome: Frustrated at the fact that my husband and son are enjoying the ice cream I crave, I become angry watching them. I yell at them for having horrible health habits, being gluttonous and never taking my feelings into account. They get upset and try to avoid me for the rest of the evening.

Coping Thought: "My husband and son don't need to try to be me to care about me. They are different people. My husband and son have no metabolic problems, exercised a ton while I sat at work, and they love ice cream. Having a little is fine for them. There are lots of treats I can have that won't hurt my health and I should make choices that are good for me."

2) "Pregnancy is tiring and stressful and ice cream would make me feel better. I deserve to be spoiled. If I don't get ice cream, I'll feel punished."

hours and I feel guilty and terrible for not taking care of my developing daughter.

Type of Thinking Error: All-or-None Thinking

Outcome: Frustrated at the perceived unfairness of the situation, I start to rationalize why I deserve ice cream and why sticking to the diet isn't that important. I give in to my craving and down a big bowl of ice cream in minutes. My blood glucose goes way above target for

Coping Thought: "Pregnancy is stressful and it is important that I feel cared for and have ways to deal with stress. But ice cream is a bad choice. I should do something else that is nice for me."

3) "This diet is a challenge, but it is important to keep my pregnancy and future daughter safe."

Type of Thinking Error: This is not an error in thinking; it's realistic.

Outcome: Recognizing the importance of the diet and my need to not feel deprived, I walk away from the table and make myself a pot of my favorite herbal tea. When I return with my warm, tasty cup of non-carbohydrate-containing tea, I'm content enough to enjoy the moment with my husband and son. They tell me fun stories from their day at the museum.

Coping Thought: "What can I do to take care of myself and my feelings and stick to my diet?"

WORKSHEET: Cognitive Restructuring Form

Directions: In the space provided, write out the situation where you found yourself having negative thoughts. List the negative thinking errors and replace them with coping thoughts. Write the likely outcome with both negative thinking errors as well as more realistic, coping thoughts.

Situation:____

Immediate Thoughts:

1) ____

Type of Thinking Error:

Outcome:

Coping Thought:

2) ____

Type of Thinking Error:

Outcome:

Coping Thought:

3) ____

Type of Thinking Error:

Outcome:

Coping Thought:

4) ____

Type of Thinking Error:

Outcome:

Coping Thought:

Notes & Observations:

Exercise 1H: Turning Values and Goals into a Plan of Action

How do we recognize thoughts and behaviors that are do not align with our values and goals? A first step is to be aware of our own values and goals. While we all have values and goals, we may not have thought about them and laid them out explicitly. If our values and goals are only hazy concepts, we may be less likely to factor them into our decisions. Taking time to identify and describe our values and goals can help us get started towards making choices that lead toward our dreams.

Recognizing the relationships between your specific thoughts and behaviors and your values and goals can help you reevaluate the benefits and costs of those thoughts and behaviors and potentially motivate change. Doing this, of course, requires that you are aware of your own values and goals. Only then can you start to consider whether your behaviors are helpful or contradictory to the things you are trying to achieve.

Step 1: Identifying Your Values

Psychologists and life coaches have come up with a variety of exercises to help you think about and identify your values. The main goal of these exercises is to help you consider what matters to you and what you value about yourself. It is fine to simply brainstorm on your own and write down what you think. Alternatively, you may find some of the thought exercises are helpful for identifying values that are important to you.

Allport-Vernon Classification

The Allport-Vernon classification of values (Allport et al., 1970) categorizes six major types of values and was designed to help people explore their own tendency toward different domains. Conspicuously missing from this classification is the value of Health, to which the attainment of all other objectives is secondary. Without our health, we are not fully functioning in our capacity to engage with and follow through on our personal values. However, the framework may still be useful to in identifying some of your own values and goals. The classifications are as follows:

1. Theoretical: Interest in the discovery of truth through reasoning and systematic thinking.
2. Economic: Interest in usefulness and practicality, including the accumulation of wealth.
3. Aesthetic: Interest in beauty, form and artistic harmony.
4. Social: Interest in people and human relationships.
5. Political: Interest in gaining power and influencing other people.
6. Religious: Interest in unity and understanding the cosmos as a whole.

You can explore your values in these areas by taking the online test at:
http://webspace.ship.edu/cgboer/valuestest.html

Thought Experiments

Additionally, we have generated some thought experiments to help you make a list of values that you feel play some role in your life. You may find it helpful to phrase your values in terms of "I" statements.

1. Imagine someone is going to give a speech about you in the future (e.g. a eulogy, a retirement party, a 50th wedding anniversary party, an 85th birthday party). What would you like them to say about you? How do you hope they see you and your life accomplishments? What matters to you most?

2. List 5 people you highly admire. Why do you admire them? What do they have in common? What aspects of these people lives or behaviors do you wish to share? What about these people do you value?

3. Pretend you are writing a resume for a dream job of your own design. What will you do in your dream job? What will you accomplish? What will your day-to-day work look like? What makes you perfect for this job? What do you want a prospective employer to know about you?

4. Imagine you could achieve your "best self," whatever that means to you. How would you live your life? What would you seek to accomplish for yourself and for others?

Step 2: Prioritizing Your Values

Once you have generated an initial list, it is important to prioritize the values you identified. Often your values will be competing for time, energy, and resources. Understanding which values are more important to you will help you design goals and action plans that avoid compromising one value to achieve another one. In this step, we will attempt to order our values based on their personal importance.

To start, let's say I (J.T.) came up with this list of personal values after doing the exercises above:
I am healthy.
I am surrounded by happy people.
I am learning new things.
I am making the world a better place.
I can provide for myself and my family.
I am not wasting resources.

Now consider these values in pairs, and think about what you would do if you had to choose between them. Go through each pair and mark the one that you would favor if you had to choose between them. For example, if forced to choose between being healthy and being surrounded by happy people, I would choose to be healthy around grumpy folks. So I would give one point to "I am healthy". If forced to choose between being healthy and learning new things, I again would choose to be healthy and stuck with my current knowledge and abilities. So I would give a second point to "I am healthy." After going through all the comparisons on the list, add up the points given to each pair of comparisons. This should clarify how you prioritize the values in your life. Although all of the values you list may be important to you, life requires choosing between them at various points. By understanding how you choose between your priorities, you can better predict places where your values may contradict and avoid creating goals and action plans that pit one value against another one.

For example, consider my (J.T.'s) choices in graduate school. While in graduate school, I had virtually endless opportunities to learn new things. There were always seminars on exciting new topics, and evening classes about new fields I never even considered. I could always keep working on my own research projects, carrying out experiments to give me answers to questions I identified. Graduate school was like a candy store for my inner nerd and I was a shameless binge eater. As encouraged by my program, I began graduate school focused on that one value (i.e. learning new things), but found myself getting more and more unhappy over time. I eventually got to the point that I did not really want to be in graduate school at all. Recognizing that I did not feel well and was not paying close attention to my health, I made some changes in my priorities, goals and behaviors to reflect my high priority on being healthy. I made myself leave the school at 5:00 to go work out at the gymnastics gym down the street. I stopped going to evening classes with less than nutritious dinners and started cooking for myself every night. With these changes, I was much happier, healthier and still learning new things, perhaps slightly more slowly, but now not at the expense of my other values. By recognizing the priorities among my values, I was able to fix my goals and behaviors so that they were in line with my values and their relative importance to me.

This example not only demonstrates the importance of prioritizing values, but also in developing goals and action plans that match these values. Just knowing that I care more about being healthy than learning new things does not help unless I come up with concrete goals and plans for becoming healthy that I can carry out in my life. Clarifying my values told me what I needed to focus on, but goal-setting and action planning was required to turn that into specific changes in behavior (i.e. going to the gym at 5:00 and cooking my own dinners). Thus, after you have clarified your goals it is essential that you take what you find and turn to the process of goal-setting.

Step 3: Turning Your Values into Goals and Action Plans

While your values may be conceptual, hazy and subjective in nature, it is important that your goals and action plans are concrete and measurable. Goals need to be specific and objective so that you can determine how to achieve them and when they have been met. As you develop a goal and an action plan to meet that goal, focus on making the goals and action plans specific, feasible, doable and verifiable. What exactly do you want to achieve? Is that goal something you could realistically achieve? Is there a behavior you could do to bring you closer to achieving your goal? Is there a way for you to know (1) when you have done the helpful behavior and (2) when you have achieved your goal? If your goals and action plans meet these criteria, then they will be useful in helping you live according to your values.

We provide you with an Action Plan worksheet to help guide you in developing a goal and an action plan to meet it. It will also help you document your goals and plans so that you are more likely to stick to the plan, and help you when you encounter problems. On the next page is a sample worksheet that describes a goal and action plan to help me (J.T.) meet my value of "being healthy". On the page following that is a blank worksheet. After you read through the example, pick one of your values and use the worksheet to develop a goal and action plan to help you live according to that value.

Sample Action Plan

The healthful change I want to make is: to eat more fruits and vegetables

My goal for next month is: to start every dinner with a salad or vegetable dish

The steps I will take to achieve my goal are (what, when, where, how much, how often):
1. I will go to the local farmer's market on Saturday and purchase fruits and vegetables for these salads/dishes for the upcoming week.
2. I will prepare a salad or vegetable dish for each dinner.
3. I will not eat anything else for dinner until I finish my serving of the salad or vegetable dish.

The things that could make it difficult to achieve my goal include: I do not have a lot of experience making tasty salads or vegetable dishes. It could be hard to think of things to make or decide what and how much to buy at the farmer's market.

My plan for overcoming these difficulties includes: I will purchase several cookbooks with seasonal recipes for salads and vegetable dishes. Before I go to the farmer's market, I will pick at least three recipes a week to try and will write down the ingredients.

Support/resources I will need to achieve my goal include: I will need time to go shopping on Saturday, so my family should not schedule other things that require my help during that time. Also, it would be helpful to have my family's support regarding eating more vegetables for dinner. It will be harder to stick to the goal if they complain about the food at every dinner. I will talk with them about my goal and see if they wish to help in choosing recipes, preparing food and shopping.

My confidence level (scale from 0-10, 10 being completely confident that you can achieve the entire plan): 7

What can you do to increase your confidence? If I find difficulty in following this plan then I will re-assess it after two weeks. I can change it to 2 recipes a week or invite a friend who is more experienced at preparing these dishes to help me learn how to make them. I know that if I keep revising the action plan I can make it work.

Plan for feedback and monitoring:

> How will you monitor actions? I will write down our dinner menu every night in a notebook.
>
> When will your actions be reviewed? My best friend (who is attempting the same action plan) and I will meet once a week to review our successes and failures, problem-solve difficulties and share solutions.

WORKSHEET: Action Plan

The healthful change I want to make is:

My goal for next month is:

The steps I will take to achieve my goal are (what, when, where, how much, how often):

The things that could make it difficult to achieve my goal include:

My plan for overcoming these difficulties includes:

Support/resources I will need to achieve my goal include:

My confidence level (scale from 0-10, 10 being completely confident that you can achieve the entire plan):

What can you do to increase your confidence?

Plan for feedback and monitoring:

How will you monitor actions?

When will your actions be reviewed?

Adapted from Jason M. Satterfield, Ph.D., University of California at San Francisco. Action plan forms in English, Spanish and Chinese can be downloaded at: http://www.familymedicine.medschool.ucsf.edu/community_service/actionPlan.aspx

Brain Challenge #2

Enriching Your Life to Tame the Need for Immediate Gratification

Challenge Introduction

I can't get no satisfaction
I can't get no satisfaction
'Cause I try and I try
And I try and I try. . .

In the song, "(I Can't Get No) Satisfaction," Mick Jagger laments his ability to find contentment while noting that he attempts to do so repeatedly ("Cause I try, and I try, and I try and I try") despite the futility. As is often the case, artists first express what scientists later explain. When we are deprived of opportunities to make life better, we are programmed to start compulsively, and even obsessively searching for immediate relief. We try, and try, and try, and try to feel better right now, neglecting all the things we need to do to create a healthful, productive, enriched life in the Future. Like the singer, many who find satisfaction elusive will become focused on feeling better in the Now. They may develop a mentality that the only thing worth working for is something that benefits them immediately.

When you are down and out, the promise of instant gratification is likely to outweigh the hope of a better future in return for years of work towards an education, job, family, or network of impressed colleagues. When a person is not sure that he can take care of his short-term needs – when his brain perceives his life as impoverished – his brain will rewire to be impulsive and focused on immediate gratification.

Humans have adapted to survive in a wide variety of physical and social environments. We may hold high status in our community or have abundant food and resources available. Alternatively, we may have low social status or live in an environment where the goods we need to survive are difficult to obtain. Our ability to shift our focus between immediate and longer-term needs contributes to our adaptability. But when we live in an environment where even those of low social status have high access to calorie-rich foods, rewarding drugs, emotionally arousing media, and sexually explicit images, the tendency to seek immediate gratification when we are relatively-deprived can lead to serious health and social problems.

Our ability to change our behavior depending on the prevalence of social and physical resources is key to our adaptability. A king and a serf would likely react differently to being offered a loaf of day-old bread. Similarly, a welfare mom would be more likely to agree to clean toilets for $50 than would a bank CEO. Sir Mick Jagger, who has secured over a billion dollars in royalties, versus Mick Jagger, the starving musician, no longer needs to compulsively seek immediate gratification. In Challenge #2, we will discuss ways to reprogram our brains to be less focused on immediate gratification, allowing us to put more effort into opportunities with longer-term benefit. In Chapter 2.1, we explain how medium spiny (MS) neurons in the nucleus accumbens hold back habits and play a key role in impulse control, what happens when these neurons are weak, and how they become strengthened. In Chapter 2.2, we present various ways in which you can enrich your life so your brain detects more opportunities and strengthens MS neurons. In

Chapter 2.3, we discuss how individuals differ biologically in their ability to strengthen MS neurons and how these differences can increase risk for addiction, mood disorders and obesity. Understanding the biological underpinnings of impulse control and need for immediate gratification will allow you to shape your environment to fit your biology.

Chapter 2.1: Reining in Maladaptive Habits: Strengthening Impulse Control

When you have lots of opportunities to make your life better, you can be picky. You can act on only those opportunities that offer a large pay-off for minimal work, and still obtain all you need. You can afford to bypass opportunities that provide short-term benefits but cause long-term problems. For example, you could turn down that fast-food burger and ask your personal chef to prepare a gourmet grilled vegetable sandwich and salad instead. When opportunities are sparse, however, you need to quickly and consistently act to take advantage of whatever opportunities are present. If it is likely that you will not have other options, then you had better accept the low-paying job and lunch on the burger and fries, despite your doctor's recommendations.

Our brains are wired to adapt our behavior to rewarding opportunities in our environments without our having to be conscious of this logic with each new opportunity. Our reward system keeps track of how many opportunities we encounter, and adjusts our responses appropriately. When opportunities are rare, our reward system becomes very excitable and works very hard for immediate rewards. When opportunities are plentiful, our reward system becomes slow and sluggish, leaving decisions to act to other parts of the brain, such as the prefrontal cortex. Only large rewards are sufficient to drive us to work for immediate rewards. Thus, living in a world that seems to offer few opportunities will increase your drive for immediate gratification and encourage automatic reward-driven behaviors. Conversely, living in a resource-rich world will lead to choices that are made more deliberately by brain circuits that consider long-term benefits and consequences as well as short-term rewards and punishments.

By now, you may be wondering: what rewards will I obtain from reading this chapter—why bother? Our answer is that we will show you how to become less impulsive and improve your control over your habits by increasing the number of ways your brain can find "satisfaction", enriching your life, challenging your mind, and recognizing new opportunities. This will free you to focus on your long-term goals.

Understanding neural control of your inner monster

In Challenge #1, we discussed the function of dopamine neurons that project to the nucleus accumbens, showing how they deliver information about the value of opportunities for immediate reward. We discussed the importance of training your dopamine neurons to accurately value health opportunities. Now we will consider the function of the nucleus accumbens neurons, a collection of neurons in the striatum, a brain region thought to play an important role in reward, pleasure, addiction, aggression, fear and the placebo effect.

Your nucleus accumbens neurons hold the reins on your reward-seeking habits. They control whether or not you habitually act when provided a chance for immediate gratification. If you have a strong grip on the reins, you will tame your habits. You can think of your nucleus accumbens as a door to the striatum – the dopamine neurons come knocking with a reward opportunity and the nucleus accumbens decides whether or not to let the striatum release the habit to perform the behavior and receive the reward. While you may still act out of habit when a really valuable opportunity arises, your nucleus accumbens neurons will slow down your reward system's habitual responses and give the rest of your brain time to consider other options. But if these nucleus accumbens neurons are weak, your habits will be given free rein, and you will seek immediate gratification at nearly every opportunity. The puff of the cigarette, the sip of alcohol, the extra cup of coffee, the extra bite out of that cookie, the giving in to social pressure, are held in check by circuits located in the nucleus accumbens and striatum.

Since the neurobiology of this system is fairly complex, it is helpful to have a clear image of the process before getting into the details (see the Figure on page 91 for further details). Functionally, the nucleus accumbens neurons listen to the information our dopamine neurons provide about the presence and value of reward opportunities. They inhibit reward-seeking habits that our striatum has learned and mastered, freeing us to act habitually only when worthwhile opportunities present themselves. Since this circuitry can be difficult to conceptualize in the abstract, we will share a somewhat ridiculous image that helps us remember how this system works.

Think of the striatum as Sesame Street's Cookie Monster™. Cookie Monster has mastered the art of obtaining and consuming cookies. Whenever there is a cookie to be had, he will aggressively find and consume it, unless he is restrained in some way. Without reins, Cookie Monster compulsively gobbles down cookies. Likewise, unless it is held back or inhibited, the striatum will seek out and obtain quick rewards at every opportunity using habitual behaviors we have learned. Your dopamine neurons provide the cookies that set the Cookie Monster into action. When your dopamine neurons fire, it is like tossing a cookie in front of the Cookie Monster. The more your dopamine neurons fire, the bigger the cookie. But the nucleus accumbens neurons hold the reins on the Cookie Monster, suppressing the striatum's habitual response. Because of how they look, these neurons are technically referred to as medium spiny (MS) neurons, but we prefer to think of them as monster suppression (MS) neurons.

These monster suppression (MS) neurons of the nucleus accumbens restrain Cookie Monster (the striatum). When they are strong, they hold Cookie Monster back and keep him from pursuing all but the best of the cookies. When they are weak, Cookie Monster runs free, impulsively pursuing all the cookies that the dopamine neurons throw his way. The striatum, originating in the reptilian brain, is capable of storing and retrieving habits we perform without much thought, including everyday addictions, such as munching on that cookie. If the nucleus accumbens neurons are weak then we may still act without much conscious thought, but if they are strong then they give our conscious brain regions a chance to remind us why we may not want to perform those habits, such as munching on a cookie.

FIGURE: Projections to and from the nucleus accumbens

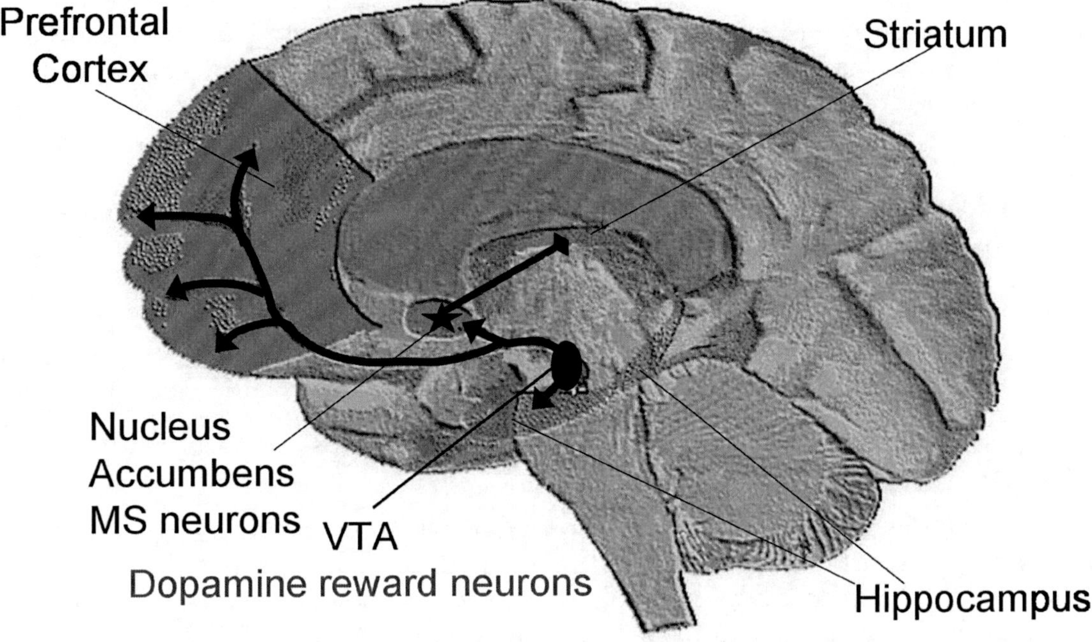

Legend: As we described in Challenge #1, the dopamine reward neurons in the VTA project to the limbic reward system and the prefrontal cortex (black arrows). These projections also go to the nucleus accumbens, located just anterior and superior to the amygdala, which determines how much work to put into seeking a potential reward. The MS neurons of the nucleus accumbens (depicted here as a black star with projections to the striatum) inhibit the behaviors of the striatum, the brain region that has learned and mastered our reward-seeking habits. In other words, if the striatum is the Cookie Monster then the nucleus accumbens neurons prevent the Cookie Monster from eating cookies all day long.

What makes MS neurons weak?

As you can imagine, strengthening your MS neurons will be helpful for getting compulsive unhealthful habits under control. If we are going to be around temptation all the time, we want to have good control over our Cookie Monster, or we will impulsively over-consume quick rewards, such as food, addictive drugs, social approval, or relief from pain or anxiety. With weak MS neurons, you would eat everything on your plate or drink the whole bottle of wine. You would be very sensitive to peer pressure and have trouble disappointing people even when it is not in everyone's best interest over the long-term. For example, you might have trouble telling your boss that you have to leave work on time today to make it to your class at the gym. You would have trouble persisting in uncomfortable social or physical situations, even when you know that the discomfort is a needed step towards an important goal. For example, with weak MS neurons you might find it hard to make it through the painful exercises in physical therapy, even when you understand the need to strengthen injured body parts to recover.

So what makes MS neurons weak? As Mick Jagger described, when we "can't get no satisfaction," we will "try and try and try and try" to get what we can. In other words, when we are not exposed to enough opportunities for immediate gratification we become more willing to take whatever we get and our MS neurons become weak. Only when a lot of opportunities are presented to the striatum do our MS neurons develop the strength to hold back reward-seeking habits. Only when lots of cookies are thrown in front of cookie monster do our MS neurons develop the strength to hold back reward-seeking habits. Notably, this strengthening is not limited to simply learning how to restrain ourselves in specific instances but changes how we respond to the prospect of immediate rewards in general. It is not simply learning how to restrain oneself in specific instances. When we are presented with enough cookies, our nucleus accumbens will develop the ability to hold back other habits as well. For example, if you were to expand your access to immediate rewards by learning better social networking skills, this should strengthen your MS neurons. This strength should make it easier for you to skip getting a second helping at dinner or keep going on a jog when your legs start to hurt a bit. Exposure to frequent and valuable options for immediate gratification will make us less impulsive over time. When our lives are enriched with the ability to take care of our immediate needs and solve our immediate problems, our MS neurons become powerful enough to keep our drive toward immediate gratification-seeking in check.

To fully understand how the sum total of reward experiences modifies our MS neurons and our responsiveness to opportunities for immediate gratification, it is important to further explain the underlying neurobiology. As we discussed, dopamine neurons that project to the nucleus accumbens indicate the value of opportunities for immediate reward through their firing rate. Because firing of dopamine neurons causes them to release dopamine, the amount of dopamine release in the nucleus accumbens over time provides information about the number and value of opportunities that you encountered recently. If you were to tally up how much dopamine was released in the nucleus accumbens, then the summary it provided would indicate the total value of all opportunities that you encountered in a given period. Our MS neurons do this tallying. MS neurons have special receptors that are activated when dopamine hits them. These special receptors are called D2 dopamine receptors. When dopamine activates D2 dopamine receptors, these receptors trigger changes in the responsiveness of the MS neurons. Specifically, they make these neurons fire more readily and make them harder to turn off (Dong et al., 2006). Thus, the total value of opportunities that you have recently encountered in your environment gets translated into the strength or excitability of these MS neurons (Trafton & Gifford, 2008). The more rewarding opportunities you encounter, the more difficult it is to turn off these neurons.

What do MS neurons do when they are on?

MS neurons are inhibitory, which means they prevent other neurons from firing. Specifically, these other neurons are the neurons they connect to in the striatum that encode well-trained or habitual motor programs. The striatum circuits have memorized all of the behaviors that you can do without thinking, like riding a bicycle, chewing gum while you walk, or eating while you watch television. Health-related habits are also part of the repertory, such as when you wake up in the morning and manage to brush your teeth without memory of having done so. In addition, there is evidence that the striatum is involved in processing rules for automatic speech. When someone says, “thank you” and you say, "you're welcome," your striatum circuits are involved (Dominey & Inui, 2009).

The key point is that in order for you to carry out a habitual behavior, you need to turn off this population of MS neurons so they can free the striatum to perform the habit. Firing of MS neurons prevents you from doing well-trained or habitual behaviors. Strengthening MS neurons so they fire more readily makes habitual behaviors harder to elicit.

What turns off MS neurons and releases habits?

This part is a little tricky. We described how over the long-term, firing of dopamine neurons strengthens the MS neurons, making them likely to fire more in the future. However, over the short-term, firing of dopamine neurons also causes the MS neurons to fire less. In an immediate sense, encountering an opportunity increases the chance that you will repeat a habitual behavior to try to get a quick reward (Taha & Fields, 2006). In other words, a reward opportunity immediately slows the firing of MS neurons, making it more likely that your striatum neurons do carry out a reward-seeking habit. But simultaneously, exposure to a reward opportunity changes the same neurons, strengthening them so that the next time you encounter a reward opportunity you will be less likely to work for an immediate reward. *While exposure to an opportunity may lead you to do a well-learned behavior to get that reward, this experience will also make you less prone to impulsive, short-term reward-driven behavior in the future.*

People often find it difficult to conceptualize a process like the one described for strengthening MS neurons, where the immediate effects favor a behavior but the longer-term effects reduce the chance that you redo that behavior. If you have trouble understanding the immediate versus the long-term changes produced when opportunities are encountered, think of weight lifting. When you lift weights, the immediate effect is to make you tired and thus weaker. So in the short-term, when you lift weights, you become less able to lift the weight and more likely to drop it as you continue. However, lifting the weight also encourages your muscles to grow and strengthen themselves, so that later, when you try to lift the weight again, it seems lighter and you are less likely to drop it. Using your muscles makes them tired and weaker in the short-term but at the same time strengthens them so that they will be less tired and weak if the same situation occurs again. The next time you lift weights, you will have to lift a greater amount of weight or do more repetitions to get as tired as you did the first time.

This is similar to what happens with your MS neurons. Let's imagine an opportunity worth $5.00 for an hour of work. The dopamine neurons presenting this value assessment to the MS neurons will 1) encourage immediate inhibition of the MS neurons, releasing your habitual behavior to get the reward of $5.00, and 2) encourage the MS neurons to get stronger so they will not be swayed by a reward for $5.00 in the future. Thus, the next time an opportunity for $5.00 for an hour of work comes along, it will be harder to turn off your MS neurons, and you will be less likely to do your habitual behavior to get the $5.00. Now it may take an offer of $5.10 for an hour of work to release the behavior, the same way you would need to lift a greater amount of weight or do more repetitions to get as tired as you did the first time. Your MS neurons have gotten stronger, and will now only release habits for more valuable opportunities.

FIGURE: How MS neurons projecting to the striatum withhold or release habits

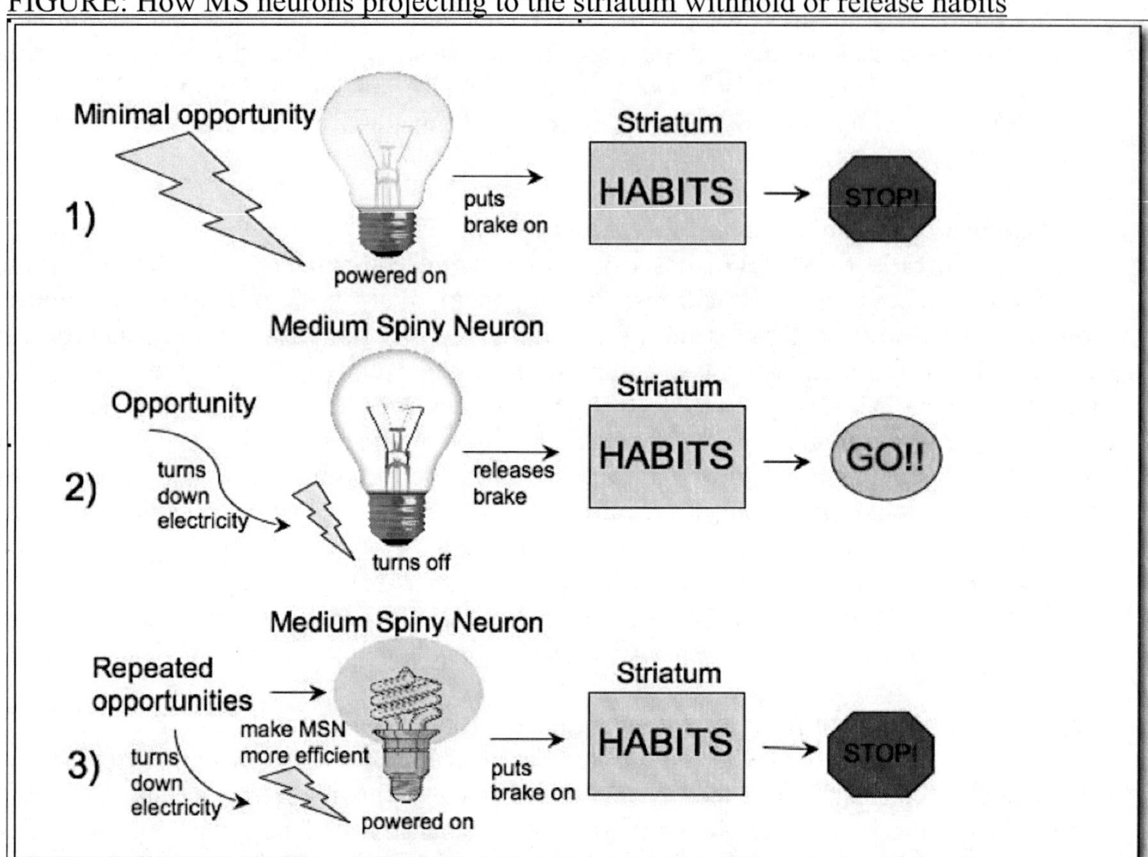

Legend: Here we depict how MS neurons connect to the striatum to control habitual behaviors, and change their activity based upon exposure to opportunities for a quick reward. In this cartoon, we depict MS neurons as a light bulb that is powered by electricity. Opportunities for quick reward turn down the electricity the way dopamine neurons can decrease MS neuron firing. 1) When MS neurons are on, they stop habits from being done, 2) When opportunities are present, they release neurotransmitters to quickly turn MS neurons off. This frees habits to be done. The bigger the opportunity, the more neurotransmitters are released, or in a light bulb analogy, the more electricity is taken away from the light bulb, and 3) When opportunities are present, they also release dopamine. With repeated opportunities presented over time, this alters the MS neurons to make them more efficient at stopping habits. In the light bulb analogy, the dopamine turns the light bulb into a type of bulb that requires less electricity to stay on (e.g. a compact florescent). With new, more efficient light bulbs, more electricity can be taken away from the light bulb before it will stop producing light. It will now take larger opportunities to release enough neurotransmitter to turn off the bulb.

Neuroscientists have a pretty good understanding of the detailed cellular mechanisms that underlie these immediate and learning effects, but explaining them in detail is beyond the scope of this book. For an overview, see Trafton & Gifford (2008). The main point is that opportunities for reward immediately alter the rate at which MS neurons fire.

On a very short time scale (milliseconds), opportunities change the immediate behavior of these MS neurons, altering the information that they send to the neurons in their network. Additionally, opportunities release neuromodulators, brain chemicals that alter the properties of the neuron by either modifying the existing proteins in the neuron or changing the type or amount of proteins the neuron produces. Because proteins function as the machinery of the neuron and determine how it responds, this changes how the neuron behaves and what it responds to later.

In short, repeated exposure to opportunities to make your life better will change the structure and function of neurons in your reward circuits, making them less responsive to the prospect of immediate gratification. Enriching your life with skills and social networks that allow you to solve problems will dampen the influence of your Cookie Monster habit system that seeks immediate gratification. When your reward system is toned down in this way, your brain will have more time and flexibility to think about non-habitual options and long-term goals. Your brain will be rewired to be more rational and less impulsive.

In sum, the responsiveness of the MS neurons in your nucleus accumbens regulates your drive for immediate gratification. If your MS neurons fire fast and furiously and are hard to distract, then you will rarely succumb to your habits and give in to the temptation of quick rewards. You probably will not eat the entire bucket of popcorn while distractedly watching a movie. Your behavior will instead tend to be driven by your long-term plans and the conscious beliefs of your prefrontal cortex. However, if your MS neurons are sluggish and readily stop their firing when carrots are waved, then your behavior will tend to be driven by your limbic autopilot. You will focus on maximizing benefit in the now, despite potential negative impacts on your future.

Exposure to opportunities for reward will alter the responsiveness of your MS neurons. Enriching your life by increasing your options for bettering yourself should strengthen your MS neurons and help you focus on long-term plans and goals.

Chapter 2.2: How Can I Enrich My Life: What Does the Nucleus Accumbens Recognize as an Opportunity?

How do you strengthen your MS neurons? Anything that adds immediate opportunities to your life will strengthen your MS neurons. If we want to increase our exposure to opportunities in our lives, the first thing we need to do is define "an opportunity" as our dopamine neurons recognize them. In its most basic description, dopamine neurons see anything that provides a chance to improve our immediate well-being, our "satisfaction", as an opportunity. But how can we achieve this?

The easiest opportunities for most people to conceptualize are basic rewards like food and water. Such primary reinforcers include air, water, food, sleep and sex. Similarly, social approval, money and increased social status also provide immediate reward, making your life better by improving how other people treat you. These are known as secondary reinforcers. The situations that you perceive as providing these secondary reinforcer rewards are learned through experience and observation rather than hardwired. Your reward system is as likely to be excited by abstract or culturally created rewards, such as money, gold or diamonds, or by the rewarding value of transformative ideas and continuing education, as by satisfying your appetite with cheeseburgers and Twinkies.

Opportunities for improvement also include situations where you can remove yourself from an uncomfortable or dangerous state to a more comfortable or safe state. This could include anything that provides relief from stress, pain, boredom, or anxiety. It could also include solving a problem that was presented to you. Thus, challenging situations and solvable problems to eliminate negative consequences operate just like opportunities to get something nice and earn positive benefits.

In sum, anything that increases your awareness of how to have nice things happen to you, anything that increases the amount of social approval you expect to receive, or anything that increases your exposure to problems that you are capable of resolving quickly will strengthen your MS neurons and reduce your drive for immediate reward. There are obviously many ways to increase opportunities in your life, and we will discuss interventions designed to do this and provide exercises to achieve this.

Social skills training and communication skills

The most readily available rewards in our environment are social rewards from others, for example being shown respect or approval during a social interaction. Social approval, a smile, kind words, helpful advice, assistance with a problem, respect, sympathy, appreciation, and so forth from others can be highly and immediately rewarding. Depending on our social and communication skills, we may find ourselves the recipient of these social rewards all the time or rarely at all. One of the best ways of expanding opportunities and enriching our lives is to improve our social and communications skills. When we know how to interact with other people in positive ways, we not only open up possibilities for pleasant, rewarding interactions with them, but also possibilities to gain access to resources and other more tangible opportunities that these people control.

Social skills training is a behavioral therapy designed to help people improve their social and communication skills. The goal is to elicit more positive responses from others. While it was designed and is primarily used to teach people with mental health disorders or clinically significant behavioral problems how to interact in ways that promote better emotional and behavioral health, the strategies and practices included in the therapy can be helpful for anyone, regardless of their starting level of social and emotional ability.

The first step in social skills training is to assess and determine the individual's actual difficulties in relating to other people. Once general problems with a social behavior are identified, the therapist can help break down the overall behavior into its smaller components. These can be worked on individually and in order of difficulty. Once specific components of behaviors are identified then they can be worked on using a variety of techniques including instruction, modeling, role-playing, and feedback. As with all behavior change techniques, successes should be reinforced.

Described more simply, a therapist, group member, or friend could tell you ideas for improving your social interactions (instruction). They could demonstrate how you might act in a situation that you find difficult (modeling). You could then pretend to be in that situation, and act out how you would behave (role-playing). Others could join the role-play as needed. A therapist or others could then give you an analysis of how you behaved, telling you things you did well, things that you could have done better, and suggestions for improving your behavior on the next try (feedback). This process can then be repeated as needed.

For example, perhaps you recognize that you feel really uncomfortable around groups of people you do not know when you are trying something new. This leads you to sit around watching television in the evenings instead of trying that Tai Chi or ethnic cooking class you thought sounded interesting. Last time you tried to go to a class you snuck in the back at the last minute, did not talk to anyone, could not really see what was going on, got really confused and left within ten minutes. You could break down your needed skills into: 1) expressing your interest in learning to an expert, in this case most likely the instructor; 2) sharing your nervousness and asking for support, 3) introducing yourself to others in the class, 4) observing the full range of expertise in the class (i.e. that there are other beginners like you) rather than comparing yourself only to the best person in the room, 5) reflecting on what you learned and how you improved during your time in the class. You could then make a plan and practice each of these skills, ideally with a supportive therapist or friend, until you are comfortable with your behavior. With a clear plan and confidence in your ability to turn going to new class or group meeting into a positive experience, you can then go to that Tai Chi or ethnic cooking class with a much better chance of having fun, meeting new friends, learning something new, and going back the next week, than you ever had before.

Psychologists have found that being passive or aggressive, as opposed to assertive, in one's communication with others is a common and harmful enough problem for people that they have designed programs that directly address this social skill. Such programs are typically called "assertiveness training". They focus on helping people learn how to express themselves and ask for what they need without being accusing or demanding, how to stand up for themselves in social interactions, and how to respect both themselves and others in their communications. The approach and techniques are basically the same as those used for other social skills training. These programs can be generally helpful for teaching communications skills that open up opportunities in one's life, particularly for people who tend to feel unsure of themselves or not respected in their day-to-day life.

To practice improving social or communication skills, see Exercise 2A (page 110) and Exercise 2B (page 114).

Progressive behavioral shaping: Breaking down a problem into smaller, solvable steps

While many of us are good at identifying final goals, rewards, or things that we would like to acquire or achieve, we may have trouble figuring out the steps involved in reaching our goals. The ultimate behavior that meets the goal or gets the reward may seem impossible when considered from your current perspective. Most goals require learning and mastering numerous smaller behaviors first, or meeting many intermediate goals before the ultimate goal can be achieved. Creating opportunities in your life requires that you begin to notice, work toward, practice and master these intermediate steps so that you can make progress toward your larger goals.

Psychologists have described a process for training complex and difficult behaviors by breaking the behaviors down into smaller, simpler parts and encouraging practice and rewarding success on these intermediate behavioral pieces. They refer to this process as progressive behavioral shaping. The basic idea is to break down a behavior into its component pieces. Then you provide rewards for completing the simplest components of the behavior correctly and repeat these rewards until the behavior is mastered and automatic. At this point, you can add another component to the behavior to make the performance more difficult again. You then reward completion of the new behavior or combination of behaviors until that has been mastered. This is repeated until the whole complex behavior has been learned. The process involves only simple reward-learning processes, but used correctly, it can be extremely powerful for shaping behavior or learning complex skills.

NOTE: If you are unfamiliar with basic behavioral theory or want to teach it to others in an entertaining fashion, there are computer games you might find helpful. Sniffy, the Virtual Rat Pro version 2.0, is a cute software program to teach behavioral theory, including progressive behavioral shaping, in a virtual Skinner box with a virtual rat. You can find out more about the software program at the following link:

http://ecatalog.cengage.com/112/lpext.dll?f=XMLHitList&qf=DCQuery&ht=catalog.xml&d=Wadsworth/0534633609&sf=item&p=&po=&q=%255Bfield%2CISBN%253A0534633609%255D&list=ProductIsbnIssnFormatted&xsl=productdescription.xsl&p1=0-534-63360-9

EXAMPLE: Progressive behavioral shaping to achieve a complex behavior

To illustrate how progressive behavioral shaping can be used to teach complex, impossible-seeming behaviors, let us consider an example from my (J.T.'s) gymnastics coaching days. Most people are fairly intimidated when I suggest to them that they could learn a back handspring (i.e. back flip). In fact, if they just attempted it, even with my help, the most likely outcome would be their landing painfully on the floor in some unpleasant position, potentially with me underneath. Thus, I always break up back handsprings into at least three component parts. These do not need to be completed in sequential order. It can be easiest to start with the end of the trick. First you need to learn to support yourself in handstand and pull your legs down to return to standing. This itself could be broken into many steps, but most of my gymnastics students have already learned all of those parts before we ever contemplate a back handspring. So first, we will practice kicking to handstand, arching slightly, and then snapping our feet back toward the ground to return to standing. This is a relatively safe but not easy exercise and can take a while to learn correctly. I will work with my students, encouraging and praising them as they make progressively better attempts toward doing this piece of the trick. While this piece itself, is not a recognized gymnastics trick and would get no credit or points in a gymnastics competition, it is nevertheless crucial to learning a back handspring and other tumbling skills. Thus, as a coach, I must find ways of providing artificial rewards for practicing and mastering this piece of the trick since it may not be independently rewarding. Once this part has been mastered, I will then switch to teaching the students the very beginning of a back handspring. They must learn to bend their knees to push off as they start falling backwards. If they lean forward instead, as is most people's tendencies, they will jump in the wrong direction and not make it safely to their hands. So second, we practice this early falling backwards part against the wall or onto a mat. I again praise improvements until this piece is mastered. Only then do I let students start to put the behaviors together as they learn the middle piece (i.e. jumping backwards from their feet to their hands). At this point, I can ensure that they safely complete this transition, knowing that they will be jumping in the right direction and are capable of finishing the trick once their hands make it to the ground. This allows us to practice the whole behavior safely until it is mastered. By breaking the trick down into pieces, a behavior that is difficult and dangerous to even try can be learned safely and consistently by the vast majority of dedicated people.

The two crucial components of using progressive behavioral shaping are: 1) breaking down your goal behavior into learnable pieces, and 2) creating rewards or reinforcers to encourage these intermediate pieces.

To practice progressive behavioral shaping, see Exercise 2C (page 115).

Enrichment activities

Getting involved in new activities will provide new opportunities for reward. New activities inherently provide new challenges and new social networks, which creates new opportunities to succeed and gain social approval. Enriching your life with new activities can seem challenging. First you must identify activities that sound interesting to you.

Next you have to find ways to learn and get involved with those activities. A trip to the library or some Internet exploration can help you find new ideas and connections. To get you started, we have provided a couple of helpful websites that provide ideas about new activities and ways to get started. Take a look, and give something new a try!

http://www.discoverahobby.com/
This website provides information on how to get started on over 100 different hobbies, from crochet to motocross. It includes descriptions of the hobby, suggestions for beginner books and videos, where to find free lessons, and links to groups, information sites, chat rooms and other helpful resources for getting going on your new hobby. Explore, pick something interesting, and get started!

http://www.hipsfinder.com/
While this page is set up with links to programs in the United Kingdom rather than the United States, this collection of information on Hobbies, Interests, Pastimes and Sports (HIPS) provides lots of new ideas for things to do. You pick an energy level, age range, environment (e.g. on the water, urban area), type of activity (i.e. individual, group, couple, family), and competition category (non-competitive, zany, competitive) and they suggest ideas, complete with links to additional information, clubs, organizations, and classes. It is a fun site because it provides suggestions far beyond the standard mix. For example, we would not have thought of belt sander racing, laser clay pigeon shooting, and greasy pole competitions on our own. This is a great place to head to for both new activities or to be reminded of activities you already know, such as gardening, hiking, or hula hooping.

To increase perception of opportunities in your life, see Exercise 2D (page 116).

<u>Chapter 2.3:</u> Reward Deficiency Syndrome: Why Having Fewer Dopamine Receptors Increases the Risk of Addiction, Mood Disorders, and Obesity

There are substantial individual differences in how fast MS neurons strengthen in response to rewarding opportunities. In other words, it takes different people varying exposure to opportunities to strengthen their MS neurons to comparable levels. This variation is caused by differences in the number of D2 receptors on the surface of the MS neurons. As we have described, reward opportunities trigger dopamine neuron firing, which in turn dump dopamine onto the dopamine receptors on the MS neurons. The dopamine sticks to and turns on these dopamine receptors, which then send a signal to the MS neuron telling it to change its responsiveness so it will be more likely to fire in the future. The more dopamine receptors are turned on, the bigger the change in responsiveness. In contrast, if MS neurons only have a few dopamine receptors on their surface, they will only receive a small signal telling them to change their responsiveness, even if lots and lots of dopamine were released. Without a lot of dopamine receptors, the MS neurons cannot detect that a lot of opportunities have been presented and will only change their responsiveness slowly. Thus, when MS neurons only have a few D2 dopamine receptors they strengthen very slowly and have trouble gaining control over our habitual behaviors.

Some people cannot make as many D2 dopamine receptors because of a difference in their genetic code for the receptor. One of the versions of the D2 dopamine receptor gene is called the A1 allele. People born with the A1 allele of the D2 dopamine receptor produce relatively few D2 dopamine receptors on their neurons. Genetic studies have shown that people with the A1 allele of the D2 dopamine receptor are more likely to develop a drug or alcohol problem, and have more trouble quitting once they have developed a substance habit. People with the A1 allele are also more likely to become obese or develop a gambling problem, demonstrating that in general they have more trouble controlling urges for immediate gratification. As we mentioned before, the limbic reward circuit cannot tell the difference between things that make life better and things that relieve immediate discomfort. People with the A1 allele also have more trouble dealing with stressful situations. For example, they may favor quick fixes or avoidance of stressful situations and are more likely to develop posttraumatic stress disorder. These associations suggest that having fewer D2 dopamine receptors makes people more prone to do automatic reward-driven behaviors. Over time this may lead to health conditions from chronic over-consumption of things that provide immediate reinforcement (e.g. cookies, alcohol or drugs) to chronic avoidance or relief-seeking from stressors. These findings also suggest that genetics can modify your risk of developing health problems due to compulsive reward-seeking.

Raised to be mild

It is important to remember that our genes alone do not determine our behavior. Although genetics clearly contributes to risk of impulsivity, the version of the D2 dopamine receptor gene that a person carries does not determine his or her tendency to seek reward on its own. For example, the A1 allele was shown to increase novelty-seeking, a personality trait associated with high-risk or impulsive behaviors such as substance use, in adults ages 24-39 only when they were raised in a punitive child-rearing environment. Interestingly, this same population of adults with the A1 allele was not at greater risk of novelty-seeking if they were raised in a more positive environment (Keltikangas-Järvinen et al., 2008). In other words, when children with this same genetic vulnerability were raised by parents who provided lots of attention, chances to succeed at things, and praise for their efforts, they did not develop a novelty-seeking personality. This study highlights that genetics alone rarely controls behavior, but rather modifies people's reactions to their environment. People with the A1 allele may need a more enriched environment than most to avoid being impulsive, but within such an environment, they may not develop a tendency to reward-seek.

Social hierarchy and need for immediate gratification

In addition to genetics, environment has also been shown to affect how many D2 dopamine receptors are made by your MS neurons. Some very clever experiments in monkeys suggest that your experiences, particularly in your social environment, may change the number of D2 dopamine receptors in your nucleus accumbens (Morgan et al., 2002). In this study, researchers started by keeping a group of macaque monkeys housed alone in cages – basically in solitary confinement– for several months. They then used positron emission tomography (PET) imaging to examine how many D2 dopamine receptors the monkeys had in their brains. They found that all of the monkeys had low levels of D2 dopamine receptors in their striatum (the region of the brain in which the nucleus accumbens resides). They then moved the monkeys to a shared living environment where they could interact for a few months. Like humans, macaques are both very social and very competitive. A group kept together will create a dominance hierarchy very quickly. The monkeys at the top of the dominance hierarchy get all the spoils of being top banana. They get first choice of food, and lots of positive attention and grooming from the other monkeys. The monkeys at the bottom do not have as pleasant a life. They get other monkey's leftovers, rarely get help picking off the parasites and, worst of all, bear the wrath of everyone else's bad days. The researchers observed the monkeys' behavior, and determined each monkey's rank in the social hierarchy. They then put the monkeys back in the PET scanner and looked at their D2 dopamine receptors again. They found that the monkeys at the top of the dominance hierarchy had greatly increased the number of D2 dopamine receptors in their brains. The monkeys at the bottom had just as few D2 dopamine receptors as they did when they were housed alone. Being dominant and having lots of resources at their disposal increased the monkeys' D2 dopamine receptor levels! The researchers then looked at whether this change had any impact on the monkeys' desire for cocaine, a potent drug reward. They found that while the monkeys on the bottom of the hierarchy would make very liberal use of the cocaine they were offered, the dominant monkeys used much less and decreased their use over time. Apparently, the extra D2 dopamine receptors helped them adapt to become less and less interested in opportunities for immediate gratification.

Dopamine deficiency and consuming passions

The US economy is driven in large part by consumption, based on the notion that having more goods and services will make us happier. This is fueled by over-valuation of a wide variety products that our reward centers have been conned into purchasing. Interestingly, compulsive buying, a condition known as oniomania, is related to dopamine activity. In clients with Parkinson's disease, a disorder of rigidity and tremor related to loss of dopamine neurons related to movement, drugs that increase total dopamine activity are also associated with compulsive buying, gambling, and sexual activity (Weintraub, 2008; Lee et al., 2009). Drugs such as these that modify overall dopamine levels have revealed greater insights about the relationship between dopamine and risky behaviors.

Dr. Larry Koran, a Stanford psychiatrist, had the opportunity to test clients who had been identified as compulsive shoppers by setting them loose at the Stanford Shopping Center, a vast mall owned by Stanford University. Citalopram, an antidepressant that inhibits the uptake of serotonin (i.e. a selective serotonin reuptake inhibitor or SSRI), also increases expression of the D2 dopamine receptor. Clients receiving this drug significantly reduced compulsive buying (Koran et al., 2002). This suggests that compulsive buyers have low dopamine activity and, like others with dopamine deficiency, compulsively reward-seek, in this case buying objects in hopes of instant gratification. A similar effect was observed by using haloperidol, a drug that mimics dopamine deficiency by blocking the D2 receptors. In pathological gamblers, haloperidol increased the self-reported rewarding effects of gambling and the desire to gamble (Zack & Poulus, 2007). These studies suggest that dopamine deficiency may contribute to our financial decisions, potentially encouraging risky financial choices as well as risky health behaviors.

Why would you want to be more driven by need for immediate gratification?

If impulsivity is risky and self-destructive, why aren't our brains simply wired to be risk averse? There are times when it makes sense for your brain to focus on the short-term. Think about the circumstances in which your MS neurons become weak. You become driven by immediate needs when you have few rewarding opportunities in your life, or are at the bottom of the social hierarchy. When you are in a situation where you may not have many chances to make your life better, or chances that you have right now may not be available next week, your brain readjusts itself to make sure that you take advantage of all the opportunities that appear. When you may not get another opportunity to get food for dinner, impress your higher ups, or make yourself feel better, you do not stop to think about whether taking that opportunity is really the best in terms of meeting your long-term goals. You take the opportunity while it is there. Only when you have plenty of opportunities to make your life better does your brain bother to stop and ponder which of the options is best for your future. Thus, our brains are wired to let our reward circuits take over when we are in a resource poor environment, or at the mercy of our dominant peers.

But what about those people who are born with a genetic predisposition for reward-driven behavior (i.e. have the A1 allele of the D2 dopamine receptor)? We cannot know for sure, but possibly their ancestors lived in an unstable environment, where plentiful opportunities could quickly disappear. For example, food and water might be plentiful in summer but sparse in winter. In this case, you would not want to start worrying too much about how you look in your swimsuit in the summer. You would eat while you can, and store up fat and supplies for the winter. You would not leave those nuts on the trees just because you already had plenty to eat today. You would pick them and store them, either as fat or preserved for later. If the number of opportunities in your environment could rapidly decrease, you would not want to reduce your drive for immediate rewards too much while they are present. Thus, when times are bad your brain will want to more slowly strengthen your MS neurons and reduce your tendency to work for immediate reward only slightly when times were good.

In other words, in environments where resource availability is unstable, it is beneficial to seek out and consume or store as many resources as possible during times of plenty, as you will need these resources later when resources are scarce. Consider a temperate northern environment with a productive summer growing period with lots of food and resources followed by harsh winter with little to eat. Those who ate or collected lots of food during the summer will be more likely to survive the winter than those who sought out only what they needed in the summer. In such an environment, people with the A1 allele will do better. In environments where resources are consistently plentiful, however, those who only seek out and consume what they need will do better, as they avoid the health problems caused by chronic over work or over consumption. Consider a tropical rain forest where food is plentiful and available all year round. People who felt compelled to eat or even collect and store all the food they could possibly find would eventually suffer from obesity or at least exhaustion from never-ending hard labor. Here, those without the A1 allele will do better. As modern society turns most environments into ones where resources are consistently plentiful, those with the A1 allele are have increasing tendencies towards health problems.

The problems arise when your brain is wired for impending scarcity, but you live in an environment where reward opportunities are everywhere all the time. This mismatch is obviously problematic when you think about positive reinforcers like food. Habitually eating most of what you come across is a good idea if you live in an extreme environment and food is scarce. But, this strategy will leave you morbidly obese if you live in a place where food is always available and you are bombarded with advertising to remind you of that fact. The same problems occur when you have a genetic tendency towards reward-driven behavior and negative reinforcement opportunities are everywhere. Let's say you live in a high-pressure environment where potential threats are everywhere. You run into people you do not know and thus do not really trust all the time. You have deadlines for being everywhere (e.g. your work, your kid's soccer game, closing time at the grocery store). News media lets you know about every upsetting problem that is occurring anywhere in the globe. If your brain habitually spends its time trying to escape from or solve every one of these problems that it encounters, you will wind up spending all your time hiding from, fleeing from, or obsessing about threats that you could realistically ignore. You may wind up with an anxiety disorder. The point here is that having a genetic predisposition for reward-driven behavior is not really a problem of having a mis-wired brain, it is a problem of mismatch between your environment and your brain's expectations of the environment. Western society is not well-designed for people with the A1 allele of the D2 dopamine receptor. Consistent exposure to too many opportunities is problematic for people genetically designed to survive in unstable and potentially dangerous environments.

FIGURE: Match between D2 dopamine receptor genetics and local environment

	Unstable Resources (e.g. summer versus harsh winter)	**Stable High Resources** (e.g. tropical rain forest with year round harvest)
A1 allele (slow adaptation to plenty)	Compulsively consume when resources are plentiful. Use reserves during scarce times. **Excellent Chance of Survival**	Compulsively consume all the time. Develop problems related to overconsumption. **Poor Chance of Survival**
No A1 allele (rapid adaptation to plenty)	Consume only what is needed when resources are plentiful. Starve during scarce times. **Poor Chance of Survival**	Consume only what is needed all the time. Stay balanced and healthful. **Excellent Chance of Survival**

Legend: Different versions of the D2 dopamine receptor are well-suited to different environments. The A1 allele of the D2 dopamine receptor is a common genetic variant. People with this genetic variant produce fewer than average D2 dopamine receptors, and thus their neurons adapt less when they receive dopamine signals. Because D2 dopamine receptors are involved in readjusting reward-seeking tendencies based on the availability of resources in the environment, persons with the A1 allele adapt more slowly when resources are plentiful. They will continue to seek and consume rewards, such as food, even when there are lots of opportunities to get more later. People without this genetic variant will rapidly reduce their search for and consumption of rewards when opportunities to get more are plentiful. These different patterns of behavior are either useful or problematic depending on the characteristics of the environment in which a person lives.

Aesop's fable "The Ant and the Grasshopper" can be a helpful allegory for remembering these biological tendencies. On a warm sunny day, a grasshopper sits in the sun, playing music and enjoying himself while a troop of ants toil away storing up food in their nests. The grasshopper encourages the ants to play and the ants retort that they can't because they need to store up food for the winter. They suggest that the grasshopper does the same, but he replies that he can't be bothered as winter is a long time off and there is lots of food. When winter comes, the grasshopper is starving and begs the ants for food. The disgusted ants reply that he played all summer and he can continue to play now and do not share their food with him. The point of the story is to teach the virtue of hard work and preparation.

As we just discussed, those with the A1 allele are wired to tend to behave like the ants. Regardless of the plenty around them in summer, they will continue to work compulsively to collect up all the rewards around them, assuming that those rewards will not be available at a later time. Those without the A1 allele tend to be more like the grasshopper. In times of plenty, they lose the drive to work for quick rewards, and may spend their time attending to less necessary things. But our world is no longer set up like the harsh insect kingdom where resources are sometimes plentiful and sometimes scarce.

Ironically, it is those of us with the biological tendency to act like ants that are more likely to have health problems in our current society. Surrounded by opportunities for immediate reward, the ants among us will have trouble not over-consuming or over-avoiding. They may over-eat, over-shop, or over-work, or develop social anxiety or depression as they over-avoid perceived threats. While we value the virtue of effort and preparedness, we have set up a society where the tendency to behave like this can lead to health problems. All the advertising and pervasive opportunities for reward in our capitalist society are endangering our ant-like peers, putting them at risk of obesity, stress-related disease, addiction, and anxiety disorders.

A scientific consensus is emerging that the origins of many chronic adult diseases are found in the developmental and biological disruptions occurring during the early years of life (Shonkoff et al., 2009). Living in environments where there is an abundance of stress and emotional abuse and few resources to advance or cope, has a strong relation to the risk of developing alcoholism, substance abuse, depression, hypertension, diabetes, and coronary artery disease. Arguably, the perception of scarcity in a society where images of prosperity are everywhere in commercials, also plays a fundamental role in encouraging desire for immediate gratification. Therefore, both the poverty of emotional and psychological support and the absence of culturally-defined resources, particularly in the presence of highly available non-nutritious food, addictive substances and stressors, are key in increasing long-term risk of chronic disorders.

Shaping your environment to fit your biology

So what should you do if you or your client has ant-like tendencies? The key here is recognizing your biological tendencies and working to shape your environment into one that works with you rather than against you. If you are an ant, it is unreasonable to expect yourself to be able to learn moderation in an environment where you are exposed to possibilities for quick rewards all the time. Instead of trying to change your behavior within your existing environment, you will need to make efforts to reduce your exposure to unhealthful opportunities and cues that trigger unhealthful habits. If you are an ant and you want to lose weight, do not expect yourself to be able to eat less without changing your day-to-day environment. Get rid of the TV or only watch pre-recorded shows so you can skip the commercials and reduce advertising exposure that drives eating. Food commercials are prevalent on TV and they work. For example, in 2004, the average child watched 40,000 advertisements on TV, at least 70% of which were for food. Moreover, a community survey of adults found that each hour of watching television was associated with additional consumption of 136 calories per day (Jason and O'Donnell, 2008; French et al., 2001). Do not allow these commercials into your home if you have trouble with over-eating. Stock your kitchen with only healthful food options. If the grocery store is overwhelming, order food online or shop with a more grasshopper-like friend so that you do not have to resist the temptation of the bakery aisle or the ice-cream case. If you are an ant, do not stock a liquor cabinet or hang out at bars and expect yourself to drink in moderation. Leave your credit cards at home and do not carry cash when you are not shopping for pre-planned needs. When you do shop, make a list of what you will buy before you go. Do not experiment with drugs, because your biology will lead you toward addiction. People with the A1 allele, people with family histories of addiction, obesity, anxiety disorders, gambling problems, people with lots of room to climb on the social ladder, or people who have simply noticed that they tend to act like Aesop's ants, should not trust their behavior to willpower, or expect to be able to moderate their habits like they may see others do. It is to your advantage to identify these characteristics within yourself so you can create or seek out the environments that work best for you.

If you or your client has this background, it is important to recognize your biology and shape your environment to be more like one for which you are adapted. Just because you have a friend that can have a wine cellar and only have 3 drinks per week, or who can buy a 5-lb. bag of mini-candy bars and keep them on her desk for co-workers without eating more than one, doesn't mean that you should be able to do the same. People are biologically different and suited for different environments. Don't waste your time trying to fight your biology and certainly do not feel bad or guilty for the behavioral tendencies you inherited. Recognize your biology and its strengths and weaknesses, and shape your world to fit your genetics. Embrace who you are and do not let envy for other's biology drive you to expect the impossible from yourself.

To identify factors in your environment that encourage unhealthful behaviors and to shape your environment to encourage unhealthful behaviors, see Exercise 2E (page 119) and Exercise 2F (page 121).

It's worth noting that the 12-step program, which has been shown to be highly effective for treating addictions and maintaining healthful behaviors over the long-term (Humphreys, 2004), starts by encouraging people to accept a disease model of addiction. The disease model of addiction suggests that the compulsive use and avoidance patterns that characterize addictive behaviors stem from a biological origin and are exacerbated by environmental contingencies. The first of the 12-steps to recovery is admitting that you are powerless over your addiction. This program starts by encouraging people with addictive tendencies to stop believing that they can control their behavior in a setting that encourages their compulsive habits, and focus on surrounding themselves with people, places, and interactions that discourage unhealthful behaviors and encourage more healthful habits. Before we understood the biology underlying the disease model, creative people came up with effective ways of helping themselves and others reshape their environment to limit dangerous compulsive habits.

WARNING: How guilt and self-stigma can drive self-perpetuating compulsive habits

On the surface, perfectionism may seem like a good trait. Logically, if you are not satisfied with yourself or your behavior, then you should be really motivated to change, and that should protect you from destructive habits. But in reality, strong motivation to change isn't the key component to long-term behavior change; it takes environmental and social changes, and learning new behaviors and thought-patterns, to make meaningful changes stick. And perfectionism, particularly feeling bad about yourself when you act unhealthfully, turns out to actually encourage bad habits by increasing the negative affect and stress that triggers compulsive habits in us all.

The dangers of feeling guilty about our unhealthful habits are delightfully depicted by Antoine de Saint-Exupery in his children's book *The Little Prince* (Saint-Exupery, 1943). In this book, a young boy visits a variety of planets, each inhabited by a single quirky adult. On one planet, he encounters a man with an alcohol problem, and in his child-like way he asks him what he is doing. The man eventually explains that he is drinking to forget that he is ashamed of his drinking problem. While this circular logic is humorous in a story, it can be seriously problematic in real-life. For example, in one of our own research studies, we found that the tendency to eat things to feel better (e.g. have a piece of chocolate to cheer yourself up) was associated with being overweight only insofar as people reported feeling bad about themselves for the way they ate.

This suggests that eating to manage mood only leads to being overweight if you feel bad about the fact that you ate a treat. If you eat to feel better and then actually feel better, then it is not a big deal. But if you eat to feel better and then feel ashamed of eating, then you are going to have to eat more to treat your shame, creating a compulsive cycle of overeating. Supporting the dangers of guilt and self-stigma, a study of participants who had already completed a 6-month weight loss program showed that those randomized to then receive a day of counseling focusing on reducing self-stigma about weight showed greater improvements in body mass index three months later (Lillis et al., 2009). Being less critical about your own behavior and tendencies and accepting yourself for who you are is not a sign that you are giving up on your goals. Abandoning judgmental perfectionism is actually a key step to being able to develop and maintain healthful habits.

Brain Challenge #2 Exercises

Exercise 2A: Assertiveness Skills
(Adapted from Sorrell et al., 2005)

Social skills training is a well-tested and effective intervention for mental health disorders (e.g. Dilk & Bond, 1996), and the skills taught are likely to be helpful for most people. Because a majority of the available rewards in human culture are social or involve working with others, good communication skills are essential for creating opportunities to make your life better. Passive or aggressive communication styles can prevent people from opening up opportunities. Here we will practice an assertive communication style.

A useful technique for practicing assertive communication is the SAS technique. SAS stands for:

> State the problem and its consequences.
> Ask for what you need.
> Spell out the advantages of cooperation.

The first step of assertive communication is to state the problem and its consequences. By clearly defining the problem, you eliminate confusion or assumptions about what the people involved are thinking or feeling. Thus, you should start your assertive communication by stating what the problem is from your perspective and how this problem affects you. Be objective and do not blame or judge the other person. Because you are explaining your side of the problem and not making assumptions about the other person's motivations or their side of the problem, you should find yourself using the word "I" rather than "you".

Once you have clearly presented the problem from your perspective, the second step is to ask for what you need in the situation. You should focus on being direct and clear so that there is no misunderstanding about what you want from the interaction. Be sure to be specific, but respectful of the other person.

The last step is to spell out the advantages of cooperation. Again, it is important to remain objective and accurately and clearly describe what will likely happen if the person cooperates with you. By focusing on the good things that will come out of cooperation rather than the bad things that might result if they do not, you reduce the chance that the other person feels manipulated, resentful or bullied into doing what benefits you.

Let us consider an example situation to illustrate this technique. Pretend you are at a business meeting with a session over lunch. You have special dietary restrictions, and indicated these in the space provided on the registration forms for the meeting. The registration forms promised that special meals would be provided for those with dietary restrictions. However, at the start of the lunch session, the server delivers you the standard meal that you cannot eat and scurries off to the next table.

For comparison, let us consider what a passive or aggressive response might look like and the likely consequences of these types of communication:

A passive response would be to let the server go and sit there looking unhappy, not touching your lunch, and hoping someone will notice and intervene. The most likely consequence of this approach is that no one would notice your expression of misery, and you will end lunch feeling hungry, neglected, frustrated and unfairly treated.

An aggressive response would be to call the server over immediately, tell him he messed up, state that you clearly outlined your dietary needs on the registration forms, and that you will complain to management if you do not get your special meal right away. This approach might successfully get you a suitable lunch, but it may upset the server, create a commotion, or make others around you think that you are not a very nice person for bullying the conference staff.

Let's walk through the SAS process and consider an assertive approach instead.

Step 1 of the SAS technique for assertive communication suggests that you should clearly state the problem and its consequences. You could get the server's attention, and explain the problem from your perspective. For example: "Excuse me sir, but I have special dietary restrictions and cannot eat this meal without harming my health. "

Step 2 suggests that you should ask for what you need. You could clearly explain what you want. For example: "I had requested a low-salt, vegetarian meal on my registration because I can only eat food that meets these criteria. Could you check whether there is a special meal reserved under my name or ask the chef if there are lunch options that would meet these criteria?"

Step 3 suggests that you should spell out the benefits of cooperation. You clearly explain how this extra effort could benefit the server. For example: "If you help me get a meal that I can eat, I will enjoy this meeting much more and will recommend that we use this conference center for all our future meetings."

This approach is likely to get you your special lunch without conflicts that might upset you or others. The server is likely to leave the interaction feeling like he was able to do something special to help his company. Your colleagues are apt to see you as a nice person who stands up for yourself.

The SAS technique is relatively simple to use, but can require practice if you are not accustomed to an assertive communication style. In the beginning, it may feel uncomfortable or take effort to plan or carry out. Thus, practicing this style in relatively safe environments is key to becoming good at it and able to use it in more stressful situations. Your body language during the communication should match your words. Pay attention to your body language during the interactions. You should focus on listening to others, maintaining eye contact and positioning your body squarely toward the other person. You should maintain a confident but respectful posture, and speak firmly, clearly, positively and loud enough to be heard. You want to make sure that the other person acknowledges and respects you and feels like they are being acknowledged and respected as well. Directing your attention clearly on the other person and giving them time to interact and respond will help ensure that this happens and that the interaction goes well.

Find a friend or partner and role-play assertive communication styles with them. It may be useful to brainstorm situations in which you have previously been unable to articulate your needs. Try responding assertively to a request for you to do something you do not want to. Practice asking for something others did not notice you needed. Share feedback with your partner about the choice of words and body language during the interaction.

The form on the next page may be helpful for you as you begin to practice using the SAS technique by yourself or with a friend or partner.

WORKSHEET: SAS Assertive Communication Practice

In the space provided, write the situation, the **stated problem** and its consequences, **ask for** what you want, and **spell out** the benefits of cooperation.

"SAS" Communication Technique
State the problem and its consequences.
Ask for what you want.
Spell out the benefits of cooperation.

Date:

Situation	Stated Problem	Asked Wants	Spelled Benefits

Date:

Situation	Stated Problem	Asked Wants	Spelled Benefits

Date:

Situation	Stated Problem	Asked Wants	Spelled Benefits

Date:

Situation	Stated Problem	Asked Wants	Spelled Benefits

Exercise 2B: Tips For Resolving Disagreements

There are a number of books and resources on healthy communication styles. Although they differ in various ways, a consensus of experts in clinical psychology agree on the following "rules" of engagement that can facilitate communicating what matters in a way that leads to meaningful change (Reis & Rusbult, 2004).

1. Agree to discuss one particular issue at a time. When multiple issues are raised while trying to deal with the problem at hand, the discussions can become counterproductive.

2. Agree on a time and place to have the discussion.

3. Agree to take a break if the discussion gets heated.

4. Use the word "I" instead of the word "you".

5. Avoid attacking the other person; instead, discuss how you feel.

6. Avoid defending your own position, even or especially when you feel attacked.

7. Agree on rules of disengagement; for example, if after 30 minutes we cannot come to a resolution, let's resume at a later time to be agreed upon.

8. If you cannot agree on rules of engagement or if they fail, secure the assistance of a trained third party in whom you can both trust to help mediate and resolve difficult issues.

Consider the list and a recent disagreement you had with someone. How many of these rules of engagement did you follow? Are there things you would do differently the next time you have a disagreement with a close relationship or friend?

Exercise 2C: Progressive Behavioral Shaping

Important components of using progressive behavioral shaping are: 1) breaking down your goal behavior into learnable pieces, and 2) creating rewards or reinforcers to encourage these intermediate pieces. In the following exercise, we will practice these components for one of your goals.

Step 1: Identify the final goal.

____

____

____

Step 2: Identify the behavior you need to do to achieve your final goal. This is your ultimate target behavior.

____

____

____

Step 3: List all of the pieces of your ultimate target behavior.

____

____

____

____

____

____

____

____

____

Step 4: Reorder these pieces according to difficulty. If there are pieces that require that you have already mastered other parts of the behavior, list them as sub-parts of that piece of the behavior. You can do this by numbering the pieces you listed above.

Step 5: Choose a piece of the behavior to work on, ideally starting from the easiest, most independent piece that you have yet to learn. Will doing this piece alone benefit you? If not, set up an artificial system to reward you for doing this piece. This may mean getting a coach or friend to encourage you, or setting up rules for rewarding your own success.

Step 6: Repeat step 5 until all pieces have been learned. Keep in mind that different pieces may take differing amounts of time.

Exercise 2D: How Can We Increase Perceived Opportunities In Our Life?

There are many different ways to increase our exposure to and awareness of opportunities in our lives. Despite popular beliefs, winning the lottery, having your company go public or inheriting millions from your great aunt are not the best or most likely ways of enriching your life. A large bank account may or may not translate into day-to-day opportunities to improve your well-being. Adding healthful activities to your life is one simple way to expand your opportunities. Happily, these are accessible to all and do not require extreme luck, a favorable market or a blue bloodline.

<u>Step 1: Identifying Health Opportunities in Your Life</u>
What rewarding events can you count on in the next few days?
1.
2.
3.
4.
5.
(additional ideas after reading Step 2)

What rewarding events can you count on in the next few weeks?
1.
2.
3.
4.
5.
(additional ideas after reading Step 2)

What rewarding events can you count on in next few years?
1.
2.
3.
4.
5.
6.
(additional ideas after reading Step 2)

Step 2: Additional Ideas for Health Opportunities

Below is a list of some healthy pleasures. If these are things you do, or would like to do, make a check mark next to them. If you want, you can write a brief description next to the item as to when and where and with whom you might like to take advantage of it.

Physical/Recreational

Walking
Stretching
Workout
Gardening
Jogging
Cycling
Swimming
Hiking
Boating
Yoga
Tai Chi
Other meditation
Massage
Leisure bath/shower
Household tasks
Sit in the sun
Rest

Creative

Arts
Crafts
Listening to music
Singing
Playing an instrument
Going to the theatre
Watching a film
Writing music
Photography
Writing in your journal
Writing essays, books, or poetry
View a video about art/music/theatre

Charitable

Attend a volunteer group
Attend a religious meeting
Donate your time
Donate clothing, goods, etc.
Support non-profit organizations
Help others in need

Prosocial
Calling a dear friend
Expressing gratitude
Inviting guests over
Sharing books, arts, crafts, healthy recipes
Playing golf, tennis, baseball, ping pong
Playing board games or cards
Join a club, band, choir, or orchestra
Workout with a friend
Express love
Start a group
Start a non-profit
Make someone laugh
Comfort someone who is sad
Plan and take a shared vacation

Educational/Cognitive
Help someone solve a problem
Teach knowledge and wisdom
Acquire new computer skills
Acquire a new language
Take a class in something you want to learn
Take a class that will provide you valuable skills
Read this book

<u>Step 3: Additional Health Opportunities in Your Life</u>
Now revisit Step 1 and add to the lists for the next few days, weeks and years based on the additional ideas for health opportunities that you selected in Step 2.

<u>Step 4: Incorporating and Remembering Your Health Opportunities</u>
Looking at your compiled list in Step 1, which now includes both health opportunities you can count on in the next few days, months and years as well as additional ideas for things you do or would like to do, you now need to come up with ways to remind yourself of these opportunities. This is not about convincing yourself to do something new, just reminding yourself of the things you already do or plan on doing.

Come up with a system to increase your perception of the goals you may take for granted. For instance, you could write your daily goals into your paper or electronic planner so that you have the satisfaction of crossing it off your list each day. You could keep a checklist on the wall of your kitchen or living room that you run through each day, month and year. You could place sticky notes around your home or workplace. You could keep a diary to track your health goals regularly. Each of these serves as a tangible reminder of the ways in which you are actively involved in your own health – even if it does not feel as active as these behaviors become habitual.

Exercise 2E: Avoiding Non-Ideal Environments for an Ant

The main question to consider here is whether a strategy of moderation versus abstinence is right for you. Is moderation is realistic for you? Consider your past behavior and your family's habits. Do you or your relatives have trouble with alcohol, tobacco, substance use, compulsive spending, gambling, obesity or mood disorders? Do you find yourself or relatives buying things you did not intend to when you go shopping, or overspending on your credit card? When you start eating or drinking, do you have trouble stopping? Do you compulsively work long hours, even though your family wants you home and you do not realistically need the money? If your honest answer to some of these questions is yes, then there is a good chance that you are biologically wired to act like Aesop's ant.

You may find that you have to change or even give up some of your current lifestyle or friends, but with some effort you will find alternatives that are just as, if not more, enjoyable. Do not try to learn to eat less at the all-you-can-eat buffet, just do not go to all-you-can-eat buffets. Try a different restaurant that provides smaller portions or use small plates at home. Do not try to buy less when you watch the shopping channel, just do not watch the shopping channel. Entertain yourself with a workout video instead. Do not try to drink less when you go to the bar, just do not go to the bar. Try taking a class or going to a community event to be social. Yes, there are people who can go to buffets, watch the shopping channel and go to bars and not overeat, over-buy, or over-drink. But if you are not one of them, do not beat yourself up trying to be someone you are not. Just avoid those situations. Get out of there. Not all environments in this world are good for all of us. Is it possible for everyone to maintain a healthy weight? Yes. But is it possible for everyone to do so while eating at all-you-can-eat buffets every meal? No.

It can be daunting to think about avoiding or giving up all of these familiar environments at the same time. If you know you have a tendency to overindulgence or excess, you can work one by one to remove tempting situations from your life. Below we give you an opportunity to brainstorm some situations, and then start by picking one to change.

If you think you have this biology, think about situations where you tend to overdo it. List some of these situations here:

____

____

____

____

____

Pick one of these situations and consider ways that you can reduce your exposure to these temptations. List ways you could avoid this situation here:

____

____

____

____

____

Lastly, for the situation you should probably avoid, think up an alternative enjoyable thing to do. List this new, and hopefully safer, alternative and then give it a try. When you are ready for more change, return to your initial list and repeat for another situation.

____

____

____

____

____

Exercise 2F: Creating an Ideal Environment for an Ant

Shaping your environment can be a powerful way to improve your habits. Here we will walk you through methods for changing your environment to discourage unhealthful habits and encourage healthful alternatives. Even subtle changes can shift your behaviors in healthful directions.

List the habit you want to limit: ____
Example: I want to stop eating a lot of sweets in the evening before bed.

1) Make it harder to do your bad habit.
If you increase the amount of effort required to do your bad habit, and insert steps that slow down your ability to carry out the bad habit, you will disfavor your habit in two ways. First, your nucleus accumbens will be less likely to determine that the effort is worth the pay-off. Second, your prefrontal cortex will have more time to notice and actively inhibit you from doing your bad habit.

Consider ways in which you can add in purposeful inconveniences to doing your habit.

Describe ways that you could make the habit harder to do:

____
____
____
____

Example:
I could not keep sweets in the house, and force myself to go out to get sweets for dessert. I could also find places to go out where I can get a reasonably sized single serving of dessert, so that my trips out are not that problematic. I could only let myself buy basic ingredients to make desserts, such as flour, sugar, baking soda, cocoa power, nuts, and fruit, so that I would have to cook or bake in order to have sweets to eat.

3) Make it easier to do the right thing.
If you reduce barriers to doing an alternate healthful behavior instead of your habit, you will increase the likelihood that you do the healthful behavior instead.

Consider ways in which you can simplify doing something healthful instead of doing your bad habit.

List the healthful behavior you want to do instead: ______________________________
Example: I want to have a cup of herbal tea and some fruit for dessert.

Describe ways that you could make the healthful behavior easier to do:

____
____
____
____

Example:
I can buy a variety of appealing herbal teas and display them prominently in the kitchen. I can keep a teapot on the stove and fill it regularly so that I just have to turn on the burner to start the tea. I can purchase fresh fruit for the week, and keep it on the counter along with a cutting board and paring knife to encourage me to prepare and eat the fruit.

3) Remove cues that trigger your bad habit.
When you are reminded about the possibility of doing your bad habit, you must actively stop yourself from doing the habit. It is much easier to stop doing a habit if you never consider the habit in the first place. Removing reminders can reduce the frequency at which you consider doing your bad habit.

Consider ways in which you can remove reminders that encourage your bad habit.

List things that encourage or make you think about doing your bad habit:

____

____

Example:
Cookie sheets on the counter make me think about baking cookies. TV commercials make me think about eating something fun. Seeing my husband looking for dessert makes me start searching too. Feeling tired and hungry makes me start looking for food.

Describe ways that you could remove or hide these things in your environment:

____

____

____

____

Example:
I could store the cookie sheets in the back of the cabinet. I could record my favorite TV shows and skip through the commercials, or not watch TV late at night. I could make my husband tea and fruit before he starts searching for food. I could eat more vegetables or drink more water at dinner so that feel full longer after I eat. I could go to bed when I start feeling tired and just get up earlier to finish things, instead of trying to stay up late.

4) Add cues that trigger your good behaviors.
Adding reminders to do alternate healthful behaviors can help you to automatically initiate these good behaviors. And if you are already doing the alternative behaviors, you might not even consider doing the unhealthful habit.

Consider ways in which you could add reminders that encourage your healthful alternative behaviors.

List things that encourage or make you think about doing your healthful behaviors:

____

____

Example:
Seeing my teacup makes me think of tea. Feeling a bit chilly in the evening makes me want tea. Soft lighting and a soft chair makes me want a cup of tea. Bright colors and tropical scenes make me want to eat fruit. Seeing trees makes me want to eat fruit.

Describe ways that you could add or showcase these things in your environment:

____
____
____
____

Example:
I can always leave my teacup on the counter, or in the living room. I can turn down the thermostat so the house is a bit colder. I can get lower wattage light bulbs with a warm color balance and put pillows and a blanket on the chair that I tend to sit in after dinner. I can decorate my kitchen or buy dishware with bright colors and images of fruit and tropical settings on them. I can put a small tree or maybe a picture of an orchard in the living room or kitchen.

<u>5) Avoid situations where consuming or doing too much is encouraged or even possible.</u>
There are many places that have been specifically designed to encourage gluttonous indulgence in our bad habits. Don't go to these places, or at least don't go often. Go somewhere else instead.

Consider places that encourage you to indulge your bad habit.

List these places here:

____
____

Example: All you can eat ice cream bar. The restaurant with the giant dessert portions. My grandmother's house. My friend's potluck dessert parties. The donut store.

Consider whether there is an enjoyable alternative place you could go.

Describe such places here.

____
____
____
____

Example:
The organic frozen yogurt place that has all sorts of fruit toppings. The restaurant with the better dinner food and smaller dessert portions. I could bring my grandmother to my house. I could encourage my friend to change up her party format, and help with suggestions and organizing. Maybe we could all go to a yoga class, do a group hike, or have an exotic fruit tasting. I could go to the bagel store instead.

Brain Challenge #3
Enhancing Resiliency to New Threats and Chronic Stressors

Challenge Introduction

Let's consider the last time I (J.T.) tried to stick to a diet. I started Saturday morning, and got myself off to a great start. I made it through the whole weekend eating nothing but small portions of healthful food every few hours. I was committed to my goal of losing five pounds, was excited about all the fresh local produce I was going to be eating, and felt great after two days of success. I went to work Monday morning with my food for the workday all packed, sure that it would be easy to stick to my diet locked in my office with nothing but good things to eat in appropriate amounts. I got to work, made myself a cup of tea, and started to go through my e-mail. First e-mail is a message from my boss in the national office. It is an absolute emergency. They need complicated data for a Congressional briefing by noon Eastern Standard Time, two hours from now, and my Californian programmers who know how to do the analysis won't be in for another hour and a half. I start to plan, but stop to read another e-mail from a journal that has been reviewing a paper I submitted four months ago. The e-mail contains ten pages of frankly mean and not very constructive criticism about my last two years of work. I feel my anxiety rising. Maybe I would feel better if I have a snack. Next thing I know I've eaten all my food for the workday and it's not even 8 am. What was I thinking? What happened to my well-planned diet? How is staying fat going to help me when I'm at risk of failing at work and being rejected by the scientific community? Why did I turn traitor on all my long-term goals the second I was stressed?

Feeling stressed and helpless increases the value of all immediate reinforcement opportunities. Stress makes feeling better urgent, and more important than competing long-term plans. Developing resilience to stress can increase your ability to make good long-term choices and stick to your health goals. In Challenge #3, we will explain how stress can ruin even the most well intended plan, and encourage you to act impulsively. In Chapter 3.1, we first describe stress and what triggers the stress response then discuss how stress increases your need for immediate gratification. In Chapter 3.2, we investigate why some people are more vulnerable to stress-driven impulsive relief-seeking. In Chapter 3.3, we discuss ways that you can become more resilient to stress. Patterning and pacing your activities can help. Moreover, learning that you have control, or the ability to keep yourself safe in the presence of stressors in your life, can buffer the effects of stress exposure.

Chapter 3.1: How Does Stress Increase Your Need for Immediate Gratification?

Why do we have a stress response?

Stress is a physiological response to being threatened. Situations that endanger your well-being alert your brain about the potential need to respond. When things in your environment or your physiological state indicate that your well-being may be at risk, your brain activates a series of protective mechanisms. We refer to these mechanisms as a stress response. This stress response alters your physiology and behavior to focus on addressing this immediate danger at the expense of other goals, thus ensuring that you prioritize getting yourself to safety.

This stress response changes hormone levels to redistribute energy to body systems needed to respond or escape. Body systems that focus on longer-term goals, like growing bigger and stronger, repairing damaged tissues, and having children, are slowed down to divert energy to these "fight or flight" systems until the threat is addressed. This part of the stress response is supposed to be a temporary and short-term change in response to an acute stressor, and can have wide-reaching and negative effects on your health when stress becomes chronic (see Robert Sapolsky's *Why Zebras Don't Get Ulcers,* 2004 for a very enjoyable and accessible description of this stress response and its health consequences). When long-term maintenance and growth systems are neglected by chronic focus on emergencies, physical and mental health problems may develop.

In parallel with these hormonal changes, your brain activates circuits that make you seek immediate relief from the threat. Among other things, these circuits talk to your limbic reward circuit, including the nucleus accumbens, as described previously, and the amygdala, a structure involved in the rapid detection of threat even before one is conscious that a threat exists. When you are threatened, the brain decides that any opportunity to improve your well-being in the immediate moment is one you should take. Immediate rewards are prioritized over long-term goals. In the case of my diet, my lunch made me feel momentarily better when important people challenged me. This temporary relief was prioritized over my long-term goal of weight loss. The logic behind this brain response is simple. Why worry about the future when you are threatened now? If that threat is not addressed, there might not be a future. This logic is highly adaptive if the relief solves the problem. If I were stressed because I was starving, then eating my lunch would be a great response. If I was being attacked and I dropped what I was doing to run to safety, that would also be helpful. *The problem is that stress prioritizes anything that will make you feel better right away, whether or not it actually eliminates the stressor.* Stress can make you drop your long-term goals, not to save your life, but for nothing greater than the fleeting feeling of calm offered by a quick treat or escape.

What triggers a stress response?

Truly threatening situations, like being attacked with a knife, nearing starvation, or being caught in the wilderness unprotected in a blizzard, will trigger this stress response. In these cases, it is obvious that this stress response is appropriate, helpful, and even crucial for your survival. However, many much more subtle and potentially threatening situations can also trigger a stress response. Thus, having your boss give you a dirty look, getting stuck in traffic when you have an important meeting, speaking in public, or talking to someone you find attractive, can all also trigger a stress response. Moreover, very subtle changes in your bodily state will trigger a stress response. When you miss a scheduled meal, do not get enough sleep, let your blood glucose get too high or too low, or have your muscles work without enough oxygen, your brain will trigger a stress response. In these situations, you may not really be in any immediate danger, but your brain will start that same stress response just in case. Since such situations may occur every day or even multiple times a day, this can lead to chronic stress and thus consistent focus on short-term fixes rather than long-term plans. As we will describe later on, most people learn to shut off the stress response when they feel they have control over these daily stressors. However, this chronic focus on the now can sabotage our attempts to improve our futures.

To assess whether your typical stress symptoms and their triggers, see Exercise 3A (page 147).

How chronic stress can alter your reward system to favor immediate gratification: The serotonin connection

Many of the behavioral effects of stress, such as depressive behaviors and altered response to reward, have been associated with the brain chemical serotonin. Notably, selective serotonin reuptake inhibitors (SSRIs), a class of medications that effectively treat depression and PTSD, modify the brain's serotonin system to produce their therapeutic effect.

Where in the brain are these serotonin neurons located? Neurons in the dorsal raphe nucleus (DRN) provide the majority of serotonin released in brain regions that regulate stress-related behaviors. The DRN is a cluster of neurons in the brainstem that connects with many other parts of the brain, including the limbic reward system and the prefrontal cortex (see the Figure on the next page for further details).

FIGURE: Projections of the serotonin neurons in the DRN

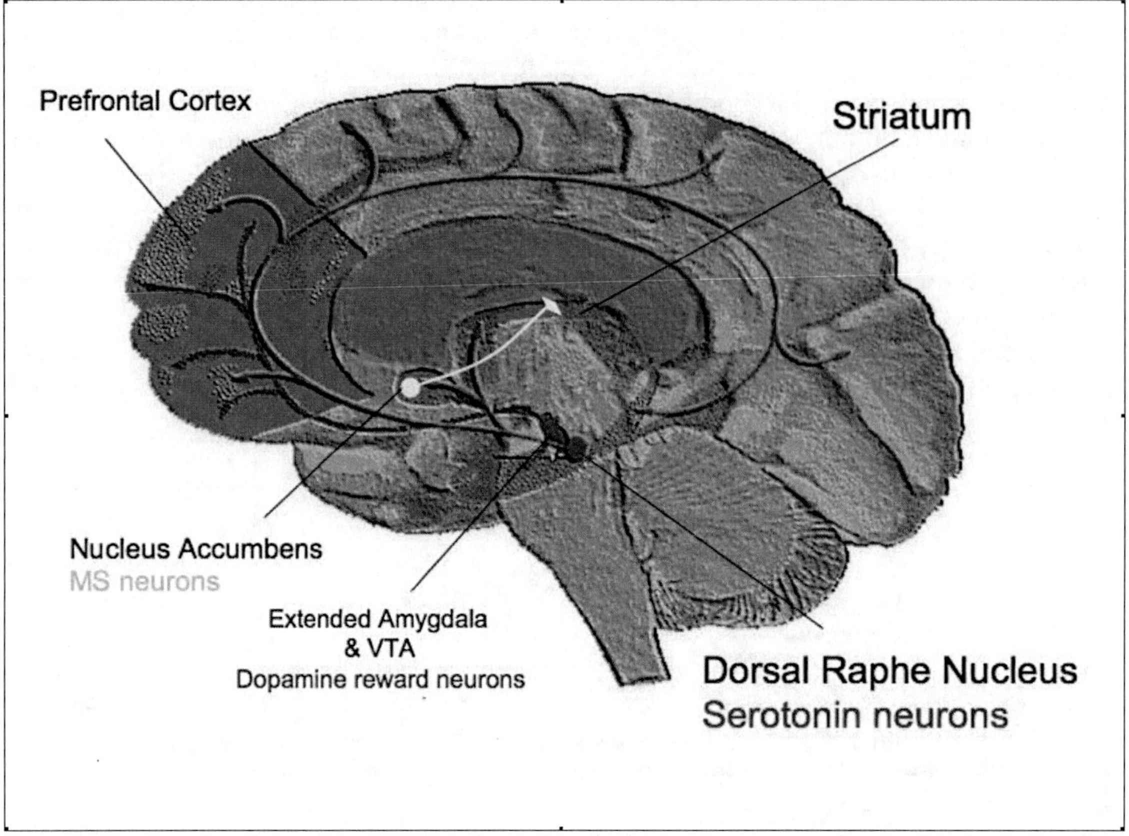

Legend: The dorsal raphe nucleus (DRN) is located in the brain stem, an area involved in basic functions such as attention, arousal, and control of autonomic functions such as breathing and blood pressure. The serotonin neurons in the DRN (in black) project to a variety of brain regions involved in reward learning, habit formation and habit inhibition including the nucleus accumbens and the prefrontal cortex.

The DRN is activated by a variety of stressors. For example, the DRN is activated during social defeat where an animal's territory is invaded and an aggressive intruder defeats it, during inescapable pain, and when an animal is forced to swim without an escape route (Abumaria et al., 2006; Kirby et al., 2007). Note that in all of the models, the animal is forced to endure social or physical threats, no matter how the animal responds to the situation. They have absolutely no control over their stressors. After experiencing these stressors and DRN activation, animals exhibit more submissive, helpless, and defensive behaviors, and increased anxiety (e.g. Cooper et al., 2008, Christianson et al., 2008). For example, DRN activity following these stressors has been shown to reduce social exploration in young rodents, indicating that they are more anxious in social situations (Christianson et al., 2008), and enhance anxiety-related startle responses (Meloni et al., 2008).

The same principle applies to humans. When stress activates the DRN, we become anxious, defensive and less likely to stand up for ourselves. We become very sensitive to pain and will do things to make it go away quickly. This might include taking potentially addictive drugs, disengaging from our lives and interests, or doing directly self-destructive behaviors to activate our bodies' inner pain control systems.

We can now alter activity in the DRN and reduce these effects using SSRI medications. The way these medications modify the serotonin system may seem confusing at first. These drugs increase the level of serotonin by blocking the reuptake of released serotonin by the serotonin neurons. This, in turn, decreases the activity of the serotonin neurons because of their built-in feedback system: when they detect that serotonin levels are high then they decrease their activity. Thus, giving drugs that increase serotonin levels reduces the stress effects in DRN serotonin neurons. In other words, SSRIs reduce symptoms of anxiety and depression, at least in part, by blocking activity in the DRN.

How a sense of control over stressors prevents the effects of chronic stress

To help prevent everyday situations that are not really a threat from causing chronic stress, our brains have a circuit that can stop these potential stressors from making our reward circuits more focused on immediate gratification. This circuit is driven by a part the medial prefrontal cortex, a part of the brain that may give us a "sense of control" over events in our lives. Some very important experiments in rats have demonstrated how this circuit is activated and what it does, and these lessons from stressed out rats can be applied to the human rat race.

Steve Maier and Linda Watkins have studied the psychological factors that determine the impact of stressors on behavior and physiology as well as the underlying brain mechanisms involved in influencing those states. They discovered that the degree of "control" which animals can exert over a stressor determines whether the stress will alter the brain and behavior. Exposure to uncontrollable stressors (e.g. a predator) sensitizes the serotonin neurons in the DRN, resulting in exaggerated release of serotonin in the areas of the brain to which the DRN neurons project.

Exposure to stressors can increase the expected value of immediate rewards (as in Challenge #1) and encourage reward-seeking behaviors. For example, stress is known to alter addictive reactions to drugs of abuse. This research team has shown that uncontrollable stressors, but not controllable ones, exaggerate the rewarding properties of opioid drugs such as morphine (Rozeske et al., 2009). In addition, they found that this effect is influenced by serotonin neurons in the DRN.

Maier and Watkins found that having control over a potential threat activates a medial prefrontal circuit that can turn off the DRN response. The researchers studied the effect of variable control on stress by setting up a system where rats would receive a shock to their tail to stress them. (Maier et al., 2006). In order to study the difference between experiencing controllable and uncontrollable stressors, they connected rats in pairs so that they would both receive the exact same strength, pattern, and number of shocks. They gave both rats a wheel that they could spin. For one rat, spinning the wheel would turn off the shock. For the other rat, spinning the wheel would do nothing. Thus, both rats would get the same shocks, but only one rat would have control over the shocks.

The rats showed very different effects on their stress response and behavior. The rat whose wheel did not stop the shocks displayed classic signs of stress, such as anxiety and submission and weight changes. In contrast, the rat that received the same shocks but had control over when the shocks stopped exhibited none of these signs of stress. Having control over the stressor prevented the shocks from causing these stress-related changes in behavior and physiology. This occurred despite the fact that the two rats experienced the exact same shocks. When the rat recognized that he had the power to turn off the shock, he realized that it did not actually pose a threat. Thus, the prefrontal cortex turned off the stress response.

Maier and colleagues then combined this shock stressor paradigm with a technique that turns on or off small brain regions to investigate exactly how having control over stress alters the response to stress. They found that activation in the ventromedial prefrontal appears to be both necessary and sufficient for control over the shocks to prevent the effects of chronic stress. Turning off the medial prefrontal cortex eliminated the control effects even when the rat actually had control over the shocks. Likewise, turning on the medial prefrontal cortex mimicked the control effects even when the rat did not actually have control over the shocks. Moreover, this part of the brain appears to be activated when a rat is given control over a stressor.

Interestingly, once a rat had been trained that it had control over the shock stress, the rat started to generalize its sense of control to other stressors. The rat acts as though it has control (i.e. does not show a stress response) even when the animal does not actually have control over the new stressor. Once a rat experienced a sense of control over stressful situations, it starts to activate ventromedial prefrontal cortex in response to a variety of stressors, thus preventing the negative effects of stress exposure. In other words, when the rat experiences control over potentially dangerous elements of its world, it stops viewing difficult situations it encountered as immediate threats. This suggests that developing a sense of control over our own stressors may help protect us from responding to everyday stressors, even those that objectively are not within our control (e.g. traffic or bad weather).

FIGURE: The effects of controllable versus uncontrollable stress

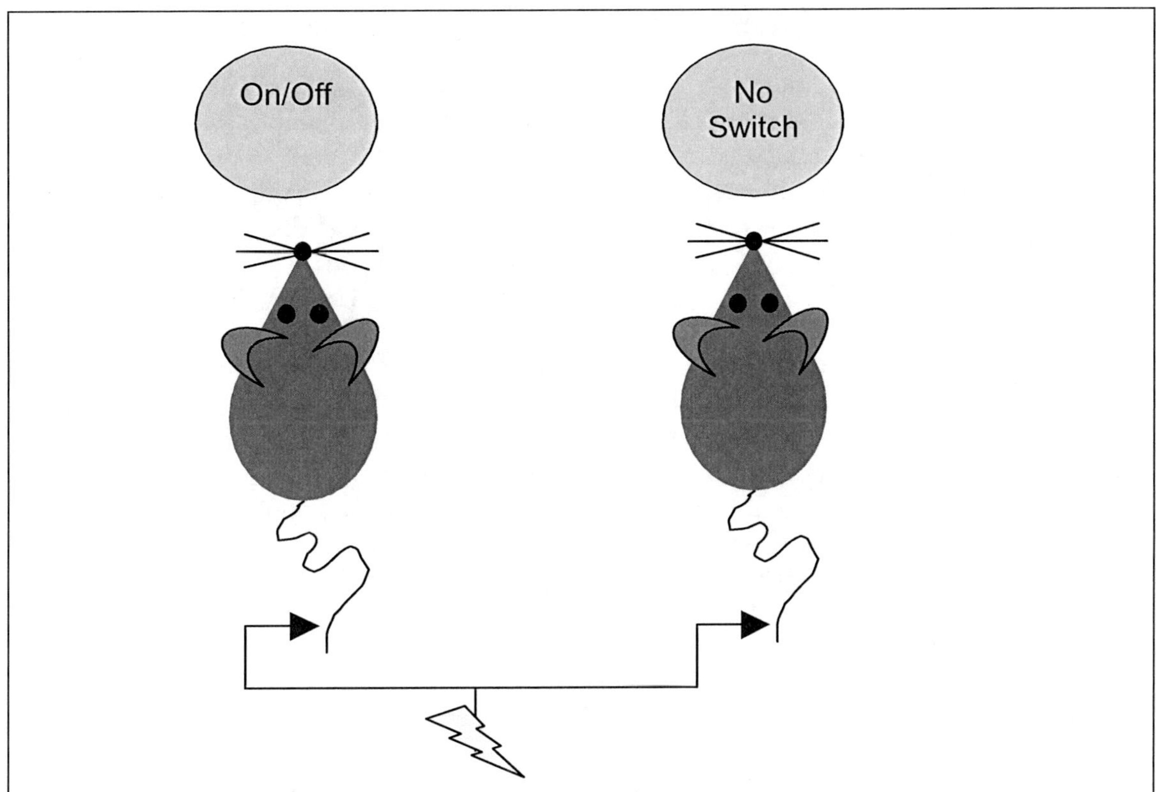

Control over stressor	No control over stressor
Little to no effect of stress exposure	Fear conditioning – *develop fear and avoidance of similar situations* Learned helplessness – *stop making efforts to solve the problem causing the stress* Exaggerated drive for immediate reward – *overvalue things that provide short-term relief or reward* Neglect of physiological responses that maintain long-term health and growth – *increase risk of chronic diseases and health problems, such as diabetes, heart disease, depression, cancer, and infertility*

Legend: Maier and colleagues (2006) experimental paradigm for determining the effects of controllable versus uncontrollable stress. The effects of this exposure are summarized in the table above. Pairs of rats were connected such that both would receive the exact same intensity and duration of tail shock. In addition, they were both provided with a wheel. For one rat, the wheel acted as a switch to turn off the tail shock. This rat was shocked, but was able to turn off the shock at will. For the second rat, the wheel was inactive and had no effect on the tail shock. This second rat was thus shocked exactly the same amount as the first rat, but did not have control over when the shocks were turned off.

Posttraumatic stress: Horror frozen in memory

The effects of control over stress observed in rats are also observed in studies of people with posttraumatic stress disorder (PTSD).

PTSD may occur in people who experience or observe a terrifying or horrible event. Greater chronicity and severity of stress may increase the likelihood of developing PTSD after a trauma. For example, an estimated 31% of Vietnam veterans and 20% of Iraq veterans developed symptoms of PTSD (National Institute of Health and the friends of the National Library of Medicine, 2009). Rape, torture, natural disasters, car accidents, and other traumatizing events produce PTSD in a proportion of the people exposed, resulting in an estimated 7.7 million people with PTSD in the US.

PTSD is characterized by a number of symptoms including: 1) feeling jumpy or on guard against impending threats or danger (hypervigilance), 2) avoiding situations or things that remind you of the traumatizing event (avoidance), 3) being unable to stop thinking about the event, oftentimes having nightmares about it (re-experiencing), and 4) feeling disconnected from people and your environment (numbing). People with a history of childhood abuse or neglect seem particularly vulnerable to developing persistent symptoms of PTSD. In addition to these symptoms, people with PTSD have been shown to have substantially greater than normal risk of developing other co-existing disorders, including substance and alcohol use problems, obesity and chronic pain (Vieweg et al., 2007; Perkonigg et al., 2009; Defrin et al., 2008; Shipherd et al., 2007; Brady et al., 2000).

Notably, these co-existing disorders are all thought to stem from compulsive behaviors to feel better immediately. People with these co-existing disorders may tend to use substances and alcohol to feel better in the next few minutes, even though it makes them feel worse a few hours later and causes additional problems. They may eat a whole bag of cookies because they taste good for a couple of minutes, even though doing so may make them feel sick 20 minutes later and gain weight for life. They may rest or take pain killers the minute they feel pain, even though they need to exercise and get involved in life to help recover from their injury. In all of these disorders, the afflicted individuals choose short-term relief with long-term consequences over longer-term benefits. These behavior patterns may result from over-active reward circuits, stemming from under-activation of the circuits in the prefrontal cortex that cancel the impact of stress-related activation of the DRN.

Interestingly, a series of brain imaging studies have shown that potentially threatening stimuli evoke a pattern of brain responses similar to that observed in the rats given uncontrollable tail shocks. As noted, the amygdala, a "watch dog" of the brain, is critically involved in sensing threat or danger, such as that signaled by a fearful voice or face. Researchers examined the response to fearful versus happy faces in trauma-exposed men with and without PTSD (Shin et al., 2005). Using fMRI, they found that the men with PTSD showed greater activity in the amygdala and lesser activity in the medial prefrontal cortex when shown fearful faces. Moreover, a greater severity of reported PTSD symptoms was related to a greater decrease in activity in the medial prefrontal cortex when viewing fearful faces. A similar pattern of brain activity was found using PET to compare responses to personal trauma stories in combat-exposed veterans with and without PTSD (Liberzon et al., 2003).

Recall that the amygdala also works as part of the limbic reward circuit to identify the importance or value of an opportunity to respond habitually, and greater activity in the amygdala indicates that the person highly values and has an exaggerated drive to escape from terrifying situations. Meanwhile, the medial prefrontal cortex is activated when you feel you have control over stressors, and a lack of activity likely indicates that you feel like you do not have the ability to keep yourself safe in scary situations. Thus, when you have a lack of control over stressors, you will have a robust stress response that increases your drive for short-term reward when exposed to potential threats. The finding that the severity of PTSD symptoms is related to a lack of activity in the medial prefrontal cortex when a person is in distressing situations suggests that lack of activity here may be partially responsible for the disorder (Maier et al., 2006). Just like the rats that had no control over when and how long they were shocked, people with PTSD have full-blown responses to threatening situations. This may lead to the exaggerated fearful and escape responses that are part of the disorder, and may explain the co-occurrence of other disorders that include compulsive searching for immediate gratification. Extrapolating from the rat studies, these findings also suggest that people who do not learn that they have control over threats or stressors in their environment may be at greater risk of developing PTSD.

How great is your sense of control over the stressors in your life?

A useful way to consider a person's sense of control over what happens to them is their "locus of control", or their belief about what causes good or bad things to happen to them. People who tend to believe that they have control over what happens to them have an internal locus of control. Presumably, like the rat with the wheel that turned off the shocks, people with an internal locus of control have learned that decisions and actions they make can change what happens to them. In contrast, people who tend to believe that an outside power, such as a god, the environment, or fate, controls what happens to them have an external locus of control; they have learned that good or bad things happen to them regardless of what they do.

Many studies have examined the impact of having an internal versus external locus of control on changing health behaviors. In general, having an internal locus of control has been shown to be beneficial for changing health behavior when other factors for health behavior change are in place. For example, having an internal locus of control seems to be helpful if you: 1) understand and believe in the connection between the behavior and health outcomes, and 2) believe you are able to achieve the behavior (i.e. have self-efficacy for that behavior).

Locus of control influences health-related behavior in clients with chronic disorders. Cancer clients with an internal locus of control were more likely to take healthful steps that prevented recurrence of the cancer (Park & Gaffey, 2007), and diabetic clients with an internal locus of control predicted better attendance at dietitian visits (Spikmans et al.,

2003). Although locus of control is not the only factor influencing behavior, these studies suggest that people who believe that they can influence what happens to them are more motivated to try to change their behavior and more successful in their attempts to change. To some extent, this finding may seem obvious. Of course, people who think that their decisions change what happens to them are more likely to change their decisions to try to change their health. However, the rat research on controllability of stressors both gives us insight into how someone might develop an internal versus external locus of control and also helps explain how an internal locus of control might make behavior change easier. A sense of control over what happens to you, by increasing your resilience to stress, can reduce drive for immediate relief and thus allow you to make decisions that are more aligned with your long-term goals rather than your short-term desires. To assess your own locus of control for health in general (Forms A/B) or for a specific health condition (Form C), check out the Multidimensional Health Locus of Control (MHLC) Scales created by health researchers at Vanderbilt University: http://www.vanderbilt.edu/nursing/kwallston/mhlcscales.htm

In review, the serotonin-driven dorsal raphe nucleus (DRN) plays an important role in overvaluing quick fixes during times when we feel threatened. Chronic activation of the DRN can lead to learned helplessness and stress-related disease. Further, we have demonstrated that the effectiveness of SSRIs for treating mood disorders may relate to their effect on serotonin activity in the DRN. The ventromedial prefrontal cortex can prevent activation of the DRN during stress, thereby preventing the negative effects of stress on health-related choices and chronic disease. The ventromedial prefrontal cortex is activated when one feels that they are in control of the stressors in one's life, and PTSD is a disorder that includes an impairment of ventromedial prefrontal cortex activity and a sense of not having control over the stressors in one's life. It is therefore not surprising that SSRIs are effective as a treatment for PTSD (Ipser, et al., 2006). Lastly, an individual's locus of control – whether he believes what he does can change what happens to him or that it depends on external factors beyond his control – also plays a role in how he responds to stress.

Chapter 3.2: The Effects of Early Childhood Experience on Stress Systems

The environment that you experience early in life can substantially affect how you respond to stress later in life. Early experiences and exposure to stress have lifelong consequences. Stress in early childhood contributes to childhood obesity and the subsequent risk of type 2 diabetes mellitus, hypertension, and coronary artery disease. Even high-quality health care is unable to eliminate the stress-mediated and significant disparities in health outcomes that stem from socioeconomic and racial inequalities (Marmot et al., 1984).

The brain is the primary organ that perceives stress, and chronic stress can leave an enduring effect on the hippocampus and prefrontal cortex. The effects of stress on these brain regions have enduring consequences for susceptibility to chronic anxiety, aggression, mental inflexibility and poor short-term memory.

Prolonged stress is associated with a reduction in the volume of the human hippocampus (Shonkoff et al., 2009). Further, chronic conditions such as diabetes, major depression, Cushing's disease and posttraumatic stress disorder can all impair the human hippocampus' ability to regulate short-term memory. The prefrontal cortex has been found to be smaller in individuals who self-report a lower socioeconomic status and in individuals with major depression. Changes in activation of the prefrontal cortex are also related to stress. Functioning in the prefrontal cortex can be impaired, at least temporarily, by increases in stress, such as that observed in medical students studying for their board examinations. Activation of the prefrontal cortex can lead to a sense of impending danger, and increase blood pressure.

What prepares us for stress: The stress hormone cortisol

Adult conditions such as heart disease, stroke, diabetes, and cancer were once regarded as the result of adult behavior and lifestyles; however, advances in the understanding of the effect of cumulative exposure to stressful experiences, including prenatal events and traumatic childhood events, have made it abundantly clear that these disorders have childhood roots. Contributing to all of these chronic conditions is the hormone associated with stress: cortisol. This hormone, while crucial for adaptively preparing us for fight-or-flight survival responses in the wake of tangible stressors, can also drive body systems into unsustainable states that wear out these systems and lead to damage over time. Cortisol endangers the hippocampus, making these neurons vulnerable to damage during otherwise survivable moments such as brief oxygen deprivation or seizures. Cortisol also suppresses the immune system, which can be beneficial for preventing acute inflammation following injury; however, chronic immune suppression leads to chronic immune-related disorders. Chronic elevation of cortisol is associated with narrowing the arteries supplying the heart and brain, and with hypertension, leading to both an increased risk of myocardial infarction and stroke (Sapolsky, 2004).

This basic stress-response mechanism developed to aid survival in an age of famine and scarcity, but now, in a time of plenty, causes disease by encouraging people to overeat to add to their fat storage and protect against the potential risk of insufficient food. Chronic stress and excessive cortisol activity leads to the accumulation of fat, especially at the midline (belly), which in turns greatly increases the risk of developing insulin insensitivity and type 2 diabetes. Onset of obesity and type 2 diabetes is occurring at earlier and earlier ages in our stressful society.

The enduring effects of maternal anxiety and separation

Research with animal models shows how the stressfulness of one's early environment influences how one's stress system develops and responds later in life. A key component of this environmental effect is the level of anxiety and type of care behaviors that one's mother shows early in one's life. If your mother acts highly stressed when you are young, you will develop exaggerated stress responses. Your response to stress adapts to match your mother's assessment of the stability and safety of your early environment. Because of this process, you tend to inherit your mother's reactions to stress. This inheritance is not genetic, but mediated through your early experiences with your mother.

Research on the effects of mothering style on children's stress resilience, or the ability to be healthful even in challenging conditions, has been beautifully reviewed by Champagne and Meaney (2001). The majority of studies of the effect of early environment have used a rodent model where newborn pups are removed from their mother for a short (15 minute) or long (usually hours) period each day. When the pups are only removed briefly, it is referred to as "neonatal handling", and when they are removed for a longer period of time, it is referred to as "maternal separation".

Interestingly, neonatal handling and maternal separation tend to have opposite effects on stress responsiveness and adult response to immediate rewards such as drugs of abuse. Neonatal handling reduces stress responsiveness, anxiety behavior and drug and alcohol use later in life. In short, rats removed from their mother for about 15 minutes a day become resilient to stress and less driven to obtain immediate rewards such as drugs or an escape from scary situations. Maternal separation increases these same behaviors. Rats removed from their mother for longer periods of time each day become more reactive to stress, showing larger, more prolonged stress responses and greater drive for immediate rewards or relief.

Maternal separation alters the development of the medial prefrontal cortex, a key brain region that we have described as critically involved in reducing stress effects when we feel in control. Specifically, maternal separation leads to changes in development of inhibitory neurons and changes in connections from serotonin and dopamine neurons in the medial prefrontal cortex (Helmeke et al., 2008; Braun et al., 2000), increases reward-seeking with preference for places where the rat was previously given opioid drugs such as morphine (Michaels & Holtzman, 2008), increases self-administration of alcohol and cocaine when the rats are adults (Moffett et al., 2007; Roman & Nylander, 2005; Francis & Kuhar, 2008), and increases response to a painful tail pinch, showing that these rats are more driven to escape from stressful situations (Brake et al., 2004). Maternally separated rats cope with social defeat by showing more passive or submissive behaviors and fewer proactive coping strategies (Gardner et al., 2005).

Differences between brief versus long maternal separation

So what is the difference between repeated brief separations versus long separations from one's mother? Why would a little time away from your mother make you more resilient but a longer time away make you more vulnerable to stress? It turns out that when pups are briefly removed and then returned to the cage, most mother rats greet their returned pups by fawning over them, licking and grooming them and giving them protected time to breast feed. Thus, the brief separation gains the rat pups extra attention from their mothers and makes them more resilient to stress. In contrast, when the pups are removed for longer periods it means more time away from mom and less attention. With longer separations, the pups receive so much less attention during the separation that a bit of extra grooming upon return cannot make up for the time away. This suggests that the level of care and attention the pups receive from their mothers might alter how they respond to stress later in life.

To test this possibility, researchers used natural differences in the attentiveness of mothers to examine the relationship between amount of licking and grooming and later stress response without actually removing any of the pups from the cage. Pups raised by mothers who were highly attentive and naturally licked and groomed their pups a lot were more stress resilient, just like those who had been exposed to neonatal handling. Pups raised by mothers who were not very attentive and ignored or avoided the pups a lot, were less stress resilient and extra responsive to stress as adults, just like the pups who had been exposed to maternal separation. Notably, when the pups grew up and had pups of their own, they tended to mother just like they had been mothered. If they had received a lot of attention, they did a lot of licking and grooming. If they had received less attention, they in turn paid less attention to their pups. Mothering style appears to be passed down from generation to generation.

Does this mean that mothering style is genetic? It turns out that it is not. If you cross-foster the pups so those born to less attentive mothers are raised by more attentive mothers and vice versa, then the pups mimic their foster mother and not their birth mother. In other words, if pups born to less attentive mothers were raised by very attentive mothers, they grew up to be resilient to stress and very attentive to their own pups (Huot et al., 2004; Champange & Meaney, 2001). Moreover, a study in monkeys showed that changing environmental conditions can affect mothering styles. If changes in the environment make it harder for mothers to care for their young ones, then the mothers pay less attention to their children and these children then grew up to be more anxious and show signs of stress (Rosenblum et al., 1994). Just by varying how hard the mothers had to search to find food, the researchers changed both the mothers' ability to dote on their babies and their babies' later responses to stress. Growing up with a mother who is stressed all the time, either because the environment is difficult or because the mother was trained to be anxious and highly reactive to stress when she was young, will encourage your brain to respond more to stress and be more focused on short-term choices.

How do you escape your past?

Is there anything you can do as an adult to make your stress system less responsive if you did grow up in a stressful environment or with an anxious mother? We do not know if you can reverse the changes in the brain that encourage larger responses to stress. But you can certainly pay extra attention to developing the other redundant systems that dampen the effects of stress. For example, you can learn to attend to and recognize your control over stressors to better activate your medial prefrontal cortex. This perception of control will decrease the impact of the stress. You can also learn to recognize, make use of, or increase opportunities in your environment to strengthen the MS neurons in your nucleus accumbens (see Challenge #2). As we previously described, this increased exposure to opportunities for immediate reward will reduce your drive to respond to short-term rewards, and make it easier to consider longer-term goals.

Increasing opportunities for reward can reduce the effects of early life neglect on stress response and behavior. With the rodent models, enriching the cage environment of pre-teen rats that had been "maternally separated" as pups normalized their stress response and reduced their anxiety behaviors when they were adults (Francis et al., 2002). Notably, these changes in stress response and behavior occur without changing the effects of "maternal separation" in the brain. In other words, the brain changes that occurred as a result of the "maternal separation" were still apparent in the adult rats after environmental enrichment. While adult enrichment did not erase the developmental changes produced by less attentive mothering, it did correct the body's response to stress and reduce anxiety behaviors. The neurobiological "memory" and stress vulnerability from early stress were still there, but the brain compensated for them and they no longer caused unhealthful effects on the body or behavior.

From a public health perspective, we can help future children grow up to be resilient to stress by supporting programs that reduce stress on mothers and give them more time to attend to their babies. Observations suggest that mothering style in humans is similarly related to stressful environments. For example, a study of mothers in the WIC program found that those that reported greater levels of stress, depression or anxiety fed their children in a less attentive, supportive manner (Hurley et al., 2008). While it has not been directly tested, we would expect that better maternity leave policies and programs to ensure that new mothers have food, shelter and support would reduce their stress, increase their attention to their children, and decrease later stress in their children.

Chapter 3.3: How We Can Develop Greater Stress Resilience

Since stress can sabotage our ability to focus on long-term goals, finding ways to avoid stress can make it easier to stick to healthful behavior plans. While obviously you cannot stop all your daily activities to avoid many stressors, there are a number of relatively easy things you can do to greatly reduce stress in your life. We describe three stress control techniques that have been successfully used in psychological interventions to facilitate behavior change.

Various scales have been proposed to assess the magnitude of life events that produce stress (see www.fulbrightelem.org/Nurse/images/Stress%20Test.pdf). At the top of the list of stressful events are the death of a spouse or child, followed by divorce and marital separation. Positive events can also be stressful, including an impending marriage, marital reconciliation and retirement. Increasing the predictability of stressors or our control over them can improve our ability to mange stress. The techniques explained below can increase your ability to experience a greater sense of control over important events in your daily schedule and overall life.

Pacing, scheduling, and self-care: The sleep connection

Our bodies and brains do their best to predict when we will eat, sleep, be active or rest. This allows our bodies to prepare for these events so that they produce less change in our physiology and thus less stress. For example, if our brains expect a meal to come soon, they can plan and release insulin to ensure that our cells are ready to absorb the sugar we eat as soon as the meal is eaten. This prevents this sugar from floating around in our blood where it might clog up or damage our blood vessels. The easiest way for our bodies to know what is coming is for us to follow a regular schedule, especially for sleep.

Not following a regular schedule has been associated with a number of health risks. This has been studied in shift workers, whose inconsistent schedules lead to greater rates of sleep disturbances and altered eating patterns. Studies have found that shift workers, especially those with night work, have higher rates of gastrointestinal problems such as irregular bowel movements, dyspepsia, heartburn, abdominal pain, flatulence, chronic gastritis, gastroduodenitis and peptic ulcer (Costa, 1996). In addition, some studies have suggested that shift workers also have higher rates of cardiovascular problems, such as hypertension, angina, myocardial infarction and other heart disease, but these are less conclusive.

Additionally, not following a regular sleep schedule may lead to poor decision-making. For example, sleep deprivation changes the way the brain, including the ventromedial prefrontal cortex, makes decisions in a gambling task (Venkatraman et al., 2007). Specifically, sleep deprivation increased activation in the nucleus accumbens and made it more sensitive to risky decisions. This suggests that lack of sleep exaggerated the value of immediate rewards. At the same time, sleep deprivation made the prefrontal cortex less sensitive to losses, thus reducing avoidance of losses and increasing the likelihood for risky behavior. Both of these changes would encourage higher-risk, short-term decisions at the potential expense of longer-term benefit. Similar effects are observed during food deprivation, when people are more likely to choose an unhealthful (junk food) versus a healthful snack (fruit) when they were hungry (hours after lunch) versus not (immediately after lunch) (Read & Van Leeuwen, 1998). Again, this is consistent with people making more short-term decisions when their bodies are stressed.

Habitual lack of sleep has been associated in some epidemiological studies with becoming overweight or obese (Marshall et al., 2008; Patel & Hu, 2008). These findings are particularly strong in children. Presumably, this is because being over-tired is a stressor, and people tend to over-eat while stressed. Partial loss of sleep (i.e. sleeping 5-6 hours instead of 7-8) can disrupt a variety of hormone levels, disturbing maintenance of safe levels of glucose in the blood-stream and altering levels of the appetite hormones leptin and gherlin to favor increased hunger (Knutson & Van Cauter, 2008). These hormonal disruptions might not only increase the risk of weight gain, but also the risk of developing Type II diabetes. Notably, associations between sleeping for less than 5 hours a night and developing diabetes have been observed (Gangwisch et al., 2007). A shift towards risky, short-term decision-making when sleep-deprived may have long-term consequences for health, potentially contributing to obesity and metabolic disorders. While good long-term studies still need to be done to prove this hypothesis, we would expect that fixing one's schedule to allow for sufficient rest and sleep should reduce risk for a wide variety of problems related to making short-term decisions focused on immediate gratification.

<u>WARNING: Do not let consistency turn into monotony</u>

One common pitfall in trying to develop a consistent schedule of healthful practices is confusing regularity with repetition. Doing the exact same thing every day is boring. Very few people can do the same thing over and over without craving something new. Monotony will lead you back to unhealthful patterns simply for the thrill of novelty. The key here is that it is important to have a consistent pattern to your health behaviors, not repeat the same behaviors over and over. While it is good for you to eat at the same times everyday, it is important to add variety into what you eat. The consistent pattern will allow your body to be prepared for the work of digestion, and the novelty in your actual food choices will keep your life full of the variety and flavor that we all require to stay interested and challenged. Similarly, it is important to exercise consistently every day, so developing a stable schedule where you do some sort of physical activity at a set time each day will do wonders for your health. But if you try to walk on a treadmill in your living room everyday at 6 for an hour, there is a good chance that you will be bored to tears with exercise within a few weeks at best. Take that same idea of walking for an hour every evening and vary aspects like the setting, companionship, and pace, and you will find that the pattern brings new exciting challenges, relationships, and places to your life. Monday, hike through a park you have never explored. Tuesday, briskly walk through the mall with a friend you have not seen in a while. Wednesday, chase your kids (or your neighbors' kids) around the playground. Thursday, take a social dance class. You will still be exercising every day at 6 for an hour, but you won't suffer the déjà vu and misery from tedium that brings an end to so many well-intentioned attempts to develop patterns that promote wellness.

Because maintaining a consistent schedule is important for reducing stress, many successful behavioral interventions have included a focus on improving consistency in one's schedule. A whole treatment program has been developed to help reduce sleep disturbances and insomnia that can lead to sleep deprivation. This program is typically referred to as cognitive behavioral therapy for insomnia, but may also be referred to by the name of a component of the treatment, "sleep hygiene". It uses simple behavioral techniques to effectively reduce insomnia and normalize sleep patterns. These techniques include ensuring your bed is only associated with sleep, restricting sleep time and napping to ensure that you are tired at bedtime, relaxation training, reducing use of substances (e.g. caffeine, alcohol, sleep aids) and exercise shortly before bedtime, and using cognitive strategies to reduce anxiety about sleep and insomnia. These strategies help people make the most of the time they leave for sleep, and have been shown to be highly effective for treating insomnia (Morgenthaler et al., 2006). Even better, they avoid the use of medications to induce sleep. Use of sleep medications can lead to greater sleep problems over the long-term. Charles M. Morin, Ph.D., the developer of this program, has written a book that provides a comprehensive description of this program and how to deliver it for treatment professionals (Morin & Espie, 2003). For a review of best practices in the behavioral management of chronic insomnia see Trafton & Gordon, 2008a.

To assess your need for better sleep hygiene, see Exercise 3B (page 148).

The detrimental effects of overwork and sleep deprivation

Of course, treating insomnia and improving sleep efficiency will only solve sleep-deprivation-related stress problems if you give yourself enough time to sleep. In our fast-paced society, it is very common for people to convince themselves that they do not have time to sleep and have to keep working when they should be resting. The unspoken assumption underlying these decisions to forgo rest and overwork is that one will be able to keep working effectively and get more done if they keep going. In many cases this assumption is wrong, and the extremes of this problem are fairly obvious. Overworking can lead people to make bad decisions that at a minimum can be difficult and time-consuming to correct. Overworking can lead to injury that can take months to rehabilitate. Overworking can lead to mood disorders (e.g. depression) that can reduce productivity for weeks to months. Pushing yourself when you need rest can be dangerous and can lead to difficult-to-correct problems. Even when overwork problems are not as extreme and obvious they can lead to similar problems. Working too hard one day will tend to make you require more rest or be less efficient the next. Moreover, the consequences of overworking can be exaggerated if you have a chronic health condition.

Concerns about overwork have been formally recognized and incorporated into effective cognitive behavioral therapy programs for a variety of chronic health problems. These programs focus on teaching clients how to pace themselves, and help them learn to recognize how much work they can do without worsening their disorder or becoming tired and inefficient. The therapist then helps the client design a work-rest plan that optimizes their ability to get things done and minimizes exhaustion and worsening of health as a result of work.

The concept that being unrested can worsen efficiency and safety is leading several industries to experiment with on-the-job naps as a way to improve work quality and efficiency. A number of hospitals are encouraging nurses and physicians with long hours or inconsistent shifts to take sleep breaks in special designated rooms in an attempt to reduce medical errors and increase client safety. It has been recognized that the work requirements of nurses and medical residents and students can leave them extremely tired. Surveys of nurses and physicians have found frankly scary rates of self-reported fatigue-related errors and falling asleep while driving home. A survey of over 1300 junior physicians in New Zealand found 24% reported falling asleep driving home since becoming a doctor, and 42% recalled a fatigue-related clinical error in the past 6 months (Gander et al., 2007). Similarly, a survey of 70 physicians in the United States who were sometimes on call found 49% reported falling asleep while driving, with 90% of these dangerous "naps" occurring post-call (Marcus & Loughlin, 1996). Physicians working traditional shifts of longer than 24 hours were more likely to make a serious medical error or be injured in a car accident than those working shorter shifts. Compared to residents working 16-hour shifts, physicians working traditional shifts made 36% more serious medical errors and 300% more fatal medical errors (Lockley et al., 2007). In short, overworked physicians are a danger to themselves and others. While shorter shifts are obviously necessary to fully ameliorate the effects of overwork-related fatigue, even a brief nap during the shift has been shown to have benefits. One study looked at physicians and nurses working 12-hour night shifts who either did or did not take a nap at 3AM. Clinicians who napped only slept about 25 minutes on average, but showed some improvements in performance at 7:30AM (Smith-Coggins et al., 2006). Specifically, they had significantly fewer performance lapses, more quickly performed an intravenous insertion, showed less dangerous driving in a driving simulator, and reported less fatigue and sleepiness and more vigor.

While a short rest cannot completely compensate for an excessive work schedule, it does produce substantial and measurable improvement in both emotional state and behavior. By incorporating this concept in your life by adding sufficient time for rest to your day, you may reduce stress and decrease high-risk habitual or unplanned behaviors.

To work on pacing and developing better rest patterns, try Exercise 3C (page 149), Exercise 3D (page 151) and Exercise 3E (pages 153).

Pre-planning and problem-solving

As we discussed, potential threats are only stressful if we feel like the outcome of the situation is out of our control. In contrast, encountering a problem for which we have a solution is not stressful because we know what to do to keep ourselves safe and healthy. In fact, encountering problems that we can solve is rewarding. Just the idea that you can find a new way to solve your problems can be a means of temporarily relieving stress.

While the threat of the problem may activate our stress systems and turn on our DRN neurons, our sense of control over the situation can activate our medial prefrontal cortex and help negate the effects of the stress. Solving the problem will provide relief that is not only reinforcing but will generally make us feel good about ourselves. Challenging situations are good to experience, so long as we have a solution to keep ourselves safe and in balance. Healthy stress is stress over which we have a good deal of control; however, it may still have a level of uncertainty regarding the outcome. Can I hike this mountain? Can I beat my best time? Can I solve this problem? Avoiding stress does not mean avoiding situations where we might fail. It means setting yourself up such that failure does not put you in serious danger. It is okay not to make it to the top of the mountain, as long as you have a back-up plan that leaves you safe come nightfall.

But how do we ensure that we only run into problems that we know how to solve? Obviously, this is not completely possible. However, in most cases our environments are predictable enough that we can make reasonable guesses about the types of problems that we may run into in the near future. By walking through scenarios in our heads, we can usually identify the majority of problems that we may encounter in our day-to-day lives. With a little practice, we can imagine possible impending problems before we actually experience them. If we can accurately predict and imagine the problems we might soon experience, we can start to figure out and plan solutions in advance to either avoid the problem in the first place or remedy it quickly when it occurs.

Some effective stress management programs include a problem-solving component. People with poor problem-solving skills often have more difficulty coping with life challenges, and training in problem-solving skills can reduce stress in individuals or families dealing with a life-threatening disease. For example, six sessions of problem-solving skills training reduced the number and severity of difficulties experienced by women with breast cancer, as long as they had at least average problem-solving skills (Allen et al., 2002). Presumably those with poor problem-solving skills required a more intensive training.

While there are many different ways to solve problems, having a simple standard strategy for addressing everyday challenges may encourage more deliberate and rational decision-making. The structure provided by training may be particularly useful for people with severe mental illnesses such as schizophrenia, and has been shown to improve functioning and even reduce symptoms in these populations (Barbieri et al., 2006, Liberman et al., 2001). These studies trained clients to use a simple six-step strategy for solving their problems, focusing on individual goals that they identified in the training sessions. These steps were:

1. Identify the specific problem and goal.
2. List all possible solutions.
3. Highlight the advantages and disadvantages of each solution.
4. Choose the best solution.
5. Plan how to carry out the solution.
6. Review your progress and change plan as needed.

This simple strategy may be helpful to anyone. Running through these simple steps to pre-plan responses to problems we anticipate in our day-to-day life may help us feel more prepared and in control as we encounter life's inevitable challenges. That increased sense of control should reduce our stress response and further prevent us from making impulsive choices. Adding a pre-emptive problem-solving routine to your mornings may be a simple way to decrease stress. We will talk about problem-solving and pre-planning solutions more in Challenge #5.

To practice problem-solving and pre-planning solutions, see Exercise 5A (page 210).

Relaxation

Exercises that use breathing, imagery, focused attention on bodily sensation or meditation to reduce stress are components of Western and Eastern wellness programs, including cognitive behavioral therapies and comprehensive yogic practices. Such practices have been demonstrated to reduce immediate stress and improve mood within weeks of regular practice. For example, participants who received a single session of abbreviated progressive muscle relaxation significantly reduced heart rate, subjective feelings of stress and anxiety, and cortisol levels after the intervention compared to participants who sat quietly in a room for the same period of time (Pawlow & Jones, 2002). Five weeks of daily practice using progressive muscle relaxation produced relaxation states and increased levels of mental quiet and joy (Matsumoto & Smith, 2001). Similarly, a pilot study found that six weeks of daily practice of Sudarshan Kriya, a form of yogic breathing exercises, reduced self-reported anxiety, depression and stress and increased optimism (Kjellgren et al., 2007). Pilot studies suggest that using relaxation techniques can help some people correct compulsive stress-related habits such as binge eating at night. Twenty minutes of progressive muscle relaxation practice for a week tended to help people with night eating syndrome, a condition where people have trouble eating in the morning, eat more than half their calories after 6 in the evening, and have trouble falling or staying asleep, eat more for breakfast and less at night (Pawlow et al., 2003). The effects of using these specific relaxation exercises alone have not been investigated sufficiently to recommend for or against them as treatments for chronic disease or mental health problems in their own right. However, cognitive behavioral therapy programs that often include these exercises have been shown to be effective treatments for a wide variety of conditions, including depression, substance use disorders, chronic pain and insomnia (Trafton & Gordon, 2008a).

While a variety of relaxation techniques exist, they all share a focus on ending or counteracting physical responses to stress. Stress can cause you to tighten up your body, causing tension in your muscles. Stress can shorten your breathing, making it inefficient. It can cause your heart to race, and your skin to prickle. These physical reactions can make you feel even more threatened and lead you to panic or have dark thoughts about catastrophic consequences. When repeated regularly, these feelings and thoughts of threat and stress can contribute to chronic pain, depression, anxiety, and other mood disorders. These feelings and thoughts can even worsen physical health; for example, potentially worsening the symptoms of heart disease and diabetes. Your physical and emotional responses to stress can become stressors themselves, leading to chronic stress-related problems. Relaxation exercises help people learn to control and limit these physical and emotional reactions to stress. By learning to notice your feelings of stress, and using techniques to dampen these responses, you may recover more quickly from short-term stressful situations and break the cycle of chronic stress response.

To practice using simple relaxation techniques, try Exercise 3F (page 155).

Brain Challenge #3 Exercises

Exercise 3A: Identifying Stress Symptoms and Their Triggers

As we have noted, lack of control is a critical element in the stress response. We achieve greater control over the environment by being able to predict when stressors reach a critical mass and cause stress-related symptoms. I (W.G.) hypothesize that stress-related symptoms may be a kind of language that reflect the acute effects of distress and the chronic effects of stress.

Step 1: To help you identify stress-related symptoms, review the following checklist to see which apply to you during your typical stress experiences:

Musculoskeletal Symptoms

__ Tension headache
__ Orofacial pain: bruxism and TMJ
__ Upper back and shoulders (trapezius region)
__ Lower back (sacral region)

Cardiovascular/Cerebrovascular Symptoms

__ Hypertensive headache
__ Shortness of breath
__ Chest discomfort, angina
__ Dizziness, sweating

Immune System Symptoms

__ GI symptoms: e.g., IBS, colitis
__ Allergies: respiratory, bronchial, dermatological
__ Autoimmune symptoms: e.g., rheumatoid arthritis, lupus, thyroid
__ Immune-related fatigue: e.g., fibromyalgia

Sleep Symptoms

__ Difficulty fall asleep
__ Difficulty maintaining sleep
__ Difficulty feeling rested

Step 2: Can you identify situations that initiate stress-related symptoms?

Step 3: Can you identify resources that can help manage stress-related symptoms?

Step 4: Below is a list of health professionals that can help manage stress-related symptoms and help develop skills to assist in stress management. Consider these in addition to the resources you identified above.

Somatic Resources	**Mental Health Resources**	**Medical Resources**
Acupuncture	Psychologist	Primary Care MD
Athletic Trainer	Marriage and Family Therapist	Nurse Practitioner
Chiropractors	Social Worker	Cardiologist
Health Coach	School Psychologist	Pulmonologist
Massage	Psychiatrist	Allergist
Physical Therapy	Mental Health Counselor	Osteopath
Tai Chi	Pastoral Counselor	Rheumatologist
Yoga	Human Resource Specialist	Orthopedist

Exercise 3B: Do I Need Better Sleep Hygiene? Creating a Sleep Journal

Although it is difficult to know how many hours of actual sleep you obtained, it is not hard to tell how tired you feel and if you had difficulty falling asleep or remaining asleep. There are many different forms of sleep disorders. Problems with pain, discomfort, anxiety, altered sleep-wake schedules and interruptions can cause problems with initiating sleep. Difficulty in maintaining sleep can follow mood disorders such as low grade (dysthymic) or major depression or bipolar disorder. If a person (or spouse) discovers long respiratory pauses, loud snoring and multiple brief awakenings – signs of sleep apnea – he or she should be referred to a sleep disorders clinic. Restless legs syndrome is another common cause of difficulty in maintaining sleep. The list goes on.

In most cases, there are environmental factors that worsen sleep quality and duration. Here we encourage you to identify these factors. By keeping records of sleep quality and duration, you can provide your primary care physician, psychiatrist, sleep specialist or other mental health professional with key information to diagnose and treat sleep problems. It is also possible it will help you see trends on your own. Perhaps you always have difficulty falling asleep when you consume caffeine after 6:00pm. Sometimes things can become so ingrained in our habits that we do not even realize the adverse consequences they may be having.

If you go online, you can find several different templates that can be downloaded without charge under the search terms "sleep journal" or "sleep diary".

Using your preferred form of documentation, each day when you get out of bed estimate and document the time you went to sleep, how long it took to fall asleep, how many times you remember awakening during the night, the time you woke up, your total sleep time, and the time you got out of bed. Keep notes about your emotional state, thoughts or environmental factors that may have altered your sleep.

There are some relatively simple rules, commonly referred to as sleep hygiene, that can help correct the majority of insomnia problems. These focus on creating a regular pattern of sleep and associating your bedroom only with sleep. These rules include establishing and sticking to a regular bedtime (even on weekends), creating a relaxing routine before bed, finishing all eating, exercise, drinking and smoking at least 2-3 hours before your bedtime, avoiding caffeine within 6 hours of your bedtime, only using the bedroom for sleep and sex (no TV, computer, work desk, reading, etc.), exercising regularly and avoiding naps, and leaving your bed if you do not fall asleep within 10 minutes (e.g. go to another room and read and come back when you are sleepy). If you find you are not sleeping well, work on improving your sleep hygiene by following the rules above.

Exercise 3C: The Power of Structuring One's Life

Structuring your day-to-day life to ensure you get regular and adequate nutrition, exercise and rest as you achieve your goals is key to minimizing stress in your life. The first step in setting up a healthful structure is becoming aware of your current patterns. An activity diary can help you identify areas and patterns in your life that may be stressful.

Use the Daily Activity Sheet on the next page to help you get started. Keep track of your diet, sleep, work, rest, exercise and mood for a week. Review the diary to identify areas in which you are not getting what you need or where there is a lot of variation in whether or when you eat, rest or exercise. If you are not sure what a healthful diet looks like, or how much sleep is enough, consult with a health professional. Once you have identified problem places in your schedule, make a plan to make one schedule change to improve your health.

WORKSHEET: Daily Activity Sheet

Date: ______________________

Hours of Day	Activity	Type of Activity (check)				Notes
		Rest	Rec/Fun	Work	Exercise	
Midnight - A.M. 12-1						
1-2						
2-3						
3-4						
4-5						
5-6						

Upon Awakening: Mood ____________________ Stress level (0-10 scale) _____

Hours of Day	Activity	Type of Activity (check)				Notes
		Rest	Rec/Fun	Work	Exercise	
Morning – Noon 6-7						
7-8						
8-9						
9-10						
10-11						
11-12						

At Noon: Mood ____________________ Stress level (0-10 scale) _____

Hours of Day	Activity	Type of Activity (check)				Notes
		Rest	Rec/Fun	Work	Exercise	
Noon – P.M. 12-1						
1-2						
2-3						
3-4						
4-5						
5-6						

At Dinner: Mood ____________________ Stress level (0-10 scale) _____

Hours of Day	Activity	Type of Activity (check)				Notes
		Rest	Rec/Fun	Work	Exercise	
Evening 6-7						
7-8						
8-9						
9-10						
10-11						
11-12						

At Bedtime: Mood ____________________ Stress level (0-10 scale) _____

Exercise 3D: Give Us This Day Our Daily Self-Monitoring

Having a schedule helps us plan out events and perform healthful behaviors on a daily basis. But even with a schedule, we may continue to make bad choices. Do you feel compelled to make the same mistakes day after day? Imagine if you had a way to record your mistakes and learn from them. Developing a system to learn from your own experience can increasingly improve your ability to cope with events and help you acquire ever-greater control. Any system to learn from experience starts with self-monitoring of daily events.

We modified the Daily Activity Sheet from Exercise 3C so you can use it as a structure to record problems or stressors you encounter each day. By reviewing this log of problems over a longer time period you can identify problems that repeat, and start to experiment with different solutions. Note what you tried and notice the impact on your mood, stress level and resolution of the problem itself. If the new solution works, repeat it. If not, abandon that idea and try a new one. To the extent that you are able to dedicate five or ten minutes a day to this pursuit, it will give you an added sense of power to shape your life. Moreover, it will protect you from things that have gone wrong before by giving you the opportunity to develop a plan of action well in advance of the time you encounter the familiar threat. You can tailor the daily activity sheet to meet your needs. Most stationary stores have a variety of daily planners that can be adapted for personal use.

WORKSHEET: Daily Self-Monitoring Sheet

Date: ____________________

Hour of Day	Problems/Stressors	Mood (0-10 scale)	Stress (0-10 scale)	Resolution & Level of Success
Midnight - A.M. 12-1				
1-2				
2-3				
3-4				
4-5				
5-6				

Upon Awakening: Mood ____________________ Stress level (0-10 scale) _____

Hour of Day	Problems/Stressors	Mood (0-10 scale)	Stress (0-10 scale)	Resolution & Level of Success
Morning – Noon 6-7				
7-8				
8-9				
9-10				
10-11				
11-12				

At Noon: Mood ____________________ Stress level (0-10 scale) _____

Hour of Day	Problems/Stressors	Mood (0-10 scale)	Stress (0-10 scale)	Resolution & Level of Success
Noon – P.M. 12-1				
1-2				
2-3				
3-4				
4-5				
5-6				

At Dinner: Mood ____________________ Stress level (0-10 scale) _____

Hour of Day	Problems/Stressors	Mood (0-10 scale)	Stress (0-10 scale)	Resolution & Level of Success
Evening 6-7				
7-8				
8-9				
9-10				
10-11				
11-12				

Exercise 3E: Work/Rest Balance and Activity Pacing

As we have discussed, it is important to get enough rest and not overdo work or activities so you can reduce stress, prevent burnout and avoid unhealthful decision-making. The first step to finding a proper work/rest balance is recognizing when you are pushing yourself too far. Consider the activity diary you kept in Exercise 3E. Is your level of activity fairly stable from day-to-day? Can you keep up that level of activity without becoming tired, depressed, or needing a day-off to sleep or escape from life? Do you feel like you are able to get enough done in the day to feel good about your life and your progress towards your goals and priorities? If so, congratulate yourself. You have done a reasonable job of balancing work and rest in your life and are likely already skilled at activity pacing.

Alternatively, do you find that you work really hard on one day (or a part of the day or week) and then become so tired, stressed, sore, sick or unmotivated that you cannot get anything done the next day? Do you work so hard during the week that you cannot get out of bed on the weekends, and feel like you are neglecting your family, friends and personal goals? Do you exercise for hours on Monday, only to find yourself skipping your planned exercise for the rest of the week because you are just too sore to move? Do you sleep only four hours on Monday, but then require twelve hours on Tuesday to catch up? If you notice patterns like these in your life or activity diary, then you may benefit from improving your ability to pace yourself.

Pushing yourself too hard and maintaining inconsistent activity levels or schedules are stressful on your body and mind. Moreover, patterns of overwork followed by exhaustion tend to be inefficient. You get more done when you work at an even pace with rest and recovery time included than when you push until you can not go any further and then crash from exhaustion. As the tortoise and the hare fable famously illustrates, the stress you endure from over-doing it does not even help you get ahead.

So what can you do to help improve your pacing skills and improve your work/rest balance? The first step is to set yourself a plan describing a reasonable amount and duration of activity followed by a planned but time-limited rest period. You will likely find that you will need to set up these work/rest plans for various activities you do throughout the day and for various time scales.

For example, on workdays when I (J.T.) am expected to write for 8-10 hours per day, I have a set writing/rest plan. I attempt to write in a focused manner for 30-45 minutes and then give myself 5-10 minutes to distract myself and think about something completely different. While this may seem like a waste of time, this rest period not only invigorates my writing, but also breaks me away from what I am doing for just long enough that I am able to more objectively consider what I have written. It also makes me more able to see errors in my grammar and recognize badly written sentences. In short, these frequent breaks keep me writing efficiently and help me reengage my thinking skills so that I can persist without tiring over the course of the day. I also have plans for work/rest balance for the day; for example, a set wake-up goal and a set bedtime goal. Goals for balancing time for household chores versus playtime, and activity/rest goals for exercise sessions (note these are typically more on a seconds to minutes time scale) are also useful and helpful to plan. Setting these goals requires you not only to recognize your priorities, but also to be observant of your own abilities and limits. It may take multiple rounds of revising your activity/rest plan until you reach a proper balance that allows steady, gradual progress towards your goal and eliminates stressful work binges. It is helpful to continue with your activity diary as well as self-monitor your emotions/stress as you make these revisions so you can keep track of all the outcomes these changes influence.

Basic strategy for developing an optimal activity/rest plan

1. Set a goal in minutes for moderate activity.
2. Set a goal for a time-limited rest period.
3. Repeat the activity/rest cycle throughout the day.
4. Notice your energy and stress level at the end of the activity and rest periods. You should be ready for a rest, but not exhausted, at the end of the activity, and invigorated at the end of the rest.
5. Adjust your activity and rest goals as needed until you reach a pattern that allows for steady repetition of the activity pattern over the day or from day-to-day without need for catch-up activity or extra rest to prevent stress due to either overwork or underwork.

Exercise 3F: Relaxation

Here we describe some of the most commonly used simple brief relaxation exercises and provide links to guided exercises where you can practice these techniques. Relaxation is a skill and requires lots of deliberate practice to master, so we encourage you or your clients to try a variety of exercises and then set a goal to practice the appealing versions at least several times per week. If you or a client wish to extend their relaxation practices beyond these brief exercises, classes in yogic practices, Tai Chi, Qi Gong, or mindfulness meditation provide more extensive practice in relaxation skills and can be found in most communities.

Breathing Exercises
Perhaps one of the simplest techniques for learning to relax involves practicing deep, controlled and intentional breathing. By bringing attention to your breathing, engaging your diaphragm, and taking long, deep, full, even and measured breaths, you will 1) stop the rapid, shallow and stressful breathing that enhances the feeling of stress, 2) reduce tension in your body, and 3) bring your mental focus to a calm place. As you attend to your deep, measured breathing, you eliminate negative thoughts by moving your attention away from them and toward the feelings of safety and calm that slow, full breathing induces. Notably, many yogic practices include breathing exercises as part of training in relaxation and health.

Progressive Muscle Relaxation
Progressive muscle relaxation adds a focus on muscle tension to the relaxation practice. Typically, this technique is used in conjunction with a focus on breathing. Like breathing exercises, progressive muscle relaxation encourages attention to your internal state and feelings. By intentionally correcting bodily responses triggered by stress, you help the feelings of stress fade. The general idea behind progressive muscle relaxation is simple. You work through the body, piece by piece, deliberately contracting each muscle to bring attention to it and then slowly releasing the muscle to relax it completely. For example, you may start with the right hand. Clench it tightly and slowly count to five, focusing on the feeling of tightness that flexing the muscle produces. Then slowly release the muscle, often in conjunction with release of your breath, noticing the difference in feeling and the relaxed sensation in the muscle. Repeat this sequence with your left hand, then your right forearm, then your left, and so forth until you have covered all the main muscle groups in the body. It can be helpful to focus some extra attention on muscles where people tend to become habitually tense with stress, such as neck and shoulder muscles, and even the muscles of the face and forehead. To ensure that progressive muscle relaxation is done safely and effectively, it is important to remember to breathe calmly and consistently throughout the exercise. It is good to remind clients or yourself to breathe at the outset, as the effort of tightening and focusing on muscles can make people forget to breathe or hold their breath. Not breathing can cause stress and reduce the impact of the exercise.

Guided Imagery
Guided imagery exercises encourage the participant to imagine that he is in a deeply relaxing, safe and beautiful setting. Imagining the sights, sounds, smells, sensations and

feelings of the imaginary environment helps draw attention to the safe, comfortable surroundings and induce feelings of relaxation and calm. Focusing on the sensory illusions of the imaginary setting can help the participant leave behind the physical, emotional and cognitive feelings of stress built up in his or her day-to-day life. Incorporating breathing exercises can intensify the relaxation experience. Different imaginary settings may work best for different people. Everyone has his or her own special safe places, and these may work best for imagery exercises. The key is to be able to imagine the setting in enough detail to feel like you are there. Good examples could be warm, sandy beaches, a peaceful forest, a soft rug in front of a fireplace, or even a fresh snow on a mountain retreat, depending on your personal experiences and associations. Focusing simply on a sense of warmth and comfort in your body can work similarly.

Practice Exercises

There are a number of websites with scripts and exercises that you can use to practice or teach relaxation skills. Below are a few to get you started:

http://www.allaboutdepression.com/relax/
Provides written scripts and audio files with a variety of relaxation exercises led by clinical psychologists. The site includes all of the techniques mentioned above.

http://www.innerhealthstudio.com/relaxation-scripts.html
Provides a good number of written scripts for relaxation exercises that you can record for yourself or use with a client. The site also offers free audio recordings of relaxation exercises, a weekly podcast with relaxation exercises, and some video clips to help with relaxation exercises.

Brain Challenge #4

Training Your Addiction Circuits To Make Healthy Behaviors Habitual

Challenge Introduction

My husband keeps nagging me (J.T.) to join him for morning workouts at the Master's swim team he joined last year. "It's so nice in the water," he says, "the rhythm of the swimming is so soothing, it's almost like you are still asleep but flying through the water". "You'll love it. It is such an energizing way to start a day." Always in need of energy, but feeling nervous because I have never swum with a group before, I agree to come the next morning. That morning, I drag myself out of bed, scramble around the house looking for the things I need, go to the pool, bumble around the locker room trying to get my suit on and my goggles to stay on my face, and jump in the pool flustered and already tired just from trying to prepare. My husband is already there, looking calm, confident, eager and ready to go. He gives me some quick pointers on how to follow the workout and I join the group. He moves gracefully, with long coordinated strokes propelling him smoothly forward. I, on the other hand, cannot get both arms to work evenly together, let alone synchronize them with what my legs are doing. Ugh, what are my legs doing? This is exhausting, I can hardly breathe, and as far as I can tell, I am at best getting in the way and likely to hit a team member with my flailing crooked attempts at swimming. Is my husband just a natural? Am I just uncoordinated? No, his one year head start has completely transformed swimming for him, from a discombobulated, difficult, tiring exercise into an efficient, relaxing activity that he can do while he basks in the beauty of the sun rising over the warm pool. He has learned to swim properly and practiced regularly, and now can do it, nearly in his sleep, with his attention elsewhere. He has taken a difficult but healthful activity and made it easy. I have a lot of learning and practice ahead of me before swimming has a chance of becoming a personal morning meditation, but his example helps me see the great rewards such hard work can bring.

New and unpracticed behaviors require thought, effort and planning to carry out. With repetition, these behaviors become mastered and automatic. Different brain regions take over and can run through these behavioral programs without conscious thought and sometimes even without our awareness. This habit learning drives much of our behavior, from brushing our teeth and tying our shoelaces to binge eating and substance abuse. With training, it may be easier to do a behavior than to prevent yourself from doing it. That's why it is important to develop healthful habits. Once you develop habits to the point of becoming automatic they become really hard not to do. Whether they are good or bad behaviors, it is easier for you to do learned habits than less practiced behaviors. Too often this means doing learned bad habits over less practiced healthful behaviors. You will need to practice new health behaviors until they are as mastered and automatic as your old unhealthful behaviors in order to maintain meaningful behavior changes. In Challenge #4, we will discuss how our brains most efficiently learn new behaviors and turn them into habits. Then we discuss psychological techniques to help us make more attempts, repeatedly practice, and eventually master new behaviors. In Chapter 4.1, we describe what behaviors can become automatic, and what happens in the brain as behaviors become automatic. In Chapter 4.2, we discuss how we learn new behaviors and the importance of modeling, observation and practice. In Chapter 4.3, we explain how to turn a new behavior into a habit through practice, support, monitoring and rewards.

Chapter 4.1: The Abilities of the Human Autopilot

Skilled movements and even complex behaviors, although initially requiring effort and concentration, can become automatic through sufficient practice. These automatic behaviors are learned and performed using the basal ganglia, a brain region involved in habits and movement. The basal ganglia are critically involved in remembering automatic patterns of movement or habits, such as swimming, riding a bicycle, driving your car, brushing your teeth, washing your hands or preparing your cereal for breakfast. Once learned by the basal ganglia, all can be performed with minimal awareness. In contrast, it is impossible to train the brain to automatically do something new, determine the fastest way home through traffic or rearrange your schedule to fit in a new exercise class because these are different skills that the basal ganglia is not equipped to learn. These behaviors require controlled processing. Behaviors that use controlled processing require focused attention to the task, and multitasking or stress will impair your ability to do them. The behaviors that the basal ganglia automatize as habits can be extremely complicated, but they must use specific learning and logic rules. You will never be able to count calories without deliberate thought nor will you be able to plan group meals without focused awareness. But you can learn the habit of drinking a full glass of water before starting dinner and of stopping eating when your stomach feels full. These habits are essential for maintaining stable health, particularly during busy or trying times.

It is important to understand the distinction between automatic processing and controlled processing (see Schneider & Chein, 2003) as we attempt to design and learn new health habits. Automatic processing is fast, more efficient and accurate, occurs in parallel and does not require explicit attention. In other words, you can do tasks that require only automatic processing quickly and correctly, at the same time as you attend to other things in life, and without purposely paying attention to them. Riding a bike after you have already learned and practiced is an example of automatic processing. Controlled processing is slow, serial, and requires attention. In other words, you can only do tasks that require controlled processing if you take your time, only do one thing at a time, and pay attention to what you are doing. Composing new written text or doing long division are examples of tasks that always requires controlled processing.

Not all behaviors become effortless with practice. Consider long division, for example. While you can have some improvement in accuracy and speed through practice, new strategies, and some memorization, you can never do it automatically. Because there are infinite possibilities for numbers to divide, we cannot learn them all and must continue to rely on controlled processing to use multiple and variable cognitive strategies to determine the correct response. And when we use these processes, trying to do other things at the same time or getting stressed impairs our ability to do the behavior.

Automatic processing is less flexible but faster, and only develops with lots of practice. Importantly, it is less likely to be disrupted by stress, fatigue or other distracters (Schneider & Chein, 2003). In other words, once a behavior is automatic, you can continue to do the behavior even when you have other things on your mind, are focused on doing something else, or are feeling too tired or out of sorts to focus on what you are doing. This feature of automatic processing is key for maintaining and consistently sticking to healthful behaviors. You cannot spend all of your time thinking about eating right, getting exercise, and eschewing unhealthful options. But if you can make those behaviors automatic then you will do them preferentially as you go about your everyday life. Finding ways of making healthful behaviors automatic can improve your ability to adopt and maintain practices that keep you healthy over the long-term.

What behaviors can become automatic?
As we discussed, not all behaviors can be automatized, so what is the difference between behaviors that can versus cannot become automatic with practice? Research indicates one main requirement for behaviors that can become automatic is that there has to be a consistent response to a consistent cue (Schneider & Chein, 2003). Automatic behaviors consist primarily of rules indicating, "when you encounter X, do Y". Whenever there is a given problem or set of inputs, there must be a consistent response that solves the problem. If you do the same thing every time, the problem will be solved. On the other hand, if the correct response varies or the situation requires using multiple or variable cognitive strategies to determine the correct response, then you will never be able to make that choice without paying some attention to it.

Automatic behavior can be something as simple as "notice the cue". For example, you might train your brain to notice signs for stairs when you enter buildings, which might cue you to think about using them instead of the elevator. Even if a health behavior involves a problem that will require multiple strategies (for example, taking pills while on vacation), you can still use automatic processing to consistently draw your attention to or away from a particular cue. For example, you might learn to habitually place your pills in a location that is conspicuous. This can help you notice specific opportunities or solvable problems in the environment that you might otherwise ignore. When decisions are more complex, it can still be extremely helpful to have trained yourself to notice opportunities to make a healthful choice or avoid an unhealthful one.

What happens to brain processing as behaviors become automatic?
All new behaviors require controlled processing to complete. You need to practice new behaviors repeatedly in order to make them automatic. You will not train automatic responses until you have tried them enough to figure out the constant relationships between cues or problems and solutions. Only with practice will you be able to do the new behavior without paying direct attention to the choice you are making. *In other words, practice and training is key for taking a new behavior that uses controlled processing and turning it into a habit that uses automatic processing.*

Repeating new behaviors via controlled processing strengthens brain connections that recognize the relevant situation and carry out the successful strategy. This strengthening of response behaviors becomes hardwired in brain regions outside the controlled processing system; in particular, the basal ganglia. With repeated strengthening, these behaviors will get triggered and performed as a sort of autopilot system run by brain circuits that are happy to do their work without your direct attention (Graybeil, 2008). Eventually, the controlled processing system may not even be engaged as you perform these well-trained solutions to your day-to-day problems.

To observe the difference between the brain processing required in early learning (i.e. using the controlled processing system) versus after practice (i.e. using the automatic processing system), researchers conducted a review of many imaging studies where brain activity was recorded 1) during early learning of an automatable behavior, and 2) after repeated practice of the behavior (Chein & Schneider, 2005). They looked across these studies to see what brain regions were highly active during early learning and much less active once the behavior was practiced, which would suggest where these "controlled processes" might take place. Because they were merging and averaging across studies, this provided a big but somewhat blurry picture. They found that in all these studies, activity in several areas of the brain (i.e. the lateral prefrontal cortex, medial frontal cortex including the anterior cingulate and pre-supplementary motor area, and the posterior parietal, occipito-temporal and cerebellar areas) showed consistent and significant decreases in activity over time as tasks were practiced and controlled processing diminished.

These brain regions, which are known to be involved in directing attention and motivation, problem-solving, and movement planning, were found to be active during early learning but much less so after practice. In other words, it takes many more areas of the brain when learning a new behavior but many less once the behavior is learned. A follow-up brain imaging study showed the same decreases in brain activity observed earlier. In particular, activity in prefrontal cortex areas such as the dorsolateral prefrontal cortex and anterior cingulate decreased to the point that activity in these areas when people were doing the well-practiced task looked the same as when they were just sitting around. Once the behavior had been practiced, the participants no longer needed the problem-solving abilities of the prefrontal cortex in order to correctly solve and answer the problems. This means that once you have learned how to do something, you can do so without any observable activity in the controlled processing areas.

Learning to ride a bike is a classical example of a task that requires attention, motivation and problem-solving when you first begin but becomes simple and effortless with practice (see the Figure on the next page). Just keeping the bike upright is a struggle at the start. Trying to do so while turning the pedals and manning the brake feels near impossible. But as we practice, riding the bike becomes easy. We can eventually maneuver the bike without even paying attention to the mechanics of the task. As you can imagine, if you are no longer thinking about the behavior when you perform it you will not longer be engaging the same brain regions. This automaticity of habits performed by deeper brain regions like the basal ganglia frees up our brain so we can complete multiple behaviors. On the bike, this means we can now talk to a friend, avoid traffic or plan out a travel route.

FIGURE: Brain regions involved in controlled but not automatic processing

Legend: Learning a new behavior requires conscious effort and activity in brain regions involved in motor planning, problem-solving and coordinated action. Highlighted in white are some of the general brain regions that are highly active when learning a new behavior, but show greatly decreased activity after the behavior has been practiced and becomes automatic (adapted and simplified based on Chein & Schneider, 2005). From right to left, these include the lateral prefrontal cortex, the pre-supplementary motor area, the posterior parietal cortex and the cerebellum. After behaviors become automatic, deeper brain structures (i.e. the basal ganglia, not pictured because it is not on the surface of the brain) can carry out the behavior without conscious attention and with little to nor help from the cortical brain regions. When learning to bike (on the left), we would expect activity in these regions to be required to successfully ride the bike. When bike riding has been well-learned (on the right), substantially less activity must occur in these regions to successfully ride the bike, freeing up these higher processing areas to focus on other tasks, such as socializing with friends, shopping or navigating busy city sidewalks.

EXAMPLE: How simple automatic rules can help in adopting and maintaining even complicated healthful behaviors

Automatic behaviors can guide us as we focus on other things and deal with other stressors in our lives. But healthful behaviors can be pretty complicated. There is not always a single correct choice every time, which means we do need to use multiple strategies to make many health decisions. How can simple automatic rules help maintain healthful behaviors when the overall decisions and behaviors are complicated? To illustrate, I (J.T.) will give you an example from my own life: how I decide what to eat every day. By supplementing my detailed knowledge of nutrition with some simple automatic rules for noticing and picking foods, I do a decent job of maintaining my nutrition without having to obsess about it all day long.

While I personally have a pretty extensive knowledge of nutrition, food composition, metabolism, endocrinology, and the physiological consequences of food choice that I could and do use from time to time to make choices about what to eat, this knowledge is far too complicated to think about every time I need or want to eat. Instead, I will admit to relying fairly substantially on some very simple hardwired rules that I developed in my teenage years. These help me filter down my food choices and avoid making particularly bad decisions even when I am too stressed or tired to think about it.

My father's side of the family has a disturbing history of heart disease and truncal obesity. My grandfather and uncle died of heart attacks in their early 50's and 30's, respectively. So when my dad had his first triple-bypass when I was a pre-teen, I concluded that products high in cholesterol and saturated animal fat were not options that should be a part of my future and switched to a vegetarian diet. With practice, I trained a couple of simple rules that are basically as follows:

1) When fresh vegetables and fruit are available, notice and eat them.
2) When meat or poultry are in or around food, ignore and avoid them.

I note that these rules are extremely simple and not very sophisticated. They also do not tell me what to do when exposed to a whole lot of foods, and there is still plenty of room for me to make bad decisions. For example, what do I do when I encounter a bran muffin or a Pop-Tart? I still need my controlled processing system to help me make those choices. Nevertheless, these two simple rules shape my perception of my environment to make it much more conducive to heart-healthy eating. By eating fresh vegetables and fruits when I find them, I keep myself from feeling hungry as often. This helps me make better choices when I need to think about them because I am not as stressed by hunger. And this, in turn, may make my controlled processing system do a better job when considering things like Pop-Tarts. By ignoring and not even considering products containing meat, I cut out many types of food that could send my cholesterol levels through the roof. My brain filters out whole restaurants, parts of menus, and sections of grocery stores that do not meet my criteria, protecting me from bad choices and drawing me towards good ones. On occasion, I have been rather shocked when a friend points out that certain meat-focused restaurants exist on main streets in downtown areas that I frequent to get other food. It may be years before I consciously attend to the fact that an Arby's or McDonald's opened a block away from my favorite falafel store. My brain automatically ignores such options, and I never have to waste my time considering whether a quarter-pounder and fries would be a good thing to eat right now.

With the help of these simple rules, I have never had a problem with my weight or my cholesterol and lipid levels, despite my family predispositions. But it only takes a few hours with my metabolic-syndrome-plagued father to realize that, although we live in the same environment, the food options that reach my awareness are vastly different than those that gain his attention. Because he lacks these simple trained rules, he is repeatedly faced with dangerous food choices every day and has to struggle with each and every one of them. Add a little stress, and he is a dietitian's worst nightmare.

Training simple behavioral habits, particularly teaching yourself to notice and gravitate towards options for healthful thoughts and behaviors and ignore and avoid unhealthful thoughts and behaviors can set you on a path towards health that requires very little focus and effort. Our environment consists of what we attend to much more than what actually exists. Thus, training ourselves to habitually notice good choices and ignore bad ones can have a huge effect on our everyday behavior. By training ourselves to only attend to opportunities that align with our long-term goals and values, we can change the environment we experience without going anywhere.

Chapter 4.2: How We Learn New Behaviors

Imitation, mirror neurons and the importance of modeling

If we consider the complex physics of getting a body to move in a coordinated, goal-directed fashion, it is frankly amazing any of us ever get up off the couch. So how do we learn complicated new behaviors everyday without big struggles? We are extremely good at learning via imitation. While it is relatively rare for someone to develop a truly new behavior pattern, once one person has done it, it can spread through a population like wildfire. Theoretically, we can plan out new behaviors in our heads and enact the movements, but we are not all that great at doing so. But if we see it done, we can imitate it. Our brains allow us to imagine ourselves in other people's bodies, and the movements we observe activate the same neurons that plan our movements. When we see someone else move in a coordinated manner, we can relate their movements to moving our own bodies, and record the movement pattern to try later.

Taking advantage of our human ability to mimic behaviors has been shown to be a crucial component of effective interventions to encourage health behaviors. Interventions that demonstrate and model health behaviors (i.e. let the trainee watch someone do the behavior and try it themselves) are much more likely to successfully train people to perform and adopt the health behavior (Trafton & Gordon, 2008a; Trafton & Gordon 2008b). Understanding how this system works can help us more efficiently learn new health behaviors on our own or design training programs for others that truly work.

Our ability to imitate other people and learn how to achieve goals through observation is facilitated by a group of neurons in the premotor cortex, the part of the brain that plans out actions prior to activating the neurons in the motor cortex that actually initiate muscle movement. These premotor cortex neurons are activated when you either 1) do something yourself, or 2) observe someone else doing that same thing (Iacoboni, 2008). These neurons are called mirror neurons, since their activity mirrors the activity of the same neurons in the person you are observing. Mirror neurons are specifically found in the inferior frontal gyrus and the rostral portion of the posterior parietal cortex. Mirror neurons fire when you plan to do something. They record and work out a behavior plan. Once the plan is finalized, mirror neurons can deliver the plan to the motor cortex, which instructs your body to carry out the behavior by sending signals to your muscles via the spinal cord. But mirror neurons also fire when they observe someone else doing a behavior, which means they can record any behavioral plan that they observe. Once that plan is recorded, it can also be sent to the motor cortex and acted upon. Monkey see, monkey do. Thanks to mirror neurons, we can learn new behaviors through imitation, rather than having to work out the whole movement on our own.

Studies that recorded the activity of these neurons in monkeys and imaged the activity of these brain regions in humans have provided us with an understanding of the general abilities and functions of these neurons. It turns out that a third of the mirror neurons act as described above. The monkey recording studies showed that these mirror neurons fire both when a monkey is doing a behavior or observing someone else doing a similar behavior (e.g. when picking up a pencil or watching someone else pick up a pencil). The other two-thirds of the mirror neurons are even more sophisticated than the description above suggests. Neuron recordings show these mirror neurons fire when observing behaviors that share a common goal (e.g. chopping food in preparation and actually cooking food). These neurons do not just mimic the movements they observe others make. They encode the intention of the actions as well.

A clever study in monkeys demonstrated that the activity of these mirror neurons depends crucially on the goal of the action rather than just the movements that were observed. In this study, a human researcher conducted various grasping actions in front of monkeys while recording the activity from their mirror neurons (Umilta et al., 2001). The monkey's neurons fired when the researcher grasped an object in front of them. But when the researcher made the same arm and hand motion without actually grasping an object, the neurons did not fire. This showed that the neurons did not respond to the motion of the arm and hand, but rather to the motion of the arm and hand in achieving a goal. The researchers then looked at how the monkey's mirror neurons would respond if part of the motion were hidden from the monkey. They first showed the monkey an object on the table and then put a screen between the monkey and the object. Then the researcher reached behind the screen and grasped the object. Surprisingly, half of the mirror neurons still fired when the researcher grasped the object behind the screen, even though the monkey could not actually see the grasping motion. They then repeated this set-up without the object. They first showed the monkey that there was no object on the table, and replaced the screen. Then the researcher reached behind the screen and pretended to grasp an object. What the monkey actually saw was identical whether or not the object behind the screen. But when the object was not behind the screen, the mirror neurons did not fire. When the monkey knew there was no object to be grasped behind the screen, then there was no obvious goal to the observed movement and the mirror neurons were not activated. Thus, mirror neurons encode both what people are doing and why (e.g. what they achieve by doing it). These and similar studies have led to the hypothesis that mirror neurons help us to both recognize and imitate others goals, thus allowing us to understand others' actions, join them in collaborative work, and empathize with their feelings regarding a situation and its outcome (Iacoboni, 2008).

Understanding these properties of the mirror neuron system, we can make predictions about how people should learn new behaviors most efficiently. If we understand the purpose behind someone's actions, observe them doing the action, and have personal motivation to reach the same goal, then we should learn a new behavior relatively quickly. If we supply our mirror neuron system with the information it needs to record a movement plan to meet a goal, and have reason to try the behavior ourselves, we should be on our way to trying and eventually mastering a new behavior.

This system is likely involved in the social contagion of health behaviors we discussed previously. Mirror neurons help us mimic others, often without realizing it. Thus, this system may encourage us to learn the behaviors we observe others doing even if we have no intentions or goals of engaging in those behaviors. Such effects may, for example, encourage us to over-eat like those around us or like people shown in television commercials. This influence of our mirror neurons may contribute to the potent effects of our immediate social network and television viewing on weight gain (Cohen, 2008; Christakis & Fowler, 2007; Jason & O'Donnell, 2009). Watching people do healthful behaviors is important for ensuring that our mirror neurons drive us to mimic and learn healthful rather than harmful habits. Watching people or ourselves do healthful behaviors in our mind's eye (e.g. visualizing healthful behaviors) can also help us learn more quickly.

To practice using visualization to engage our mirror neurons in learning new habits, see Exercise 4A (page 184).

The importance of observation

The existence of this mirror neuron system helps explain a consistent finding in trials of interventions to promote health behavior change. Specifically, mirror neurons explain why interventions that include an element of modeling and practice of the new target behavior are much more effective than interventions that simply educate clients about what to do. People are much more likely to adopt a new behavior if they are shown the behavior. If they have a chance to try the behavior in a safe setting with an encouraging person, they are even more likely to adopt it. When people are only told what to do, no matter how compelling the reason given, they rarely take up the recommendation. Even when the behavior seems relatively simple, people generally need help translating what to do into how to do it. *Demonstrating the health behaviors that you wish a client to practice can greatly increase the chance that they do the behavior correctly and regularly. Didactic education alone (i.e. simply telling people what to do and why) has very little to no effect on changing people's health behaviors.* However, if you add a component where clients observe others doing a behavior, and get a chance to try it themselves and receive feedback, much greater effects on behavior can be achieved. For example, programs to improve oral hygiene that demonstrate how to brush teeth have greater effects than those that simply explain what to do.

Without knowing much about mirror neurons, psychologists observed what worked for training people in new behaviors and described these strategies in their theories. One such theory that has received substantial empirical support is the theory of self-efficacy, which states that people who have observed, tried, been encouraged, and feel confident about doing a behavior are more likely to actually do it. I note that this is just what we would expect given what we know about mirror neurons. New behaviors are most efficiently learned when we can observe and receive coaching from another person who has mastered and can demonstrate the behavior. Next, we will discuss the theory of self-efficacy in more detail and explain how to use each piece in our efforts to learn and encourage new healthful behaviors.

Increasing your confidence to do a behavior: Practice, modeling, encouragement and anxiety-reduction

In his research on a concept he termed "self-efficacy", Albert Bandura, a professor of Psychology at Stanford University, identified several elements that facilitate behavior change (Bandura, 1997). These elements have been successfully used in programs to encourage health behavior change in a wide variety of domains, including encouraging physical activity, weight loss, pain management, smoking cessation, and chronic disease management (for a review of how the theory of self-efficacy has been used to change health behaviors, see McKellar, 2008). Self-efficacy refers to a person's belief about his or her ability to do a specific activity, and has been shown to be highly predictive of actual behavior in many studies. Not surprisingly, if you are more confident that you can do a specific behavior, you are more likely to do it in general, and more likely to do it repeatedly in the future. According to Bandura's theory, there are four main ways you can increase your self-efficacy or confidence that you can do a behavior: (1) enactive attainments, (2) vicarious experience, (3) verbal persuasion, and (4) observation of your own physiological state.

1. "Enactive attainments" refers to actually doing the behavior. Not surprisingly, if you have tried and successfully accomplished a behavior, you will probably be more confident that you can do it in the future. Successfully achieving a behavior is probably the best way of increasing self-efficacy. This might explain the inherent appeal of the famous Nike ad campaign encouraging would-be athletes to "Just Do It". We all know that "doing it" would increase our confidence and help us see ourselves as competent and able. If we "just do it", then we know we are capable of the same things that we might otherwise idolize in others. But one concern is that trying and failing at a behavior can be counterproductive and discourage repetition of a behavior. That is why successful training of a health behavior often requires breaking down the complex behavior into simple steps, a process that is often complicated and not obvious. It can take an expert in the behavior to be able to parse a behavior into achievable pieces. When presenting new skills that clients need to master, such as the proper use of oxygen delivery devices, asthma inhalers, complex medication or rehabilitation regimes, or use of assistive devices, it may be necessary to break down the behavior into many small pieces to avoid failure and discouragement, rather than to try to teach the entire sequence all at once.

2. "Vicarious experience" refers to watching someone else do the behavior. Seeing someone else do something can increase our confidence that we can do it too. Watching someone else do something lets us know it is possible, and provides us with an opportunity to develop a mental plan for how to do it. As we discussed, observing a behavior activates our mirror neurons and encodes the actions and motivations of the behavior in the part of our brain that plans movements. By seeing a behavior done, your brain actually wires in a plan of how to move your body to do that behavior or reach that same goal. Observation not only tells you that this behavior is achievable, but also provides you with enough information so you can probably roughly approximate that new behavior yourself by mimicking what you saw. Thus, by watching Michael Jordon dunk a basketball, I am convinced that people can dunk basketballs, and have a decent idea how it is done—however, jumping five feet above the ground is beyond what most of us can expect to attain. This highlights a major caveat of this type of learning. Observation teaches new behaviors better if the model is someone that the observer believes is "like them". As a 5'1" woman, I (J.T.) have trouble imagining myself as a 6'6" man, and thus watching NBA games has done little to teach me basketball skills. Having a model in which you can see yourself in or to whom you can relate is important for strengthening the effects of observation on learning.

This aspect of "vicarious experience" helps explain why mutual help groups are so effective for encouraging behavior change. Mutual help groups let you see and interact with people like you who are also learning and doing the behavior. They provide models for behaviors that you can do in your environment with things you know. People who are challenged by a condition can greatly benefit by finding mentors who have the same condition and have been successful in managing it. Examples where mutual help groups have been shown to benefit include children who have lost a loved one, preteens with depression, adolescents in residential settings, adults with HIV, survivors of sexual abuse, homeless women and children, people experiencing separation and divorce, parents with addictions, and elderly coping with bereavement (Gitterman & Schulman, 2005). Seeing my officemate lose all her baby weight by taking mid-day walks and making careful choices at the company cafeteria makes me confident that I can, within the realities of my world, really get back to my pre-pregnancy state. Interacting with and observing people like you doing the behaviors and reaching the goals that you wish to reach can greatly increase self-efficacy and encourage behavior change.

3. "Verbal persuasion" refers to being encouraged to accomplish a behavior. When someone tells me I can do it, I am more likely to believe I can and give it a try. Like we mentioned, simple verbal instruction is often insufficient for learning new behaviors but verbal support can be an instigator for actually doing the behavior and motivating practice of a behavior. Encouragement, cheerleading, or expressed confidence in your abilities from another person can increase your belief that you can do a specific behavior. As with modeling, the impact of encouragement on your self-efficacy will depend on who is doing the encouraging. The person encouraging you needs to be knowledgeable and credible. You have to believe that they know enough about how to do the behavior and enough about you and your abilities to make a decent judgment about your likelihood of success. Moreover, you need to respect their opinion.

4. "Observation of your physiological state" refers to being aware of your fears and your stress level about trying something. If you are terrified about doing a behavior, your self-efficacy will be lower. When you are anxious or think you could be hurt, you probably will not try the behavior. If you do try, you may quit partway through the behavior or only put a little bit of effort into it. You may be so focused on maintaining an escape in case something goes wrong that you wind up sabotaging your attempt. Gymnastics coaches warn their gymnasts against such fear-related half-attempts with the saying "when in doubt, don't kick-out". When you are upside down in the air, the last thing you want to do is quit and stop right there. Being aware of your fears and anxieties about a behavior and working to reduce them before you make an attempt can improve the chance that you really try, and thus have a chance at succeeding. And success or even surviving a feared behavior is good for your self-efficacy.

To walk through how Bandura's theory of self-efficacy can be used to increase the likelihood that someone develops and maintains a health behavior, let's consider the example of trying to get someone who has just been diagnosed with diabetes to test their blood sugar after meals. A brief visit with a nurse or educator who knows how to test blood sugar can be very helpful. The nurse or educator should demonstrate how to test blood sugar (vicarious experience), demonstrate that taking a blood sample is not very painful or dangerous (reducing the client's fear and anxiety about the needle stick), encourage the client to try and reassure them of their ability (verbal persuasion), and help them test their blood sugar themselves (enactive attainments). This simple visit uses all four of the elements to increase self-efficacy for testing blood sugar, and visits such as these are standard components of effective interventions to improve use of blood sugar testing to manage diabetes. The theory of self-efficacy and the effective interventions that use these elements highlight the importance of modeling and imitation, practice, encouragement and support, and decreasing fear in encouraging new behaviors.

Chapter 4.3: Turning a New Behavior into an Old Habit

Practice, practice, practice: Getting yourself to train a new behavior

Once you are able to do a behavior and gain confidence in your abilities, you need to find ways to make the new healthful behavior habitual. If the behavior does not come automatically, you are not going to do it very often. What can you do to make a healthful behavior a habit? Well, we know you need to practice the behavior a lot.

But how do you get yourself to practice? For example, I (J.T.) have been taught how to swim, can swim laps reasonably well, and know that it would be good for my health to swim laps regularly. But I have not been in the pool for ages. How do I turn swimming laps into a regular part of my life? How do I get myself to practice and keep myself going day after day?

As we have spent a lot of time discussing, habits are generally maintained by rewards. We do things automatically when we repeatedly experience short-term benefits from doing them. While all healthful behaviors have long-term benefits, our reward system, which drives most of our habitual behavior, is only tuned into short-term ones. The effects of exercise on my bone density decades down the road are not inherently reinforcing, and will not do a lot to encourage daily workouts on their own. Our brains simply are not set up to detect these long-term health benefits. Thus, to make a new behavior a habit you need to find or create ways of making that new behavior rewarding in an immediate sense. If you want to exercise consistently, you have to make exercise benefit you right away.

The amount of practice that is sufficient to make something habitual will depend substantially on the complexity of the skills. Simple behaviors, such as "press this key when this message shows on the screen", can be learned and become automatic in less than an hour of practice. More complex, multi-step behaviors can take years to practice and automate. One study of new health behaviors found that depending on the complexity of the habit, daily repetitions for as little as 20 to over 250 days were required to make the new behavior automatic (Lally et al, 2010). Most importantly, however, all automatic behaviors require on-going reinforcement if they are to continue. Even after you train a behavior to the point that it is automatic, the behavior must continue to provide short-term benefits or it will slowly fade from your daily behavior. Finding ways of consistently rewarding our healthful behaviors is crucial to maintaining healthful habits over long periods.

Next, we will discuss some ways in which you can improve adherence to or maintenance of newly developed healthful behaviors to turn them from a skill into a habit.

Social support

For humans, the most powerful, readily available, and modifiable rewards are social. While you may not be able to afford to reward yourself with expensive gifts every time you do something healthful, with some purposeful effort you can almost always find a group of people who support your goals and will be pleased with your efforts towards them. The best way of turning a new behavior into a habit is to make it socially beneficial. If you get social approval and support for your new behavior, that behavior will now immediately improve your well-being and you will begin to favor it automatically. If you can find a social network that encourages and is impressed by your new behavior (or disapproves and is horrified when you do not do it), you are apt to continue it consistently over time. If the healthful behavior is normative in your social network, it will be maintained by the responses of those around you (see Brain Challenge #1).

As a simple example, let's consider a lunchtime workout program started by a co-worker at my office. A colleague who was very interested in yoga and practiced it regularly herself went to the trouble of finding a teacher willing to teach a low-cost yoga class in an open conference room during the lunch hour. At the start, the class was attended primarily by staff members who were already interested in yoga and had some yoga experience. They loved having a new, convenient option where they could do their already learned behavior. Other staff members started to become more aware of the class as the initial attendees began scheduling their meetings around the class and talking about how great and important it was to them. A few brave yoga-naïve staff members decided to try it, and their positive reviews as well as the subsequent cajoling of others, encouraged a few more to try. This eventually snowballed to the point that now, every Thursday at 11:50AM, an entire troupe of employees don exercise gear and start down the hall, collecting colleagues as they head to the yoga class. This healthy new habit has spread so effectively that finding staff members to cover the phones during the class is a substantial challenge.

For an excellent and amusing three-minute narrated video demonstrating the rapid spread of a new behavior through a social group, see "Leadership Lessons from Dancing Guy" on YouTube at the following link: http://www.youtube.com/watch?v=fW8amMCVAJQ

Setting up social rewards for behaviors not only encourages them in individuals, but can make healthful behaviors spread as if contagious. Reinforcing good behaviors in one group can set up social responses that reinforce that same behavior in other connected networks of people. Linking yourself to a network that already reinforces a behavior can help you make that behavior a regular everyday part of your life.

In the previous chapter, we mentioned how mutual groups can assist in "vicarious experience" to visualize new behaviors. In addition to that, mutual help groups create a network of people with the same goals who provide support and social reward for maintaining the behavioral goal. Client support groups can be found for almost every major disease, and lists are provided online by the World Health Organization and other major national and state organizations. Moreover, health care providers can help their clients by providing names and contact information of support groups and individual members to encourage their clients to make use of this resource. For example, a study that linked new clients diagnosed with substance use disorder to volunteers from twelve-step-based support groups found that these efforts significantly increased both clients' use of these resources and abstinence rates a year later (Timko & DeBenedetti, 2007).

Interventions like these can amplify the effects of "vicarious experience" as clients learn to master the key challenges they will need to confront.

Attendance at mutual help groups has been shown to be a strong predictor of long-term recovery from addictive disorders. This demonstrates the importance of a reinforcing social network for turning a new healthful behavior into a lifelong habit. Mutual help groups have been set up to help people with many different health and behavioral disorders. The American Self-Help Group Clearinghouse provides a searchable catalog of mutual help organizations for a wide variety of health problems at http://www.mentalhelp.net/selfhelp/. This sourcebook can help people find networks of other people dealing with similar problems and with similar behavioral goals. Connecting with such organizations may be helpful, particularly when you are trying to incorporate a newly mastered behavior into your everyday life or are having trouble maintaining healthful behaviors in your current circumstances.

Including friends or family members in attempts to change behavior can also help reinforce the new behavior. For example, you may find it easier to make diet changes if everyone else in the house is supportive of the new diet and agrees to follow it as well. Not only does this help keep the home environment free of foods that the diet discourages, it also helps set up a home environment where healthful eating will be encouraged by those around you. Ideally, old unhealthful habits may be noticed and challenged by people close and important to you. Having the support of a group of people with shared goals encourages individuals to stick with their new behaviors, even though they may be time-consuming, tiring, inconvenient, or even painful or scary. A sense of obligation to the group members, the pleasure of shared effort toward a common goal, or simply knowing that other people will notice your behavior may encourage you to make the healthy choice in those moments when your old unhealthful habit sounds so much more comfortable and tempting. For example, a review of interventions to encourage people with serious chronic disease to exercise found that people more consistently stuck to their exercise regimens when programs used a group format rather than just targeting individuals (Buckworth & Sears, 2006). Studies of family involvement in weight control interventions suggest that spousal or parent involvement can improve effectiveness (McLean et al., 2003).

Behavioral Couples Therapy is an example of a therapy that specifically encourages social reinforcement of new healthful behaviors. Behavioral Couples Therapy for substance use disorders explicitly trains a significant other to reinforce and support healthful abstinence behaviors and avoid interactions that trigger or encourage old unhealthful substance or alcohol use patterns (O'Farrell, 1999). In this treatment, the therapist works with both the client and the significant other to help set up a pattern of social reinforcement that will encourage and maintain sobriety and healthful coping strategies. For example, the client and significant other may set up a contract where they agree not to bring up old substance-using behaviors or fears about future substance use outside the therapy session to discourage reminders and conflicts that may trigger relapse. Notably, Behavioral Couples Therapy is the only psychotherapeutic technique that reliably improves upon standard psychotherapies for substance use problems. The improvements are particularly obvious later in the attempt to change behavior (e.g. 6 months after a quit attempt) when people without this close social support start to slip back to their old habits. This approach also has a beneficial side-effect on relationships, further emphasizing the benefits of bringing those close to you on board during attempts to change behavior. Remarkably, this focus on encouraging supportive reinforcing behaviors within the family reduces domestic violence, child abuse, and martial separations, and increases happiness of relationships and success at sobriety (McCrady et al., 1991; O'Farrell et al., 1992). By reducing family conflicts during the difficult transition from a dangerous old habit to a new pattern of behavior and emotional response, Behavioral Couples Therapy not only increases the chance that the new behavior becomes normal and automatic but also improves relationships between family members. The success of interventions that purposely include a significant other or buddy to encourage, support and reinforce new healthful behaviors highlights the importance of consistent social reinforcement to make the new behavior a habit and maintain it once initial motivation has faded.

Note that unhealthful behaviors may also be learned and supported by our social networks. Results of the Framingham Heart Study found that both obesity and smoking were "contagious" and spread through social networks over time (Christakis & Fowler, 2007; Christakis & Fowler, 2008). Additional analysis of this same study found that happiness also spread through social networks over time (Fowler & Christakis, 2008). If the people in your social network were happy, you were more likely to be happy. If someone close to you became happy, you were more likely to become happy. Associating with a positive, healthy group of people can improve your health behaviors, and it can also improve your mood and happiness in life.

To practice in identifying and using social supports for your healthful behaviors, see Exercise 4B (page 186).

Monitoring and feedback

Setting up a whole network of people who support your behavior change or even finding a reliable buddy willing to help you learn can feel daunting. Instead, some of the same benefits of these social supports can be achieved just by knowing someone is watching and will evaluate your behavior. When interventions include a method to monitor behavior and provide periodic feedback about progress or success, people do a better job of following their behavioral plans. We have all seen people dutifully start driving the speed limit when they see a police car on the side of the freeway. Similarly, we are more likely to follow recommended health behaviors when we know someone is policing our behavior.

When we know that someone is watching, has a good and reliable way of measuring our behavior, and will respond with positive or negative feedback (in the case of highway patrol, mostly negative feedback in the form of scary intimidation and a big fine), we are much more likely to do the right thing. Thus, having someone monitor your behavior and provide feedback, even if it entails nothing more than an approving or disapproving word or look, can do wonders for changing a new behavior into an everyday one. The trick here is that the monitoring needs to be consistent. As the police example shows, a radar gun at one point on the freeway only slows down traffic for a mile or so at best. Once drivers know they are out of monitoring range, they may accelerate back up to their habitual excessively dangerous and wasteful driving speed. If we wanted people to consistently follow speed limits, we would need periodic vehicle checkpoints on the freeway where electronic monitors could track where a car was and how long it took them to get from the last checkpoint. This would allow monitoring of average speed over the whole distance, thereby catching (and potentially fining) those who drove above the speed limit consistently. While a single radar gun may slow drivers driving 90 mph down to 65 mph for maybe a mile, checkpoints would force them to keep their average speed to 65 mph, thus strictly limiting times they could drive 90 mph without punishment.

To illustrate another way, let's consider how monitoring and feedback have been used successfully to encourage other health behaviors. The effective weight loss program "Weight Watchers" uses monitoring of weight change at meetings to motivate people to stick to their diet plan, and bring attention to problems that might be stopping progress. They do not choose to take the police radar approach and watch people eat a single meal and rate them on their food choice. While this might be helpful for teaching people how to eat well in the first place, it probably would not do a lot to encourage consistent adherence. Most people would just wait for the person watching them to leave before having the big slice of pie and ice cream they were craving. Instead "Weight Watchers" chooses to monitor and reinforce a marker of average eating behavior, overall weight change. This makes sure that any pie and ice cream binges are identified, except in the rare instances that the dieter managed to eat nothing but undressed salad for their previous five meals.

Having a system where your behavior is consistently monitored and then rewarded or punished promptly after will reinforce target behaviors and encourage close adherence. Monitoring and feedback can be even more helpful if a problem-solving component is added to the feedback. Sometimes people do not stick to their target behaviors because they did not know how to do a behavior in a specific circumstance, or they encountered a stressful situation that disrupted their good intentions. While withholding rewards or punishing people in such circumstances may increase their desire to do the right thing the next time, if they do not know how to behave appropriately in that specific circumstance, they may fail again in similar situations. Instead, if failures to do the target behavior are treated as signals that the person needs additional training or help finding solutions to difficult situations, then they can be assisted with problem-solving in hopes of improving their chance of success the next time they encounter similar situations. Interventions that add a problem-solving and retraining component to the feedback can be very powerful in encouraging regular use of new target behaviors.

Let's go back to the "Weight Watchers" example. Let's say someone's goal was to lose two pounds over a week, but the weigh-in indicates that he gained two pounds instead. This obviously will not lead to approval from the counselor doing the monitoring, but it may provide useful information for problem-solving. The counselor might then ask the dieter about his eating patterns over the week and times he had trouble sticking to the planned diet. Perhaps the dieter reports that because of some impending work deadlines, he simply did not have time to grocery shop and make his lunch in the morning. Since most of the office cafeteria food was of highly questionable nutritional value, the dieter decided to skip lunch until he could get home and make something from his healthful cookbook. But then, three days this week, he got stuck at work late, and his boss bought thick-crust, greasy, meat pizza and sugary soda to keep the team focused on their work. By this point he was so hungry, tired and stressed that he wound up eating five slices of pizza and drinking a lot of caffeinated soda as he worked. With this information, the counselor could help the dieter plan solutions to prevent this from happening again. The counselor could help the dieter go through the cafeteria options to identify things that would be consistent with his diet. Then when the dieter got busy, he could still eat lunch, preventing him from getting so hungry and tired that he made bad choices later. The counselor could also work with the dieter to practice polite but assertive ways of discussing his food needs with his boss. If the boss could be convinced to order some healthful food options, or send employees home or out to eat before reconvening, then he would have a better chance of meeting his diet goals even when work deadlines made things more challenging. By using the monitoring to identify and address problems with adherence to planned healthful behaviors, you can make sure that your plans are not high-jacked repeatedly by problems you have not solved yet.

It is important to note that this monitoring, feedback, and problem-solving approach does not have to involve a second person. It is perfectly possible to set up a system where you monitor yourself, reward yourself for successes, and work on addressing problem situations you identify. Sticking with the dieting example, you could weigh yourself weekly and keep a food diary. Each week, you could allocate some time to evaluate you progress. When you meet your target goals, you could reward yourself with something you like. Maybe go see a movie in the theater, take off the afternoon to play soccer with your friends, treat yourself to a massage, or get yourself the really fancy loose-leaf tea you love. When you do not meet your targets, you could take an hour to problem-solve. Write down the problem and brainstorm solutions. Look for information on the Internet. Call a friend for advice. Schedule an appointment with a professional for help. Not having an outside person to monitor you is not a reason to abandon this strategy.

Yet another option for improving adherence is remote monitoring. The use of telehealth for remote monitoring of biological data has been used to beneficially affect clients with hypertension, depression, asthma and congestive heart failure (Trafton & Gordon, 2008b). For example, Robert DeBusk, MD, a Stanford cardiologist reported that simple telephone calls for monitoring people with congestive heart failure highly improved health outcomes (DeBusk, et al., 1994). Even if you cannot find someone in your immediate community and do not feel like monitoring yourself will be sufficient, there are still opportunities to ensure your progress is tracked and evaluated.

Typically, the hardest part of the monitoring and feedback approach is finding the right behavior or outcome to monitor. In the case of some behaviors, there are obvious things to monitor, like weight in our diet example. In other cases, it is harder to come up with something objective and measurable that is reliably associated with the behavior. For example, let's say someone wants to get his diabetes under control. He can monitor his blood glucose, but that is kind of like the police radar scenario. If he chooses to test himself only while he is following his diet and medication plan closely, then his blood glucose values will look much better than they are in reality. While selectively testing like this is obviously counter-productive in terms of meeting a goal, the reward of feeling good about oneself can sometimes favor this sort of "cheating". Just like we often want to fool the police officer who is trying to keep us safe, we often want to fool ourselves to avoid feeling bad about our failure. Thus, this individual needs a more stable marker of how well controlled his blood glucose is over a longer period.

Researchers have spent a lot of time trying to find good markers of recent blood glucose control that let you know how well blood sugar has been regulated in the last couple of weeks, rather than the last 30 minutes or 30 years. The best marker they have found is hemoglobin A1C. In this test, health professionals look at how much sugar has stuck to the proteins on your red blood cells. When you have higher concentrations of sugar in your blood, more sugar sticks to your red blood cell proteins. Since each red blood cell lives for about three months, the amount of sugar stuck to your red blood cell proteins provides a decent measure of your average blood glucose levels over the past three months. Thus, measuring hemoglobin A1C provides a longer-term measure of blood glucose control that cannot be fooled by selectively testing blood glucose levels only after appropriate meals. But three months is a long time to wait to get feedback. If you fix your behavior, you do not want to wait three months before anyone notices and rewards you for it. Conversely, if you do relapse to bad habits, you know that you have at least three months before your failure will be detected and you meet with disapproval. This time lag is terrible for encouraging adherence.

Thus, the best plan for monitoring blood glucose regulation involves using multiple methods. First, regular monitoring of hemoglobin A1C will provide a big picture of how well your blood glucose is regulated overall. Having a long-term outcome monitored will reduce the temptation to cheat on the short-term monitoring. Next, monitoring blood glucose levels in the morning and after meals will provide immediate feedback on how your diet and exercise choices affect your sugar levels. Lastly, monitoring when and how consistently you test your blood glucose will make sure that you stick with the monitoring plan such that you can catch behavioral problems. This is why blood glucose monitors record not only the blood glucose levels but also the time and date they are recorded. By monitoring and rewarding success on these three separate outcomes, you may encourage good diabetes care and not simply avoidance of criticism from your clinician or yourself.

In summary, for monitoring to be effective, it needs to catch behavior not just instantaneously, but also over time. Moreover, it must also be responsive to changes in behavior over relatively short time periods (e.g. days to weeks) so that rewards and punishments are actually associated with the behavior. In many cases, you may have to monitor multiple outcomes to meet all of these criteria. Taking time to come up with a good monitoring system can make a huge difference in the success of using monitoring and feedback to encourage consistent behavior changes.

FIGURE: Examples of immediate and longer-term monitors for common health concerns

Health Concern	Short-Term Monitors (days to weeks)	Longer-Term Monitors (weeks to months)
Obesity	Calorie consumption	Body weight
Diabetes	Blood glucose level	Fructosamine, Hemoglobin A1C
Fitness	Minutes of exercise	Maximum aerobic capacity (VO2max)
Alcohol use	Breathalyzer, Standard drinks per sitting	Carbohydrate-deficient transferrin test
Smoking	Carbon monoxide breath test	Cotinine urine drug test (only 2-4 days)
Substance use	Urine drug screening	Hair sample drug screening
Dental hygiene	Tooth brushing frequency	Plaque levels
Risky sex	Consistency of condom use	STD and pregnancy testing
Heart health	Cholesterol blood test (HDL and LDL levels)	High sensitivity C-reactive protein test

EXAMPLE: Health success based on a self-monitoring program

In 2007, I (W.G.) was diagnosed with Grave's disease, an autoimmune thyroid disorder. I was producing five times the normal amount of thyroid hormone. In addition to extreme fatigue, a racing heart rate, and weight loss, I also found myself having difficulty concentrating. In the 19th century, 50% of people with this disorder died of it. But now, advances in medicine have made it possible to radioactively ablate the thyroid gland and then pharmacologically replace the correct amount of thyroid hormone needed for proper brain and body function. With this treatment, my symptoms went away and I expected to return to normal except for one troubling statistic.

I had read that a typical client after being treated for Grave's disease gains 20 – 30 pounds in several years. I was determined not to let this happen. My father, his brothers, my mother's brother, and both grandfathers had heart disease; both grandfathers and two of my uncles developed type II diabetes. With a resting metabolic rate of less than 1500 Kcal/day, I knew I had to carefully monitor my weight, restrict calories, and have sufficient physical activity to protect myself against the risks of hypertension, heart disease, diabetes and stroke.

The first thing I did was to develop a way to monitor my weight on a daily basis. I created a daily diary in which I recorded my weight, body fat, duration and type of physical activity, and daily hints that could help me maintain this program over the long-term. I noted situations when I would overeat or forget to exercise. I kept the notebook in a location where I could not fail to notice it before going to bed.

In the first few months, in spite of my best efforts at self- restraint, I gained close to ten pounds. I realized this was going to be a lifelong challenge and I needed to improve upon my strategy. I began to identify triggers and emotional situations that led me to overeat. I learned to avoid my favorite Indian buffet. I practiced refusing seconds, and stopping eating before I felt full. It was and remains trial and error. I cannot tell you my efforts have led to a permanent cure; but for the three years following thyroid surgery, my weight and body fat percent are well below what they were prior to developing the thyroid disorder.

If I gain a pound, I make extra effort to lose it and change my eating and physical activity patterns until this achieved. I've discovered this kind of feedback is what works for me—not the kind of feedback I get from the hunger centers of my brain, which would tell me that I could be starving. If I pay careful attention to the "fullness" in my stomach, I can use that kind of feedback to indicate when I am full, even if not fulfilled. It took a year to realize that I could keep my weight constant if I either went to sleep with an appetite equal to about 200 calories, or if I exercised such that I burned an extra couple hundred of calories. My wife has been very supportive of my efforts and continues to prepare original creations that manage to remain healthy within the portion size I have requested.

Another thing I learned is that it is necessary to discover what kinds of exercise I really enjoy, and then to continuously vary them so that no one set of muscles is apt to get sore. For me, moderately-paced walking, swimming, and Hatha Yoga are the most enjoyable and relaxing, but I will use interval training to get my pulse up when running around the park or on a treadmill. I have not reached my goals, but am far closer than would be the case if I had not developed this self-monitoring. Each person needs to discover, on a trial and error basis, what works best for them. I have no idea if this will work for you.

Below is an example of what I recorded in the daily diary of weight, body fat, and other concerns that I made for myself using a simple college-ruled spiral-bound notebook.

Month: July
Goals: weight <160, body fat <20%

Date	Day	Weight	Body Fat	Duration & Physical Activity	Insights
6/20	M	164.5	22%	45 min. moderate walking	

Creating immediate contingencies for health behavior

As we mentioned above, monitoring and feedback can be helpful even when you do not have someone else to monitor your behavior and provide reinforcers. When shaping your social situation is not feasible, you can reinforce new behaviors by setting up rewards for yourself. While social reinforcement is a cheap and powerful source of reward, any sort of reward will work for encouraging your new behavior. If you get something nice or get relief from something unpleasant shortly after you complete a healthful behavior, you will be encouraged to keep doing that behavior. You can set up rules or systems so that you are quickly rewarded for doing something healthful. This method to reinforce behaviors can be helpful when a person is not particularly responsive to social cues or rewards. For example, some people with autism or psychopathy may not respond to or may have unpredictable responses to social reinforcers. These individuals may find that using other non-social rewards may more effectively train in new target behaviors.

Monitoring and feedback interventions that use short-term rewards contingent on completing a pre-defined target behavior are often called contingency management programs. These programs have been very well-tested, particularly for treating substance use disorders. There are many variations on contingency management programs that have been shown to be effective for reducing substance use, but the typical program works something like this: Clients are put on a frequent periodic urine drug screen schedule to monitor their drug use. When they provide "clean" urine samples, demonstrating that they did not use drugs in the last few days, they receive a reward, most commonly a gift card or a ticket for a lottery of goods and services held periodically at the clinic. A large number of studies have shown that contingency management programs such as these reduce substance use or increase other target behaviors, at least during the period in which the program is in place (see Stitzer & Petry, 2006 for a review). However, unsurprisingly, if reinforcement of the target behaviors ends then people start slipping into old habits over time. As such, an important element of reward-based programs should be for participants to learn how to develop ways to continue providing rewards to themselves after the program ends.

While contingency management programs have been most commonly studied for reducing substance use behaviors, this strategy can be used to encourage all sorts of behaviors and has been shown to be successful when tested for other behaviors. Notably, these interventions can be used progressively. Not only can they successfully increase the practice of a single behavior, they can also encourage practice of increasingly more difficult or complicated behaviors by adding to the behavioral goals as the original goal becomes mastered. This is referred to as behavioral shaping, and can be particularly helpful when the targeted behavior is complex or multi-part (refer the example about progressive behavioral shaping on page 99). To use our diabetes example, you could first reinforce regular glucose monitoring regardless of the result of the testing. Then you could reinforce adherence to the individual's daily insulin or medication regimen. Once this is done correctly and consistently, you could train and reinforce good breakfast eating habits and reward these. Then lunch behaviors, or exercise, or food choice at restaurants, or so forth could be used as targets. Eventually, combined together, this collection of behaviors should lead to the final outcome of stable blood glucose control, which could then be monitored and rewarded as the longer-term endpoint.

Research on contingency management programs has identified a number of elements that are crucial to the success of this strategy (Petry, 2000; Higgins & Petry, 1999):

1. The target behavior has to be doable. In other words, this is a program for reinforcing a new behavior that you have already learned but do not do consistently. A contingency management program will not help if you have yet learned to do the behavior. Strategies such as those discussed earlier on confidence and self-efficacy can help you learn a new behavior. Contingency management can only help you use it more consistently.

2. Rewards need to be provided as soon as possible following completion of the behavior. Remember, our reward circuits are not very good at associating behaviors with rewards in the distant future. The more concurrently the target behavior and the reward are tied together, the more effective the reward will be in reinforcing the behavior.

3. Bigger rewards are more reinforcing than smaller ones. This observation is pretty self-explanatory. Nevertheless, even very small or probabilistic rewards (e.g. lottery tickets) have been shown to effectively shape behavior.

4. Rewards for good behavior are more effective than punishments for failure for encouraging good behaviors. Punishments for failure tend to primarily encourage people to avoid whomever or whatever is monitoring the behavior. If a client were getting monitored in a substance use disorder treatment program, he may stop coming to treatment when he has a lapse and used drugs. If he had diabetes and wrongfully ate a box of cookies, he may conveniently forget to test his glucose after that meal. Rather than encouraging people to do the healthful behavior more frequently, punishments encourage them to avoid the systems and people who are trying to help them become healthier. Thus, punishments are not recommended, as they are just as likely to lead the person to stop trying to get better as they are to encourage better behaviors.

The contingency management concept can be used to encourage consistent uptake of new behaviors in a range of contexts. For example, self-guided smoking cessation programs encourage individual smokers to use self-rewards. Smokers making a quit attempt are encouraged to stow away the money they would have otherwise spent on cigarettes that week and get themselves something nice with the money they saved from not smoking. Some health plans offer incentives to people who take part in preventative health programs (Marosits, 1997). The government has offered tax breaks to people who purchase certain fuel-efficient vehicles (U.S. Department of Energy, 2010). Some companies encourage people to bike or take public transit to work by providing incentives or bonuses for not driving (Wikipedia, 2010). The simple concept of providing immediate rewards to encourage consistent use of behaviors that naturally have long-term benefits (e.g. reduced risk of disease for smokers and people following preventive health regimens, and fuel savings and better air quality for people driving more efficiently or not at all), is effective for increasing and maintaining goal behaviors regardless of whether the concept is applied to individuals, programs, or even whole communities.

These contingency management programs can be effective when they are as simple as the tax break programs described above but they can also be more complicated. For example, a fairly complicated contingency contract and lottery system was used to elicit substantial weight loss in a recent study where clients with a goal to lose 16 pounds were randomly placed into one of three groups: (1) a control condition consisting of only a weight-monitoring program with monthly weigh-ins and a home scale for daily self-monitoring, (2) the weigh-ins plus a lottery component where participants could win daily prizes of varying value (averaging \$3.00/day, and reported to the clients daily by text-message) but these clients would only receive the prizes if they achieved the monthly weight loss goal, or (3) the weigh-ins plus a deposit contract system where participants could contribute \$0.01 to \$3.00 per day which would be matched plus \$3.00/day. They received daily feedback on the amount they had accumulated, but would only receive the funds if they met the monthly weight loss goal. Forfeited money was split among participants who lost more than 20 pounds over the trial. While only 10% of controls were able to reach the weight loss goal, about 50% of those in the lottery and deposit contract groups successfully lost 16 pounds. Control participants lost an average of about 3 pounds, but in the deposit contract and lottery conditions, the participants lost an average of about 13 -14 pounds (Volpp et al., 2008).

Setting up artificial systems to reward target behaviors is a consistently effective strategy for achieving goals, even those as difficult as losing a substantial amount of weight or quitting a long-term substance addiction. Designing such a program for yourself can be a helpful tool. The main challenge for people using this method is maintaining the behaviors after the end the contingency management program. Ultimately, you want to set up some other type of consistent reward that exists outside the program. One of the most reliable ways to ensured continued practice of your desired behavior is to get involved in a community that supports the behavior during the time you are being rewarded through the program.

Immediate awards may also be highly valuable for helping children learn a new habit. Using a calendar, you can place a star on each day of the week your child washes her hands before dinner or remembers to brush his teeth before bedtime. Once these early habits are engrained and lifelong, their persistence is probably as valuable in preventing disease and improving wellness as more difficult-to-implement habits in adulthood.

For help in designing your own contingency management program, try Exercise 4C (page 187).

Brain Challenge #4 Exercises

Exercise 4A: Using Your Mirror Neurons to Master a New Behavior

Our mirror neurons provide a powerful system for rapidly learning ways to meet our goals through imitation. As you may remember, they are activated by what they observe and can help teach our brains how to do behaviors or solve problems to achieve goals. We can activate our mirror neurons by actively observing others solving problems or achieving goals that we wish to achieve, but also by visualizing ourselves or others solving problems or achieving goals in our imagination or mind's eye.

Visualizing yourself doing behaviors can help train in these behaviors even before you have the opportunity to try them in real life. Visualization can also allow you to practice and to try out variations without actually having to do them. For example, studies have shown that not only does mentally imagining oneself practicing a behavior improve performance on the task, but it also reshapes the brain in similar ways as does real practice (Blakeslee & Blakeslee, 2007). Real repetitive practice playing the piano increased the area of the motor cortex that was devoted to representing the fingers; one week of mentally imagining oneself practicing the piano two hours per day caused the same changes in motor cortex representation of the fingers. Visualization activates many of the same circuits as real practice of a behavior, and produces learning and brain changes that help you do the real behavior later.

This can be particularly helpful when the goal you are trying to reach involves substantial risk, extreme effort, or rare circumstances to try. Giving yourself time and space to relax, think about your goal, and imagine your way through attempts to achieve it, can be a powerful method for learning and practicing a new behavior in a safe environment.

Using visualization to learn and practice behaviors is a skill in itself and you will become better at it as you use and practice it more. There is no one correct way to use visualization, and it can be done alone or with others to good effect. Group imagination exercises can be fun, and adding others to the creative process can provide you with possible solutions that you would not have imagined on your own. It can take some added practice to be able to "see" or imagine other people's stories. But since it is generally an entertaining practice, most will find this an exercise that reinforces itself.

To get you started, let's go over the basics of individual and group visualization exercises. Then find a quiet space and give visualization a try.

1. Find a space where you feel safe and not distracted by things going on around you. Closing your eyes is helpful for most people.
2. Think about your goal or the problem you want to solve. Imagine achieving that goal. What would it be like to have already solved the problem? What would that look and feel like?
3. Think about ways that you could reach that goal. Be creative and let yourself try out ideas that may seem a bit ridiculous. Imagine yourself trying ideas you think might work. What happens as you work towards your goal? Are there other problems that come up? Are there places you get stuck? If so, step back and think about other

ways of reaching your goal or imagine solutions to the new problems that arose in your imaginary simulation.

4. If you can imagine a story in which you achieve the goal, run through it several times. Can you see yourself actually doing the behavior? Does it come out the same way when you think through it again? Are there other stories in which you also achieve the goal? Is one more appealing to you than another?
5. Let your mind wander and give yourself time to play in your imagination.
6. If you find yourself in a bad place, feeling negative, and failing repeatedly in your imagination, take a break and try again later when you are in a better mood.

Repeatedly imagining failure can train you to fail in real life. In my experience, when I (J.T.) fail in my imagination it is because there is some part of the behavior or situation that I fear. Recognizing and acknowledging my fear, taking time to assess whether my fear is valid, and finding ways of being or feeling more safe in that situation can make it easier to get past such imaginary and real life setbacks.

If you want to practice visualization with another person or a group, the basic steps are similar but you need to find a way to share what you are imagining or seeing among the group. This typically involves people narrating the story in their heads out loud. Describing what you are seeing, doing and experiencing can bring the group together into a shared visualization. The trick here is finding ways of letting everyone participate in the story-making. Sometimes, a single individual can wind up dominating the talking and crowd out others' contributions. If this is agreed upon beforehand, that can be fine. Letting a single person guide others through a visualization can be a powerful way of sharing a solution. But if the goal is for the group to create a shared experience from their collective imagination then it is important for everyone to be able to participate. Encouraging people to talk slowly and pause after sharing an observation can help in this process. Ultimately, once you have visualized the behavior or goal you wish to achieve, either by yourself or with others, you will need to implement it in real life to determine whether your visualization was successful in preparing you for the task.

Exercise 4B: Finding Social Supports for Practice

Having social support for your health behavior can greatly increase your motivation and consistency in sticking to your new behavior. But finding friends and colleagues that are expert at or committed to your new goal behavior can be difficult. It is likely that you will have to specifically search out the social support you need. Below are some suggestions to help you find or develop a supportive social group to encourage your health improvements and focus on your goal behavior.

Support groups are an obvious place to find social support for healthful behaviors, as these groups are often set up specifically for this purpose. The American Self-Help Group Clearinghouse is a directory of mutual-help groups for just about every disease and health behavior. The Clearinghouse can be searched by topic, and provides information about organizations designed to provide social support for people with a variety of disorders, health problems, or behavioral goals. The website also has links to local self-help clearinghouses organized by state to make it easier to find groups in your area. Some organizations also have virtual meetings where people can chat with others with similar goals online. The American Self-Help Group Clearinghouse can be found at: http://www.mentalhelp.net/selfhelp/

For nearly all but the simplest health behaviors, you can find classes that will teach you about a health issue or train you in new health behaviors. These will range from a simple 30-minute lecture to months of hands-on training and practice in a new behavior. Regardless, such classes are a great place to meet at least one expert in the new behavior as well as other people interested in the health issue. Classes may be offered by a variety of organizations in your local area. Good places to look for classes include local community colleges, hospitals and health care systems, athletic clubs, community centers, and after-school programs. A few helpful links are provided below.

You can find a listing of community colleges in the US with links to their websites at:
http://www.utexas.edu/world/comcol/state/

You can find local health clubs by searching at:
http://www.gymticket.com/athleticclubs-sportsclubs/
or http://www.healthclubdirectory.com/

You can also ask your health provider for the names of groups in your area that offer support for your area of interest.

Exercise 4C: Creating Your Own Contingency Management Program

New behaviors must be rewarded consistently if they are to be learned and used habitually. Sometime new behaviors are naturally reinforcing, such as eating more fruit or practicing relaxation exercises. In other cases, artificial rewards may be needed to train and maintain a new habit. In this exercise, we will help you develop a system of artificial rewards (i.e. a contingency management program) to keep you practicing a new health behavior.

Part 1: What health behavior do you want to learn to practice regularly?

____

Part 2: In order to develop a contingency management plan, you will need to define the following elements. We will walk you through each of these decisions to help you design your own program.

1. What specific behavior will be rewarded?
2. How will it be objectively assessed whether the behavior was done?
3. Who will provide the rewards?
4. How and when will the behavior be monitored?
5. What will the reward be?
6. How often will the reward be available?
7. How quickly will the reward be provided?

1&2. What specific behavior will be rewarded? How will it be objectively assessed whether the behavior was done?

In order to consistently and correctly provide rewards, you must clearly define what is to be monitored and rewarded. First, consider whether you will reward a marker of the behavior or observation of the behavior itself.

If you plan to use a marker, it is useful to consider the following:

a. How accurate is the marker? Can it reliably tell if a behavior was done or not done?
b. How often is the marker wrong?
c. For how long can the marker detect a behavior?
d. Are there ways to fool the marker? In other words, are there ways to cheat on the test?

If you plan to use the behavior itself, you will need to clarify all the parts of the behavior that must be done in order to count as successfully completed. For example, if your target health goal is to exercise, does it count if you put on your walking sneakers and walk around your house, or do you have to walk at least thirty minutes without pause to call your exercise attempt successful?

Describe the marker or the criteria for successful completion of the behavior here:

____

____

3. Who will provide the rewards?

There are only a few key criteria that the person who will provide the rewards must meet. First, they must have some objective way of assessing whether the behavior was done. If you happen to have a clear marker of whether the behavior was completed that can be observed after completion of a behavior, then anyone who you see periodically could provide the rewards. For example, a breath test on a carbon monoxide meter can be used by anyone to tell if someone recently smoked. This means a health professional, co-worker, friend or family member could do carbon monoxide testing on a regular schedule and reward non-smoking. Likewise, it would be easy for someone to check whether you consistently monitored your diet over the week by reviewing your logbook. However, sometimes it is hard to find a reliable marker of a behavior after the fact. If this is true of your health behavior, then the person who provides the rewards must be present while you are doing the behavior in order to verify that you did the behavior. In this case, the person providing the rewards will have to be someone close to you, such as a spouse, friend or even yourself.

Second, the person providing the rewards must be invested enough in encouraging your new health behavior to consistently monitor and reward it. When considering who could realistically monitor whether you did your health behavior, pick the person you can rely on to pay attention to your behavior and reward it. It is absolutely fine if you yourself are the only person who meets these criteria.

Enter the name of the person who will provide the rewards here: ____________________

4. How and when will the behavior be monitored?

It is good to consider how and when the behavior will be monitored. Is the person who is doing the monitoring and providing the rewards always around when the behavior is done? Will you need to make special efforts to have them present? Do you need to schedule special times or events to verify the behavior?

It is also important to consider the times when your behavior will not be monitored. Is there a risk that you will sabotage your health efforts during the times you are not being monitored? Are there safeguards you can put in place to prevent unhealthful behaviors while you are not being watched? For example, if your spouse is monitoring your saturated fat intake but cannot tell what you are eating for lunch at work, could you get your office-mate to monitor you at work?

Describe the times when your behavior will be monitored:

____

____

5. What will the reward be?

It is important to decide beforehand what the reward for the behavior will be. Rewards must be meaningful to you, but may or may not be expensive. If you are creating self-rewards, you might consider determining your play budget based on your success at your health behavior. Such a plan may be easiest if you happen to be giving up an expensive habit like smoking or frequently eating out at unhealthful restaurants. If someone close to you is providing rewards, there are many options for free rewards. A spouse might agree to do the dishes for each day you meet your behavior goal. Your kids might agree to give you fifteen minutes of quiet time. A friend might give you stickers to save up towards a massage. If you prefer monetary rewards but do not have a lot of money to spare, you might consider state lottery scratch cards as rewards. We tend to overvalue probabilistic rewards, so even though it is rare that these provide a substantial reward, the anticipation of the possibility can be reinforcing.

Consider your options and enter your planned reward here: ________________________

6. How often will the reward be available?

Depending on the behavior and the reward, there may be few or many opportunities to successfully complete the behavior. Thus, it is important to define how often the reward will be available. For example, if I wanted to encourage proper dental hygiene, I might consider providing rewards each time I successfully brushed and flossed my teeth after a meal. Alternatively, I could provide rewards only for each day I successfully brushed and flossed after every meal. I probably would not want to make rewards available for brushing and flossing anytime because I might encourage brushing teeth ten times before going to bed or some other strange pattern of behavior. Defining the schedule on which rewards can be obtained can help to pattern the behavior and prevent your plan from failing because rewards become too expensive or time-consuming to provide.

Enter the frequency at which rewards can be obtained here: ______________________

7. How quickly will the reward be provided?

Rewards are better at reinforcing behaviors when they are received as soon as possible after the behavior. Consider your reward plan. Is there a way to provide the reward in close proximity to completion of the behavior? Define when the reward will be delivered to prevent discouragement due to delayed rewards.

Define when rewards will be delivered here: ___________________________________

Now, pull all of these pieces together to describe your contingency plan in full! For example: My goal is to walk 3 miles per day. I will wear a pedometer daily to track my behavior. My spouse will monitor my success by checking the pedometer before bed each day. Each day that I meet the 3-mile goal, I will put $5 in a fund towards the weekend yoga and spa retreat that I have wanted to do for years. My spouse will tell me the balance I have saved at the end of each week. Once I have saved the $700 I need for the trip, I will schedule the weekend and go.

Describe your full contingency management plan here:

____

____

____

____

Brain Challenge #5

Making Flexible Decisions to Empower Your Brain to Make Healthful Choices

Challenge Introduction

I get home from work, unlock the door and walk inside my house. I am tired, hungry and really need to think about something other than work. I start to think about what I need to do. I need to call my friend with whom I promised to exercise and I need to make something decent for dinner. I head to the kitchen to look in my pantry. There are some beans, onions, broccoli, pasta, chips…. Next thing I know, I have the chips open and the TV on. An hour later, I remember I was going to make myself some real dinner and go out with a friend. But now I have already eaten about 800 calories worth of chips and my friend has probably already gone to the gym without me. I meant so well. Why do I always do this, day after day?

Our health-related habits set in motion a chain of behaviors, some conscious and some below our level of awareness. Certain brain centers have their own priorities, setting in motion actions that may surprise us. Long-term survival of our species over thousands upon thousands of years has relied on us storing sufficient fat to outlast long periods of scarcity. No wonder those chips are so appealing. There is now convincing evidence that "will power" may be no match for tempting but unhealthy foods that we encounter. In some cases, making healthful choices may require us to ban these temptations from our immediate environment.

Optimal health requires the ability to make creative, flexible decisions based upon your current condition and the local environment. To be able to adapt to the unexpected, you need to be able to problem-solve and implement novel solutions. As humans, we have impressive and rare brain circuits that can solve complex problems. However, these circuits are the last to develop, require training to become efficient processors, and are the most vulnerable to damage and dysfunction with age. Moreover, they are slow. These circuits must stall behaviors long enough to give themselves the opportunity to decide upon and plan a new behavior. In Challenge #5, we discuss how these circuits work and techniques for improving their function. In Chapter 5.1, we explain the limitations of trying to use willpower to stop unhealthy habits. In Chapter 5.2, we describe the process by which problem-solving skills develop and disappear including the role of new neuron growth. In Chapter 5.3, we provide techniques for improving problem-solving and cognitive skills so that you will be able to successfully engage in healthful behaviors.

Chapter 5.1: Delaying Automatic Unhealthy Habits to Try Something New

In order to give ourselves enough time to come up with a new plan for how to respond in a familiar circumstance, we need to be able to postpone doing our habitual response long enough to enact the new plan. The dorsolateral and orbitofrontal cortex circuits are able to stall impulsive habits, giving the prefrontal cortex circuits time to consider options and come up with new plans.

This ability to develop flexible thinking has been extensively studied by psychologists using behavioral tasks such as Go-NoGo tasks. A simple example of a Go-NoGo task is the game, "Simon Says", where one is supposed to carry out commands except when the command does not include the words, "Simon Says." In these tasks, participants are tested to see how well they can stop themselves from doing a well-practiced, automatic response.

These tasks have shown that there is considerable variation from person to person in how well they can stop a habitual behavior. Clients with impairments in part of the prefrontal cortex, specifically the dorsolateral area, do very poorly at Go-NoGo and similar tasks, as do children whose prefrontal cortices have yet to develop. Notably, even in a single person, this ability varies depending on what other things the person is trying to do at the same time. It turns out that, at least when it comes to stopping us from doing habits, our prefrontal cortex is not a very good multi-tasker.

But before we continue, let's remind ourselves what the prefrontal cortex is trying to do and why. We know from Challenge #1 that our limbic reward circuit holds learned patterns. The limbic reward circuit can identify situations where a habitual response is likely to result in short-term gain, and can initiate that habitual behavior if it seems worth the effort. Importantly, the limbic reward circuit can do this without the conscious approval of prefrontal cortex circuits. Also, the limbic reward circuit can make decisions to do a habitual behavior very quickly because they use efficient but relatively simple and pre-defined decision rules (Saling & Phillips, 2007). Meanwhile, the prefrontal cortex circuits can often take longer because the decisions they are making are relatively complex and require use of a variety of multi-stage logic processes. The prefrontal cortex circuits can calculate and weigh difficult multi-stage decisions that include consideration not only of short-term gains, but also long-term consequences, our goals and values, and special circumstances of the current situation. The more complicated the decision and the more things that need to be considered, the longer it will take the prefrontal cortex to finish processing the decision. Thus, for anything other than simple decisions, the prefrontal cortex will come up with its plan for behavior much later than the limbic reward circuit. But our prefrontal cortex's decision will be useless if our limbic reward circuit has already started our habitual response. Therefore, it is crucial that our prefrontal cortex can stop the limbic system from carrying out the habit until it has had time to finish its own analysis.

Luckily, we know that, with conscious effort, our dorsolateral and orbitofrontal circuits can work together to stall or stop the limbic reward circuit from carrying out the habitual behavior. To successfully guide our behavior, our prefrontal cortex must stall the limbic reward circuit from carrying out our habitual response long enough to finish its calculations. The more complicated the decision, the longer the prefrontal cortex must stall. In some of the examples we will present next, you can observe this stalling. You can see that most people slow down their decision-making when the instruction or task is harder to follow. Some people appear to be better at slowing down their decisions than others, and this may explain differences in people's ability to successfully overcome old habits and try new behaviors.

Why willpower is not enough

Willpower can be very helpful for getting people through a difficult task. Motivation and determination to do something can help someone keep going through an uncomfortable situation, and persist through a grueling undertaking. Like "The Little Engine That Could" who said "I think I can" over and over to get over the hill, willpower can help you make that deadline, cope through a painful event, or sprint the last mile of a run.

However, willpower is not effective for getting people NOT to do something. Trying to use willpower to stop you from eating the chocolate that you love is not likely to work, and might even lead to your eating more than normal. There are clear biological and psychological reasons for this rooted in the set up of your prefrontal cortex circuits.

Your prefrontal cortex has the ability to prevent or stop you from doing habitual behaviors. For example, your prefrontal cortex can stop you from eating the chocolate sitting in front of you, or keep you from pulling your arm away from the poor phlebotomist drawing blood from your needle-phobic veins. However, your prefrontal cortex can only do this with conscious effort. For your prefrontal cortex to inhibit a behavior, you first have to be aware of the behavior you are trying to inhibit! This is where the problem lies. Part of the process of stopping habits involves remembering that you want to avoid that behavior. Your prefrontal cortex has an ability, called working memory, to keep thoughts that it intends to use during upcoming decisions ready to access on a moment-to-moment basis. To delay a habit, you have to keep that behavior or thought in your working memory so your prefrontal cortex has access to that information when a situation presents itself. Thus, when the time comes to make a quick decision, your prefrontal cortex will include that working memory information about the habit in its rapid calculation. If your brain had to go rummaging through your long-term files to try to dig up the information about what you intended to do, your limbic system would have already carried out the habit before your prefrontal cortex figured out what to do.

The problem with keeping the thought of an undesirable habit in your working memory is two-fold. The first problem is that if you keep a thought in your working memory then your prefrontal cortex will tend to include that thought in all of its decision-making and not just for decisions related to the habit. For example, if I put chocolate in my working memory, then my prefrontal cortex will tend to include chocolate when considering all of its decisions. This may help me stick to my intended decision not to eat the chocolate that my well-meaning office-mates have left in our shared area. However, it also means my prefrontal cortex will consider chocolate in other decisions it's making. When I start feeling a bit hungry or when I get stressed out by a work deadline, my prefrontal cortex will at least consider chocolate as a possible solution. When I think about what I should get my friend for her upcoming birthday, chocolate is apt to come to mind. With chocolate in my working memory, I will now problem-solve with chocolate on the short-list of all solutions. This may actually lead me to expose myself to more opportunities where I could eat chocolate, or even make me decide to go out and buy chocolate on my own. In the majority of cases, trying to use willpower to avoid eating chocolate leads people to eat more chocolate than they would have if they never tried to stop themselves. (Note: For those who want to read more, this concept has been termed the "White Bear Effect" by David Schneider. He described and studied it by instructing people not to think of a white bear, which, of course, they were compelled think about thereafter.)

The second problem with using working memory to inhibit an undesirable habit is that this system gets slow and inefficient as working memory gets cluttered. The more thoughts you put in your working memory, the slower your prefrontal cortex is at remembering what to do with them. If your prefrontal cortex gets too slow, it may not remember what habit you were trying to block until after you have already done the habit. When I get busy and have a lot on my mind, I may already have the chocolate in my mouth before I remember that I was not going to eat any.

The limits of willpower in overcoming habits

In one brain imaging study, participants were asked to try to inhibit a habit using a version of the Go-NoGo tasks we described earlier (Hester & Garavan, 2004). Specifically, the researchers flashed letters on a screen and asked the participants to press a key every time a letter appeared. Once that task was learned, they showed the participants a letter and told them to remember it (i.e. put it in working memory) and not to press the key when that particular letter was flashed on the screen. Because the vast majority of the letters shown were not that particular letter, the participants were quickly trained in a habit of pressing the key whenever something flashed on the screen. This forced the prefrontal cortex to try to use the particular letter in working memory to inhibit the key-pressing habit when that letter appeared. Most people could do this very well. Then the researchers made it harder. Instead of just one letter, they gave the participants five letters to remember and asked them not to press the button when any of these were presented. These extra letters cluttered up participants' working memory, and most people got much worse, often pressing the button before they recognized that the letter was one they were trying to remember. Notably, most people realized shortly after pressing the key that they had messed up but the prefrontal cortex was now too slow to actually inhibit the key-pressing habit.

The corresponding brain activity may help explain what happens. Looking only at the times when people correctly inhibited their key-pressing response, increasing the number of letters to remember increased activation in parts of the prefrontal cortex (the left medial frontal cortex, and anterior and posterior cingulate cortex). Additionally, the amount of activity in the anterior cingulate was associated with doing the task correctly in the five-letter version, suggesting that activity in this region is important for overcoming the increase in working memory demand. Supporting this further, typical people increased their anterior cingulate activity as more letters were added to the task, but regular cocaine users, who have difficulty inhibiting the key-pressing, did not increase their anterior cingulate activity as more letters were added. We know the anterior cingulate is required to monitor for and assess errors in learned behavior. Thus, this study suggests that as we start to multitask and hold more things in our working memory, our brains have to work harder and harder to identify mistakes in our planned behavior. If we try to multitask too much, this will lead to mistakes in our planned behavior even if we have a very healthy anterior cingulate and prefrontal cortex. We will start to do our habitual behaviors despite intentions otherwise.

Damage to the anterior cingulate and other associated regions of the prefrontal cortex, such as that caused by years of cocaine or other stimulant abuse, can make it very difficult to intentionally inhibit habits. Further, people with obsessive-compulsive disorders, who feel as though they are constantly required to be on alert to solve working memory-types of problems, have been found to have abnormalities with the anterior cingulate. In contrast, damage to the anterior cingulate can induce a state of lethargy and motivational inertia known as akinetic mutism. Even the healthy aging brain, experiencing typical mild cognitive impairments, is more likely to have working memory problems. In other words, trying not to eat a tempting piece of chocolate may become even more difficult as we age.

Alternatives to willpower

These studies highlight the need to use other strategies beyond willpower to keep us from carrying out our bad habits over the long-term. We are going to have other things to think about in life. We will get busy and clutter up our working memory. Moreover there is great individual variation in ability to inhibit habits while multi-tasking, which means it will take different people differing amounts of clutter before they can no long inhibit their habits. Some can handle thinking about many things at once without making too many mistakes, but others start to revert to habits pretty quickly. While our ability to inhibit a habit may be crucial for preventing us from reverting to bad behavior patterns in the occasional, unavoidable, high-risk situation, relying on this system alone during attempts to unlearn bad habits is certain to fail.

Using problem-solving strategies to reduce exposure to situations where we do bad habits, as well as using the strategies discussed in previous chapters, is key to long-term success in quitting bad habits. We are much more likely to achieve success in changing our bad habits if we problem-solve before we are faced with an opportunity to do the bad habit, rather than waiting until we are in a high-risk situation and then trying to stop our habit and do something else. If I really do not want to eat chocolate, I should do my problem-solving before I am in the common room with the chocolate in front of me. Knowing that there is often chocolate in the common room, I could decide to always walk down a different hall or make sure that I never got very hungry at work by keeping lots of salad and vegetables in my office and snacking all day long. If I am forced to sit in the same room as some tempting dark chocolate, I can move it far enough away to keep it out of reach.

Problem-solving ahead of time takes the pressure off your prefrontal cortex. Without the urgency of a situation where you could get immediate rewards for doing your bad habit, your prefrontal cortex can focus on coming up with a solution without fighting to hold off your limbic reward circuit while it searches for alternatives. I am much better at figuring out how not to eat chocolate when it is not sitting in front of me, teasing my nucleus accumbens and begging to be consumed.

Chapter 5.2: How Do Our Problem-Solving Skills Develop and Fade?

Developmental stages and cognitive decline

The prefrontal cortex is a highly complex and evolutionarily recent feature found only in a small number of mammal species. It is substantially larger in humans than other primates and constitutes about 40% of the entire cerebral cortex. As noted, the prefrontal cortex is extremely slow to complete development. Cortex development involves a process where neurons insulate the connections between each other with specialized fat cells called myelin. This myelin increases the chance that a signal sent by a neuron gets successfully delivered to the next neuron, just like putting insulation on a wire makes it conduct electricity more efficiently. Additionally, cortex development starts by making lots of interconnections between the neurons until the neurons learn which connections will be useful. As cortex matures, these neurons start to get more selective about their connections. They start to eliminate connections that do not contribute to successful signal transmission or problem-solving. This pruning makes the cortex more efficient and consistent in its decisions. While some parts of cortex finish this myelination and pruning process during the toddler years or very early childhood, the prefrontal cortex continues to add myelin and prune connectivity substantially through at least adolescence. Consistent with this late anatomical development, performance on tasks that make use of prefrontal circuits improves up until one's early twenties.

For example, the Stroop task is commonly used to assess how successfully one can inhibit a well-trained behavior. Like the Go-NoGo tasks described earlier, this task requires the participants to inhibit their habitual response. This task makes use of the fact that, at least among literate people, reading is a habitual behavior triggered by the presence of words. That is, when we see a word, the first thing we do is read it, not notice the font, or the type size, or the color. We can obviously do all of those things as well, but our first instinct is to read the word. The Stroop task looks at how well a person can block this reading habit in order to report other characteristics of a word. First, the Stroop task asks people to read a number of color words, printed in black text (e.g. "red", "blue", "yellow") to get a measure of reading speed. Next, the task asks people to identify the color of a series of "XXXXX" printed in various colors to get a measure of how quickly they can identify colors. Finally, the person is asked to inhibit their reading habit. The person is asked to identify the color of the type in which a color word has been printed (e.g. "red" written in blue ink should elicit a response of "blue", "yellow" written in red ink should elicit a response of "red"). The number of incorrect responses and the change in speed in the person's ability to identify colors is an indicator of how much trouble the person has inhibiting their reading behavior in order to successfully name the colors (Stroop, 1935). To try the task yourself, go to:
http://faculty.washington.edu/chudler/java/ready.html

As we might expect given the slow development of the prefrontal cortex, people get better at the Stroop task during late childhood, and continue to improve during adolescence, reaching a relatively stable level of their personal best performance in late adolescence. This level of performance is on average maintained until about age 65, when performance on a population level starts to decline (Comalli et al., 1962). Notably, not all older adults show large declines in executive function as measured by Stroop. Researchers found that although Stroop performance generally declined with advancing age, the declines in performance were substantially greater in individuals with a lower level of education (Van der Elst et al., 2006). This emphasizes the importance of training and practice for development and maintenance of executive function. Education early in life may provide extra training of prefrontal circuits that buffers the effects of aging-related decreases in prefrontal abilities. We will discuss this more in the next section.

Risk aversion and risky decision-making

The slow development of the prefrontal cortex can lead to more impulsive and risky behavior in children and teenagers compared to adults. Prefrontal cortex function has been associated with "risk aversion", which refers to the idea that people are generally very careful not to lose things they have obtained or to subject themselves to even small risks. This trait is less pronounced in children and adolescents, as well as people with damage to ventromedial region of the orbitofrontal cortex circuits, people with psychopathy and substance use disorders, or people who have been deprived of sleep.

In his excellent book *Descartes' Error* (1994), the eminent neurologist Antonio Damasio describes a client, initialed EVR, with ventromedial prefrontal cortex damage. EVR had a meningioma tumor growing in the midline area just above his nasal cavities that compressed both frontal lobes upward. Although EVR scored in the superior range on tests of intelligence, his ability to make decisions was impaired, especially in social situations. He could sense that topics that used to evoke emotion, no longer did so. Although he had social knowledge, he now lacked feelings of embarrassment. Like other clients with lesions in this region, he was no longer compelled to avoid risky behavior for fear of embarrassment, loss of social standing, or other unpleasant consequences. In other words, the lack of these feelings eliminated his risk aversion. Thus, Damasio proposed that a reduction in comprehension of emotional consequences might underlie irrational behavior as much as alterations in non-emotional reasoning did.

The Iowa Gambling task has been used to characterize problems with decision-making, particularly in one's ability to learn and adapt their choices based on punishments or rewards. Participants are presented with four card decks from which they must choose cards. The goal of the task is to try to win as much money as possible, and typically participants are given a portion of their earnings at the end as a motivator. Participants are told that some decks are better than others and asked to make 100 card choices. Two of the decks have cards indicating a relatively large gain of money, but also occasional cards that provide an extremely large penalty loss. Consistently choosing from these decks leads to a net loss of money. The other two decks have cards with generally lower gains than the other decks, but also much lower penalties. Consistently choosing from these two decks leads to a net gain of money. The average person with high risk aversion will relatively quickly learn to avoid the decks with the extremely large losses out of fear of a future large loss. However, people who are very driven by opportunities for big immediate rewards will tend to choose more from the decks with the higher wins, even though this is a poor long-term strategy that leads to loss of money.

Individuals with ventromedial prefrontal cortex damage like EVR consistently make decisions guided by immediate possibilities rather than longer-term rewards or consequences (Bechara et al., 2000). This may be in part because they cannot use emotions associated with past losses to adjust future behavior. They will consistently pick from the high win/high loss deck, tempted by the bigger gains even though it is an overall losing deck. Children and adolescents tend to show more of this pattern of choosing than adults, and slowly improve over time as their prefrontal cortex develops. As children age, they slowly make more complex decisions in the Iowa Gambling task (Huizenga et al., 2007). First they start to consider the frequency of loss. Only later can they consider both the amount and frequency of losses in their choices.

In healthy adults, sleep deprivation leads people to choose more frequently from the high gain/high loss money-losing deck than they do when they are well rested (Killgore et al., 2006). Notably, this effect of sleep deprivation cannot be reversed by caffeine consumption (Killgore et al., 2007)! This same study observed that although age did not predict performance on the Iowa Gambling task when people were well rested, age did predict performance when people were sleep deprived, with older adults showing more immediate reward-driven choices than younger people. This suggests that older people are more sensitive to sleep deprivation than younger people and show more risky reward-driven behavior when poorly rested.

Taken together, these studies indicate that a fully functioning ventromedial prefrontal cortex is needed in order to learn and follow good strategies to maximize long-term benefit. When the ventromedial prefrontal cortex is not working well, that person will tend to make risky choices that put their longer-term well-being in jeopardy for a chance at a big immediate reward. Moreover it is not particularly rare for someone to have only a partially functioning ventromedial cortex, either because it has not developed yet (e.g. teenagers) or because it is not rested enough to work correctly (e.g. following sleep deprivation). This could lead to all sort of risky behaviors. For example, teenagers might drive dangerously fast just to experience the thrill, despite the fact that they are risking devastating injury or even death by doing so. A sleep-deprived adult might eat a whole box of cookies just because they taste good, even though they know they need to get their weight down to keep their diabetes under control or else risk heart disease or foot amputation. Thus, fostering development, training, and good up-keep of one's ventromedial prefrontal cortex is crucial for encouraging healthful behavior.

Making good long-term decisions also relies on having a well-functioning orbitofrontal cortex, and people show abnormal behavior on the Iowa Gambling task when their orbitofrontal cortex is damaged. But in this case, they demonstrate a lack of punishment learning. They do not switch to the more conservative decks after experiencing huge losses on the high gain/high loss decks. Individuals with sub-clinical psychopathy symptoms also show this pattern of decisions on this task (van Honk et al., 2002). This finding is consistent with anti-social behaviors that individuals with psychopathy display. Basically, their brains do not modify their behavior when they do something that upsets other people or even causes themselves immediate harm. Their choices are driven only by the chance of being rewarded and not by the risk of punishment. Thus, if you want to make good long-term choices, you need both the ventromedial prefrontal cortex to help you consider the long-term consequences of your decision and your other portions of the orbitofrontal cortex to help you avoid choices that lead to immediately damaging results.

Use it or lose it: The effect of novelty and activity on lifelong cognitive function
Knowing how important our prefrontal cortex is for making good long-term decisions for our health, how do we help our prefrontal cortex become strong and sophisticated? First off, it appears that the prefrontal cortex is a bit like our muscles. If you want your prefrontal cortex to work really well, you need to work it out regularly. You need to train it, and then provide it with regular challenges to maintain its fitness. But what constitutes a good workout for your prefrontal cortex?

Since your prefrontal cortex generates alternatives, solves problems and makes decisions, a good workout for your prefrontal cortex is anything that presents you with a lot of problems. More complicated and novel problems are even better for building up the prefrontal cortex. Since school is generally designed to help you identify problems you do not know how to solve and help you work toward a solution, education would be expected to strengthen your prefrontal cortex. As expected, education tends to be associated with improvements in decision-making skills. The importance of education becomes more obvious during old age when brain function starts to decline. As they age, people who received less education tend to show greater losses of problem-solving skills than more educated people. Researchers have argued that education when you are young helps create a "functional reserve" of brainpower. If you train your brain exceptionally well when you are young, your prefrontal cortex will have so much extra strength that your problem-solving skills will still be up to par when your prefrontal cortex starts to deteriorate (Fillit et al., 2002). Studies have also shown that continuing to train the prefrontal cortex can keep it "in shape" and maintain problem-solving skills. Older people who remain engaged socially, and challenge themselves with new problems on a regular basis show less loss of problem-solving skills over time. Overall, these findings are consistent with the view that continuing education throughout life is good for your brain, good for your health, and enlightening too.

While we generally lose brain cells and function as we age, this does not mean that our prefrontal cortex slows down over time. However, it may be working harder than before. Brain imaging studies have demonstrated reliable increases in prefrontal activation in older adults, indicating increased blood flow to this region that suggests the cortex may in fact work harder as we get older. Older adults who had the largest tissue losses in the hippocampus over a ten-year period showed the greatest additional activation in the right dorsolateral prefrontal cortex (Park & Reuter-Lorenz, 2009). The right dorsolateral prefrontal cortex is implicated in executive control, mental flexibility, and problem-solving. People with damage to this region demonstrate some of the following impairments: perseveration (i.e. sticking with the same strategy even when it ceases to be rewarding), impaired divergent thinking, impaired retrieval and distress intolerance (see Millder & Cummings, 2006).

Since the dorsolateral prefrontal cortex is substantially more active for older adults with greater degeneration in the hippocampus compared to younger people and older adults with less degeneration in the hippocampus, it is reasonable to assume that the additional activity contributes to compensatory processing. When the parts of the brain that normally help with memory begin to fail, other parts are recruited to help. When we start to lose brain resources, we put more pressure on the parts that remain to solve problems. And these back-up systems that rely on alternative brain pathways allow us to continue achieving our goals so we may continue to function normally even as we lose neurons with age. Ongoing challenges that require flexible thinking and exercise can help build and maintain these back-up problem-solving systems and help prevent declines in our abilities as we grow older.

How does training strengthen the prefrontal cortex's ability to problem-solve? This probably occurs through a few mechanisms, such as strengthening connections and adding new neurons. First, practicing problem-solving appears to strengthen neuronal connections in the prefrontal cortex. This practice probably teaches the prefrontal cortex specific strategies for tackling a problem. As these strategies are practiced, the connections between neurons needed to implement this strategy will be strengthened. This will make it easier to try this strategy in the future. Second, adding new neurons and support cells (glia) to the prefrontal cortex appears to strengthen it. This process is called neurogenesis (for neurons) and gliogenesis (for glia). For years neuroscience lore suggested that your brain does not make new neurons after early development, but neuroscientists have now shown that this is not true. The brain can and does make new neurons throughout adulthood, particularly in the hippocampus. New neurons, but more commonly new glia, are also generated in the prefrontal cortex. Neuroscience lore also suggested that glia have little to do with cognitive processing, but it is now increasingly clear that these cells, in addition to their role in providing nutrients and related functions, also have their own signaling system that can influence the function of neurons during learning and memory. Albert Einstein's brain was found to have exceptionally high volumes of glia, suggesting they are important for high cognitive functioning.

While it is still not known exactly how adding new cells strengthens the prefrontal cortex, birth of new brain cells has been suggested to help maintain good prefrontal cortex function and prevent mood disorders. Perhaps the new cells replace ones that get damaged with aging, or perhaps they are needed to make or strengthen new circuits that address new problems. Encouraging glia to multiply or become more effective in their supportive roles may improve cognitive function. Further research is needed to figure out how neurogenesis and gliogenesis improve prefrontal cortex function, but until then we can still encourage the birth of new cells in our brain and reap the benefits in our prefrontal cortex.

Doing your part to keep up the birthrate in your neural neighborhood

Birth of new brain cells does not appear to occur at a consistent stable pace. Rather neurogenesis and gliogenesis appear to be triggered or increased in response to environmental interactions. We have learned a substantial amount about when birth of new brain cells occurs and what prevents it from occurring by studying animal models.

The first finding regarding growth and death of new brain cells was that chronic stress is doubly problematic for keeping brains healthy and functioning. Chronic stress makes neurons vulnerable to damage, loss of connections, atrophy and cell death, particularly in the hippocampus (Sapolsky, 1999; McEwen, 1999). On top of this, chronic stress, including chronic social stress, reduces or prevents birth of new brain cells in limbic brain regions and the prefrontal cortex (Czéh et al., 2007). Thus chronic stress makes you more likely to lose brain cells and less likely to replace them, a combination that is obviously not good for keeping your brain connections intact and functioning. This means that steps to reduce stress in your life, such as those we discussed in Challenge #3, should help you keep your neuron numbers up and maintain your problem-solving functions.

Next, poor diet was found to contribute to brain deterioration. Rats only developed deterioration in the hippocampus (e.g. retraction of apical dendrites) when they were exposed to stressful social events (e.g. unstable housing and viewing a cat daily) if they were also fed a diet high in animal and saturated fat (Baran et al., 2005). A fatty diet has been associated with chronic stress and both have been linked to increased risk of cardiovascular disease and dementia. In contrast, adherence to a low fat, Mediterranean diet has been linked to a lower risk of age-related cognitive impairment (Féart, et al., 2009). Further, adherence to a Mediterranean diet, alone or in combination with regular physical activity, reduced the risk of Alzheimer's disease (Scarmeas et al., 2009).

Long-term caloric restriction also has been shown to protect the hippocampus of aging rats (Mladenovic Djordjevic et al. 2010). In rhesus monkeys, caloric restriction by 10-20% extended longevity by about 10-20%, prevented Type II diabetes, and reduced the risk of stroke and age-related cognitive impairment (Colman et al., 2009). Caloric restriction seems to be a daunting idea for most adults, and it remains unclear whether it is possible for more than a small percentage of people to exercise this kind of restraint and whether the tradeoffs are worth the effort. Interestingly, the cells in the prefrontal cortex that make informed decisions and protect us from unhealthy temptations would be preserving their own existence by reducing the risk of hypertensive stroke or age-related cognitive impairments from a diet that promotes diabetes, a key risk factor for Alzheimer's disease.

While the idea of reducing caloric intake, cutting fat from your diet, or damping down your stressful life commitments may seem like signing up for a life of perpetual sacrifice, there are an increasing number of people shifting to a more relaxed, minimalist lifestyle that embraces these goals. For example, the "Slow Movement" encourages people to "downshift" their lives, reducing time pressure and commitments and connecting in more meaningful ways with the people in their communities, the food they eat, and the work or services they provide (http://www.slowmovement.com/). Reframing stress reduction and lower caloric intake into terms of reducing time pressure to allow yourself to become more engaged in the core things you do and to savor the things you eat more deeply, can make these same behavioral changes seem highly appealing and even downright indulgent. For maintaining neurons, less is more, at least when it comes to social pressure and food consumption. And less social pressure and food consumption can be torture or paradise, depending on how you approach it.

In addition, exposure to enriched and novel environments, depression treatments, and voluntary exercise have all been shown to increase neurogenesis in the hippocampus and/or gliogenesis in the prefrontal cortex (Banasr & Duman, 2007; Mandyam et al., 2007; Olson et al., 2006). For example, old rats that lived in cages where there was plenty of visual stimulation and the opportunity to play generated more new hippocampus neurons than rats living in ordinary cages. Further, rats living in complex environments showed greater ability to learn and solve problems. Extrapolating to humans, there are good reasons to maintain a complex and stimulating environment, one that engages your mind and body.

It has been suggested that the effects of antidepressants on the birth of new brain cells is actually responsible for the reduction in depressive and posttraumatic stress symptoms that the medications produce (i.e. the ultimate effect of changing serotonin levels is to increase the birth rates of new brain cells), and researchers are now looking for new medications that increase cell birth rates in hopes of finding new treatments for depression and anxiety disorders (Banasr & Duman, 2007; Bremner et al., 2008). The birth of new neurons in the hippocampus is thought to be mediated by a growth factor known as Brain Derived Nerve Growth Factor (BDNF), which can be stimulated by antidepressants, electroconvulsive shock treatment used to treat depression, and moderate physical exercise (Castrén & Rantamäki, 2010). Notably, voluntary exercise not only stimulates the birth of new brain cells but also tends to reduce depression (Daley, 2008). This is consistent with the idea that birth and development of new brain cells actually causes reductions in mood disorders.

Overall, these studies suggest that maintaining exposure to new environments and challenges, having a rich diverse lifestyle, proactively treating mood disorders, and exercising regularly should improve and maintain cognitive abilities and problem-solving skills late in life. These predictions are supportive of a growing body of human research that suggests that social engagement, intellectual stimulation, and physical activity all contribute to maintenance of cognitive ability in older age (Butler et al., 2004). Lastly, one of the best ways to maintain cognitive performance is to not damage your brain cells in the first place. The protective helmet you wear when you ride a bicycle or the safety belt that keeps your head from striking the windshield are obvious examples. Head injuries in sports, occupational injuries, from firearms and from falls can be meaningfully reduced by taking the necessary precautions.

In addition to traumatic brain injury, there are many insidious causes of brain injury resulting from toxic, behavioral and neurodegenerative causes. These include diabetes, hypertension and vascular disease, sleep disorders, depression, alcohol, and substance and medication misuse. The benefits of regular screening for these causes of neuron loss cannot be underestimated and daily adherence to medically-prescribed exercise and drug regimes can be life-saving. For example, hypertensive stroke can be prevented in a majority of people through adequate monitoring and treatment of high blood pressure.

Chapter 5.3: Improving Problem-Solving and Cognitive Skills

What prevents problem-solving?

Assuming your prefrontal cortex is well-trained, well-rested and healthy, is there anything that would make your prefrontal cortex make short-sighted decisions? As we discussed in Challenge #1, our thoughts, expectations and learned associations about the value of immediate rewards can make our brains, including our prefrontal cortex, believe that these rewards are more important than their objective value. For example, if we are convinced that eating a gallon of ice cream will make us feel better, or expect that drinking a six-pack of beer will make us more attractive and socially adept, then our prefrontal cortex will include those assumptions in making its decisions. We will be more likely to eat the gallon of ice cream or drink that six-pack of beer if we hold those beliefs. Correcting these beliefs by consciously observing that we feel sick to our stomach after eating that much ice cream or that we wound up embarrassing ourselves while drunk can shift the decisions our prefrontal cortex makes. In order to make good decisions, our prefrontal cortex not only needs to know how to solve problems and make good choices but also needs accurate information about the choices it is considering.

In Thomas Jefferson's Declaration of Independence, he wrote about self-evident truths, justifying the rights of life, liberty and the pursuit of happiness. For some, it is "self-evident" that the freedom to make self-destructive choices is an inalienable right for the pursuit of happiness. As a society, we have chosen to put few rules around the marketing and promotion of products, such as sugar-filled food products and alcoholic beverages that provide a quick transient pleasure but ultimately make us feel worse. Many marketing dollars are put into efforts to encourage us to attend to the quick "happiness" associated with the most common self-destructive habits. With personal effort, we can train ourselves to attend to the delayed effects of our choices. Listen to your body, and practice connecting the longer-term feelings produced by a choice to the choice itself. Remember the hangover instead of the intoxication, and beer will not be as appealing.

Our bodies communicate a kind of truth through these delayed somatic symptoms (e.g. a hangover) that should help us to protect our life and liberty against the indiscriminate pursuit of happiness. However, the time delay prevents our limbic circuits from recognizing the connection between these bad feelings and the choices that caused them. It takes conscious attention to link these later consequences and unhappiness to the choices that caused them. Only your prefrontal cortex can link the hangover to the beer. *Be aware of over-valuation of rewards. Your prefrontal cortex cannot make good choices if it is starting with inaccurate information.* Pay attention and consider the longer-term consequences of choices. This will provide the prefrontal cortex with the more accurate information it needs to make decisions that lead to lasting happiness, rather than the futile pursuit of quick pleasures that ultimately make us unhealthy and sick.

Tricks for helping your prefrontal cortex

1. Be prepared. Problem-solve possible problems before the situation occurs.

Knowing that problem-solving is a relatively slow process, you can improve the chance that you make good long-term choices by pre-planning responses to situations that you expect to encounter. If you already have a solution to a problem figured out beforehand, you will not have to actually do the problem-solving during the situation. This will not only speed up your problem-solving, but also help ensure that the stress of the moment does not bias your decisions towards things that produce immediate relief rather than long-term benefit. Having predetermined solutions to situations that you expect to encounter can help your prefrontal cortex make up for its slow processing time. This helps ensure that you do not fall back on your habitual behaviors just because you did not have time to come up with a better response.

To practice pre-planning solutions, try Exercise 5A (page 210).

2. *Ask or observe respected role models.*

Although planning solutions beforehand can greatly increase your ability to make good long-term choices, this trick is still restricted by the limits of your own creativity. Pre-planning will only help you come up with solutions that you can think of based on your own problem-solving skills, knowledge and past experience. Moreover, you can only come up with solutions for situations that you can anticipate. If you are not happy with your solutions, want to come up with new ones, or feel like you are often confronted by problematic surprises, you may want to either ask others what they would do or watch people respond to similar situations.

Obviously, the new solutions that asking or observing others provide will tend to be better when the person you are asking or watching is highly skilled at solving that particular problem. Thus, finding experts or role models who have mastered the behaviors you are interested in is key to making the most of the learning opportunity. If you are trying to learn to better control your anger, talk to a person who is particularly skilled in mediation or very client. If you want to learn how to keep your diabetes under control, talk to a nutritionist or a person with well-controlled diabetes. If you want to learn how to swim for fitness, get advice from someone who has swum regularly for many years. Networking with friends, coworkers and teachers can provide powerful new solutions to stubborn problems.

If you want to observe others solving a similar problem, you will likely need to find a high-risk environment so that you can readily observe people being challenged. The difficulty with this strategy is that you will likely need to be in this high-risk environment yourself to do the observing. Thus, this is only a good idea if you can find a way to protect yourself while you are doing the observing. For example, if I wanted to observe strategies people use not to overeat when provided an excess of food, going to an all-you-can-eat buffet could provide a good opportunity to watch people's behavior and see who successfully eats in moderation and who eats more than necessary. However, I do not want to wind up over-eating myself. Making sure I am protected from eating too much, by not purchasing the buffet, going at a time when I am not hungry, or finding a restaurant where I do not like the food, is key to giving me space to observe behavior without getting into trouble myself.

Many successful therapies and interventions include a component where people are encouraged to learn from and observe experienced others. For example, therapists may rehearse new solutions with their clients and model new behaviors. Mutual help groups such as Alcoholic's Anonymous encourage people in stable recovery to come to meetings and mentor people who are still having trouble initiating behavior change. At these meetings they can provide suggestions regarding ways that they successfully navigated difficult situations or solved problems.

To learn some prefrontal mnemonics for questions to ask yourself or your role models, see Exercise 5B (page 213).

3. Play! Logic problems, games, sports, and exploration.

Finding fun and challenging pastimes is very important for ensuring that your prefrontal cortex gets regular workouts. The more practice your brain gets solving problems, the stronger and faster your prefrontal circuits will become. Since you cannot solve problems unless you have problems, this means that you need to find ways of exposing yourself to challenges. However, as we mentioned before, stress, especially chronic stress, actually weakens the prefrontal cortex. Thus, the trick is to expose yourself to problems without getting stressed.

This is where the fun comes in. You need to give yourself time to play. By play, we mean you need to give yourself challenges where your success or failure is of little consequence to your actual well-being. For example, I could try to master a new videogame. If it is a decent game, I will have to learn a number of new strategies to progress through the game and will likely learn to enact them quickly. This is a good prefrontal cortex workout. At the same time, it does not really matter if I fail at the game repeatedly. I can always just restart and try it again. Thus, the problems the videogame provides should not be stressful. I suppose I could get all worked up and stressed about the game if I tried, but with any amount of perspective, I would see that I was being silly. These are the sorts of challenges you need to create.

To really strengthen the prefrontal cortex, it is also important to make sure that you get a lot of variety in the challenges you create. Otherwise, your prefrontal cortex will get really good at solving one type of problem but be terrible at others. Diversity in your games is important! Playing videogames all day long will not make you a great overall problem-solver, it will just make you great at playing videogames. So mix it up! Try some crossword puzzles. Take piano lessons. Master Sudoku. Learn a new language. Join a debate club. Study organic chemistry. Play basketball. Attend cooking classes. Practice yoga. Immerse yourself in a new culture. Try some logic problems. Do a jigsaw puzzle. Take a multivariate calculus class. Learn to knit. Join a creative-writing group. Garden. Test out investing strategies by tracking simulated trading practices. Train to run a marathon. Teach a child to read. Figure out how to get the stains out of your living room carpet. All of these will force you to address new problems and situations that you have not encountered before. Figuring out how to successfully solve those problems will teach you how to respond when you encounter similar or analogous problems later. And in all of these cases, who cares if you fail 27 times before you get even close to a workable solution. Half-finished crossword puzzles, missed free throws, a sweater with two different length arms, the wrong answers on some math problems, and a burnt dinner are not the end of the world. So get out there and try the things that interest you. You almost certainly will not be good at them for a while after you start, but that is a good sign that you picked something you need work on. Each try on a new problem helps train your prefrontal cortex, regardless of whether you succeed or fail.

Lastly, the fun part is also important for encouraging practice and persistence. Becoming a good problem-solver takes work and repetition. If you give yourself challenging play that you do not enjoy, you will not keep at it and you will not develop your problem-solving skills. For example, I (J.T.) once decided I wanted to learn to wind-surf and signed up for lessons, thinking it would be a fabulous way to spend spring afternoons. But a couple of lessons in, I was forced to admit that I hated it. The water was freezing cold, and the lake we were learning in had big yucky weeds that got tangled in your legs and shifting gusty winds that knocked you over almost every time you started going. I am not very cold tolerant and found the whole experience miserable. Rather than ensure that I never tried the sport again in my life, I stopped going to those lessons and took up water polo instead. I was equally bad at water polo, but the pool was reasonably warm, the coach had a sense of humor (which he needed to put up with my lack of talent), and there was so much to learn that I could not help but get substantially better relatively quickly. It provided a much better environment for learning and practicing. My failures did not involve a torturous dunk in ice-cold, muddy, slimy water, and my successes were so unexpected that they excited both my supportive coach and myself. Even though the water polo lessons were exceedingly challenging for me, and I was by far the worst person in the class, I looked forward to the class and made sure to never miss one. It was fun. So follow your interests, do not be afraid to look foolish or fail, but do find challenges and a learning environment that you honestly enjoy. Otherwise you will never practice long enough to learn anything.

To practice building problem-skills by playing games and doing physical activities, see Exercise 5C (page 214) and Exercise 5D (page 216).

EXAMPLE: The value of expanding your horizons and trying new things

I (W.G.) took up yoga in spite of (or perhaps because of) substantial inflexibility. At first, I felt hopelessly overmatched by the capabilities of the students who had learned these skills and made them seem easy, while I found the poses beyond my capabilities. Although I did not "believe" yoga would do me any good, I initially persevered because my aching neck and shoulders felt much better every time after I exercised. My teacher gently reminded me, "you don't have to believe in it to benefit." Several weeks later, I quit, felt worse, returned, felt better, quit again for a shorter duration, felt much better when I returned, and soon the habit stuck. For the last couple of years, I have attended a yoga class two to three times a week and I always look forward to it.

The challenge is not only in doing the poses, which, for the most part, I am still much more deficient in performing than most of the other students, but in paying absolute attention to the constantly changing instructions. These 90-minute sessions are sufficiently focused so that there is no time to worry about the usual things on which my wandering mind usually perseverates. This experience is more than doing, but one of being. It occupies my nervous system pretty intensively to stay focused and balanced.

My experience has been duplicated by investigators who have studied the health benefits of Hatha yoga, and found that it is associated with a reduction of stress hormones such as noradrenaline and cortisol in practitioners (Ross & Thomas, 2010). Taking up a new activity can be healthy for your brain and body. Explore your choices and expand your brain.

Brain Challenge #5 Exercises

Exercise 5A: Pre-Planning Solutions to Situations Where You Have Difficulty Acting Healthfully

There are many high-risk situations that trigger learned bad habits; for example, to drink excessively or use drugs, to eat too much, to eat non-nutritious food, or to express oneself inappropriately. Identifying high-risk situations that tend to initiate your bad habits is a first step towards pre-planning new solutions to these challenges. For example, this list adapted from http://www.brighteyecounselling.co.uk/highrisk.html describes high-risk situations for drinking that are common to many people with drinking problems:

When I pass a bar
When I am with other people who are drinking
When I feel tense
When I have to meet people
When I think that just one drink would cause no harm
When I am feeling depressed
When I am not at work that day
When I am happy
When I have money to spend
When I feel myself getting angry
When I feel frustrated with my life
When I feel tired
When I feel disappointed that other people have let me down
When I remember the good times I was having
When I have already had a drink

Now it is your turn to generate a personal list of high-risk situations for the bad habit that you wish to change.

Step 1: Select a bad habit you would like to change:

____

Step 2: Brainstorm situations where you tend to do the habit. These are your high-risk situations:

*
*
*
*
*
*
*
*
*
*
*

Step 3: Develop a plan for dealing with a situation.
Now that you have identified the situations that tend to trigger your bad habit, you can begin to problem-solve new ways of preventing or responding to these risky situations.

Often preventing exposure to the high-risk situation is the simplest and most effective solution. For example, if I have trouble not drinking when I pass by a bar on my way home from work, I might simply change the route that I take to get home to one that did not pass by a bar. After getting used to taking the new route, I would be able to avoid that high-risk situation with little effort.

Pick one of the situations you listed above: ______________________________

Consider the situation you picked. Is there a way that you could prevent or limit your exposure to the situation? If so, write it here:

____

____

Sometimes, high-risk situations are unavoidable or should not be avoided. For example, if I have trouble not drinking when I am happy or have something to celebrate, it would not make sense to try to avoid being happy or successful. Here, it is important to find alternative behaviors that would be better to do in these situations. If these alternative behaviors can only be done instead of the bad habit, rather than in addition to the bad habit, the new solution may provide more protection from the high-risk situation. For example, instead of a bottle of wine, I might decide to treat myself with a massage, invite friends over to play board games, or go to a social dance event (one where alcohol is not served).

Consider the situation you picked. Is there something you could do other than the bad habit which would serve the same purpose? Write down ideas for alternative behaviors here:

*
*
*
*
*

Consider the list you just generated. Of those ideas, which can only be done instead of the bad habit?

____

____

Step 4: Practice the new solution.
Now that you have some ideas of new ways that you could handle high-risk situations, it is important to practice them a bit so that you are ready to use them.

Choose a solution that you think would work for you: ________________________

In your head, or role-playing with a trusted friend or close relation, walk through the situation as you carry out your new solution. Did the solution work out the way you thought it would? Practice walking through the situation a few times, ideally varying the context and responses of those around you, to help solidify the plan in your head and work out difficult areas where it might be easy to slip back into habit rather than continuing with your new solution.

Did you come up with any changes or revisions? If so, make note of them here:

____

____

Exercise 5B: Four Forms of Forethought for Your Prefrontal Brain

Some find mnemonics to be extremely helpful tools to remember complicated information and encourage its use in everyday life. I (W.G.) remember both key strategies for encouraging behavior change and key areas of the prefrontal cortex involved in those behavior changes through the use of some simple mnemonics:

1. Daily Life Planning (DLP, DorsoLateral Prefrontal cortex): Consider your choices. Am I making the same mistake repeatedly? What can I do that I have not tried before? What new behaviors have a reasonable chance of working?
2. Action Control Guide (ACG, Anterior Cingulate Gyrus): Consider your motivation. How motivated am I to manage the problem? Do my goals and values favor my behavior? Have I consistently tried to deal with this issue in a meaningful way? If I am not motivated, what might motivate me?
3. Valued Momentary Pleasures (VMP, VentroMedial Prefrontal cortex): Consider your impulsivity. Are you taking big risks in hopes of a big, but maybe not likely, reward? Is your excitement about what you could have jeopardizing what you have already achieved? Are you valuing momentary pleasures more than achievement of your long-term goals and maintenance of health and happiness?
4. One's Friends and Confidants (OFC, OrbitoFrontal Cortex): Consider the social context of your behavior. How does my behavior affect the feelings of other people involved in this issue? Have I obtained sufficient social support to achieve my goal? Who can help me? Have I communicated my concerns in a way that resonates with the feelings of others?

Try using these mnemonics to guide you through your assessment of a health behavior problem. Considering your choices, your motivation, your impulsivity, and the social context involved in your health behavior problem will help you identify areas where focused attention or problem-solving may improve your chances of successful behavior change.

A more comprehensive discussion of the way these prefrontal areas work together and separately as cortical-subcortical loops to create and maintain habits is described in Appendix 3.

Exercise 5C: Building Problem-Solving Skills By Playing Games

There are hoards of games, puzzles and riddles that challenge problem-solving skills and creativity. All of these can strengthen your problem-solving skills and open up new options in everyday life. Adding some of these games or puzzles to your daily or weekly routine can improve your ability to find answers to seemingly complicated problems you encounter. Remember, solving a problem is a reward and a problem with no solution is a stressor.

Some tips

First, do not get upset if the puzzles seem hard or impossible when you start. That is a good sign. It suggests that these puzzles use skills you have not learned yet or are difficult for you. There is a lot to be gained by playing with a type of puzzle that completely stumps you. Problem-solving skills grow by practice, so you will get better at them if you just keep trying.

Second, when you are stuck on a problem or a new type of puzzle, it is OK to "cheat" and look at the answer, so long as you go back and work out how to get from where you were stuck to the answer. Working backwards from the answer to figure out the strategy for solving the problem still teaches you the problem-solving strategy and can sometimes be the only way to figure out new types of problems. So when you get stuck, do not give up. Look at the answer and figure out where it came from. You will be better at the next problem.

Third, do not be shy about asking others for advice or help if you get stuck. Sometimes other people notice things that you have not seen. It is always nice to have someone who is really good at a particular type of puzzle around to ask for advice or walk you through a complicated bit of logic. If you do not have such a person handy nearby, I note that many of the puzzle websites on-line include forums for people to post-questions and comments to one another. With an internet connection you should never find yourself lacking assistance and guidance from others.

Links to puzzles and games

There are many websites that provide brainteasers and puzzles that can be done online or printed and completed. To get you started, try the sites below. Most break the different types of puzzles into varying levels of difficulty. Start with the easier ones to help you figure out the general puzzle strategy and then work your way to harder ones!

www.brainbashers.com

www.brainden.com

www.braingle.com

http://www.rinkworks.com/brainfood/

For the brilliant among us

http://www.mensa.org.uk/puzzles/

Mensa, a society "for people with IQ's in the top 2%" includes weekly brainteasers on their website and sells games and puzzles which challenge problem-solving skills.

Designed for kids

http://kids.niehs.nih.gov/braint.htm

National Institute of Environmental Health Sciences (part of the National Institutes of Health (NIH)) has a page of puzzles, riddles and brainteasers meant for kids, but which are fun for adults too!

http://www.hoagiesgifted.org/brain_teasers.htm

This page, intended to provide stimulating activities for gifted children, includes lots of links to sites with games, puzzles, and brainteasers. There are hours and hours of fun problems to solve here that would be enjoyable for anyone.

Designed for pairs or groups

Many board and card games include substantial problem-solving challenges and test your skills. Any of these can be great ways of learning and practicing new strategies in the context of fun with friends. The key here is to be deliberate as you play. Think out your options and their immediate and longer-term consequences. Deliberately choose a strategy and observe the outcome over several plays or games. This will not only develop your frontal cortex, but also make you a better, more successful game player! There are lots of games to choose from and playing a variety is probably a good idea. Some suggestions include Mastermind, Chess, Checkers, Card Games (e.g. Bridge, Cribbage, Hearts), Scrabble, The Game of Go, and Mahjong, but there are many, many great others.

Exercise 5D: Mixing Physical Activity with Problem-Solving Skills Development

For those of you who already spend enough time sitting, additional quiet time spent doing puzzles may not be very attractive. There are plenty of options for mixing problem-solving skill development with physical activity, although in most cases it may require that you pay deliberate attention to focusing on problem-solving during the activity.

Below are some activities that can be used to develop problem-solving skills. These are only examples; if none of them are appealing, use your creativity to come up with ways to exercise your prefrontal cortex and body at the same time.

Orienteering
Orienteering is both a sport and a pastime basically consisting of a race to an endpoint or endpoints over unmarked terrain guided by only a map and a compass. It is most commonly done on foot, but can be done in combination with just about any form of locomotion (e.g. mountain biking, skiing, canoeing, horseback riding, or a mix). The main problem to be solved is how to most quickly reach the target destinations. Solving this overall problem will require solving many smaller problems and considering your options, strengths and weaknesses, and ability to pass obstacles, as well as those of your competitors. It also requires developing navigation skills. Where are you on the map? What do your compass readings tell you about where you are and where you are headed? Should you take the shorter route up the hill or go around? Should you run up this trail or will that only tire you out and slow you down for the subsequent six-mile trek? What is the best way around or through this stream?

A nice thing about orienteering is that it gets you outside in new and often very pretty places. It can be done competitively or casually, independently or in groups, and by young and old. It can be a great activity for a family, group or class. Adding a group dynamic brings in all sorts of additional social interactions and decisions that must be solved. What do you do when people disagree about strategy? There are associations with national and local groups and teams where you can learn more about orienteering and find other interested people to share the fun. See the US Orienteering Federation at: http://www.us.orienteering.org/

A more recent variant on the "get outside and test your navigation skills" concept is "Geocaching". In this game, people hide small "treasures" all over the world in outdoor spaces and then provide clues and latitude and longitude markers online for other treasure seekers. You can look up treasure clues in your area and head out with a GPS device to try to find them. A website provides space to log your successes. For anyone who has ever had pirate treasure hunting fantasies, everything you need to get started can be found at: http://www.geocaching.com/

Bouldering
Bouldering is a variant of rock climbing where the object is to figure out and execute a climbing strategy for a specific route. Because no ropes are used, the endpoint is typically not far off the ground. Otherwise, the inevitable failures involved in problem-

solving would be too painful. Bouldering can be done wherever there are things to climb, assuming you can get a mat or crash pad underneath. It is most commonly done at rock climbing gyms, outside on the base of rock faces or large boulders, or even on roughly textured buildings or other architecture (although this can sometimes anger the owners, especially if you get chalk marks and shoe smudges all over the structure). Solving a bouldering problem involves figuring out a pattern of movements that will get you up a challenging route. Importantly, there is no one solution to any boulder problem, and your personal solution will require considering both the specifics of the problem and your own height, weight, reach and balance, and strengths and weaknesses. Watching others can give you ideas, but what works for another person may not work for you. Because the route is short, you have the opportunity to try out lots and lots of potential solutions. With each try, you not only sharpen your problem-solving skills, but also improve your strength and coordination.

Indoor rock climbing gyms are a great place to get started, learn skills and meet other people with whom to practice and share ideas. They also tend to be staffed by rock climbers and bouldering enthusiasts who can direct you to good places to boulder outdoors. A directory of indoor rock climbing gyms can be found at: http://www.indoorclimbing.com/worldgyms.html

Team Sports

Team sports offer a variety of physical challenges catering to people with different body types. Most share some general problem-solving challenges. How can we best organize, focus and motivate a group of people to meet a goal? For example, how do I organize a group of people with varying abilities and skills to most consistently get a ball into a goal? There are questions of overall game strategy. For example, should we play all our best players hard at the start of the game or save some until later so they are fresh and energetic at the end of the game? There are questions about immediate game strategy. How should the team move the ball (or whatever) to best score or prevent the other team from scoring in the next thirty seconds? There are questions about interpersonal dynamics and motivation. How do we keep our star player from getting frustrated and quitting while he is being guarded by a much larger and very aggressive defense? The fact that team sports are almost universally played against a second team which changes from game to game means that the most effective strategy and organization is apt to change from game to game based upon the skills, strengths and weaknesses of the challenging team. In short, there are endless opportunities to practice problem-solving skills in team sports.

The big problem with trying to use team sports as a way to practice problem-solving skills is that coaches typically do 95% of the problem-solving. Thus, with normal team sport dynamics, the coach practices his problem-solving skills and the players practice carrying out his instructions in the immediate setting. Thus while players may have to do a lot of quick, reflexive, improvised problem-solving on the field, the coach does nearly all of the deliberate planning and strategizing that challenges the frontal cortex. Notably, a coach's abilities at general problem-solving seem to be related to the success of the team. For example, a study in Germany found that national top-league basketball and team handball coaches out performed local-league coaches in problem-solving challenges unrelated to their sport (Hagemann et al., 2008). Finding ways of sharing in the coaching duties can turn team sport participation into a great problem-solving exercise. You may find that taking over the role of coach may be easier to do in small pick-up games with friends than in actual organized leagues.

Surmounting the Challenges: The Example of Weight Loss

Example Introduction

Even when you know things, it takes practice to understand how to apply them. To help illustrate how the concepts we discussed in the five brain challenges can be put to practical use, we now go back through each process and consider how it might be used to target a common problem; specifically, how to lose weight and keep it off. We hope you will not only find these tips helpful for weight loss, but also better understand how seemingly unrelated or small behavior or environment changes can have a big impact on achieving a large, long-term health goal. What may initially seem like overwhelming or intractable problems are often best solved by constantly doing the little things you can do right now rather than feeling like you must run at the whole problem head-on.

Challenge #1: Valuing Health

Social reinforcement and peer pressure

Misconceptions and biases about healthful and unhealthful foods are substantial barriers to healthful eating. People often do not know what is and is not healthful to eat. And even when they do, they often have biases and expectations that discourage eating well. Healthful foods are often assumed to taste bad or be unsatisfying while unhealthful foods are assumed to be delicious and rewarding to eat. In reality, this is not true. Healthful food can be amazingly delicious, tempting, satisfying, and craving-inducing, particularly when you know how to prepare it well. For example, my husband and I (J.T.) eagerly await fresh fig season every year, when we tend to gorge ourselves on giant arugula, fresh fig and gorgonzola salads to the exclusion of the rest of our planned meal. Having spent years trying healthful vegetable-focused recipes out of cookbooks and off the Internet, I now view fresh produce as a wondrous treat that offers up numerous options for combining and cooking into joyous meals.

To make meaningful changes in your diet that will encourage weight loss and long-term weight maintenance, it can be helpful to challenge your beliefs about healthful and unhealthful foods. First, there are many cultural misperceptions about what constitutes healthful food. It may be helpful to take a nutrition course to learn to think about food from a more objective perspective. Next, challenge ideas that healthful food will taste bad or be torture to eat all the time. If you do not know how to prepare tasty dishes made with healthful foods, consider taking a cooking class or asking a healthy friend to share recipes. Whenever you eat a healthy meal you enjoy, learn the recipe so you can replicate it yourself. Conversely, challenge ideas that unhealthful foods are truly flavorful and make you feel good. Reflecting on how you feel 30 minutes after eating unhealthful foods can help to correct beliefs that eating unhealthful foods will make you happy, content or satisfied.

The power of suggestion: Placebo and nocebo effects

Food as medicine

Food is often presented as a "cure all" for problems of all sorts. "Eat this, it will make you feel better." Some suggestions for foods that will make you feel better are so frequently repeated that they may be considered American cultural clichés or even alternative medicine. Examples include eating chicken noodle soup for colds and flu, indulging in ice cream when you have a sore throat or relationship problems, or having a glass of warm milk to help you sleep. Generally, these expectations are helpful lore, providing harmless interventions that, via placebo, will make people feel better and give concerned loved ones something to do to help. However, when the occasional use of food as medicine transforms into a habit of eating to feel better, this helpful placebo effect can become a significant driver of obesity. Expectations that food will elevate your mood, when combined with frequent experiences of negative moods, can lead to chronic overeating. If you find you yourself eating to feed your feelings rather than true hunger, you may benefit from learning and practicing new strategies for managing mood or stress. A psychologist or other health professional may be helpful here.

Weight loss panaceas
The American advertising landscape is littered with products promising to solve all weight problems with little effort in a short period of time. Driven by great hope that these miracle cures will work, people may achieve rapid initial weight loss with these diets, pills and services, but this rarely lasts and can lead to rebound weight gain. While great expectations may allow us to persevere through unhealthful treatments or behavioral plans to drop a few pounds quickly, these stressful attempts at a quick fix tend to encourage binge or over-eating. The typical person who tries these crash diet plans will, after losing a few pounds in the short-term, regain the weight plus a bit not long thereafter. Do not be fooled by the hype and avoid these placebos. Only patience and true stable changes of behavior and diet will take off a substantial amount of weight over the long-term.

Marketing your own expectations and rewards
As we discussed, advertising is extremely effective for increasing consumption, thus justifying the billions of dollars spent by corporations to encourage consumption of their products. Cutting back on exposure to TV and thus advertising has been shown to reduce weight gain in numerous studies in children (Jason & O'Donnell, 2008). Direct food cues (images of food) and the positive cues (happy families, sex, fun, success, plenty) that have been linked to food by advertisers are everywhere. Once these associations have been created, it will be difficult to avoid exposure to cues. But if we become more aware of the associations that are presented to us, we may be able to reduce our exposure and challenge the assumptions underlying the associations. Will eating a hamburger make me sexy? Will my family get along better if we eat at a particular restaurant? Will drinking a soda lead to world peace? Casting doubt on these associations may help to devalue some of the cues that advertising has encouraged us to overvalue.

Work to create cues to encourage healthful eating. Put a refillable water pitcher in the front of your refrigerator so that you always have cold water as an option. Make sure your kitchen is filled with healthful snacks so that you eat these before you get too hungry. Put cookbooks with healthful options on your bookshelves so that you do not fall into bad habits or go out to eat just because it is too hard to think of something healthful to prepare. Plan your menus in advance so you can get the fresh ingredients you need. Think about positive associations you have with healthful foods. Link good times you have had with positive eating habits. Barbecues can be fun, but it is not the over consumption of beer and beef that makes them so. Focus on the fun you had with friends, or the naturally sweet fresh corn on the cob that you grilled, or the amazing pitcher of fresh iced peppermint tea that you shared. Go beyond the standard stereotypes to create associations that help drive you toward healthful eating habits.

When helpful is hurtful: Rescuing, doting and enabling

Do loved ones in your life feed you to soothe your emotions? Do others "give you a cookie" when you are upset? For example, my (J.T.) sweet Italian grandmother found it hard to see family members upset and loved to cook and feed people. When anyone showed signs of negative emotion around her, she was likely to have their favorite food ready and waiting shortly there after. My two cousins, whom she cared for frequently, developed significant obesity problems as kids as her treats trained their reward circuits. They would get upset, she would feed them in response, and that would encourage them to get upset again, creating an unpleasant cycle for all. The combination of my grandmother's discomfort in seeing loved ones upset, her tendency to dote, and my cousins' poor emotional regulation, fueled my cousins' weight gain.

Because patterns like these are driven by the reward systems of both the person doing the doting and the person being doted upon, they are automatic rather than conscious responses. Thus, they can often continue unacknowledged and unaddressed for years or even decades. In trying to achieve and maintain a healthy weight, it is important to recognize these patterns and discuss them with those who tend to feed you when they are uncomfortable with the emotions you are experiencing. Help them come up with more helpful responses to your bad moods. Might they give you a hug instead? Maybe they could walk you through some breathing exercises? Perhaps they could help you problem-solve or reframe your situation? Work with them to help them respond to you better. Then work with yourself to try to come up with better ways of expressing your emotions to others. Are you catastrophizing or exaggerating how upset you are? Are you getting upset around your loved ones to get sympathy, attention, special treatment, or food? Try to tone down the cues you present to others that lead to their attempts to feed you into sedation or contentment. As you work with your loved ones to try to address these patterns (if they exist), be wary of your own tendencies toward extinction bursts. Work with your loved ones when they try responding to you in a new way. Do not escalate your bad mood or emotion-fueled behavior.

These sorts of interacting habits can be difficult to break. Sometimes, altering the context of your interactions with doters and rescuers can be more effective. For example, my grandmother was more likely to overfeed people when she had her own kitchen available. Spending time with her in settings other than her home would be another way of reducing the impact of her tendency to dote on others' weight. While other people's behavior is not usually in your control, creating or choosing the situations in which you interact with them can allow you to reduce the likelihood of certain unhelpful and unhealthful behaviors.

Comparing against others: Correcting perceptions through normative feedback

As we discussed in Challenge #1, weight gain is contagious. We pick up the habits that lead to weight gain from the loved and respected people in our social networks. Our social circles can normalize unhealthful eating patterns and encourage us to conform to these local norms, leading to weight gain. Being aware of these social influences is an important first step to preventing the spread of obesity. Even simple awareness that bad eating habits within one's immediate social circle are not shared by the broader community can help counteract some of this social pressure. For example, as a teenager, the "cool kids" in my (J.T.'s) neighborhood used to meet at the local convenience store on the way to the bus before school, where they would purchase and consume big bags of chips and bottles of soda for breakfast. I was thankfully buffered from this rather unappealing routine by the fact that I spent much of my free time outside of my neighborhood with a group of gymnasts from all over the region, who I knew would be horrified by this choice of breakfast fare. My exposure to a broader sampling of social norms protected me from more local pressure to adopt poor dietary habits. Aware that not all of my peers ate this way, I felt confident in my choice not to join this group practice, and simply ate my bran flakes before leaving the house. Taking a hard and critical look at your everyday behaviors, especially those that "everyone does", may help you identify and correct bad habits that you picked up from those around you.

As you begin to make healthful changes to your diet and eating practices, be prepared for the near inevitable discouragement that you will receive from your peers. Your successes at improving your diet will almost certainly be punished by some members of your inner network. "You always used to eat the triple burger with cheese. Why not now?" "If you are going to insist on eating your home-cooked food, maybe you shouldn't join us for lunch anymore. It's embarrassing having you eating that with our group." In responding to these challenges, we have found some strategies to be helpful and others problematic. On the helpful side, explaining your deviance from the normative eating practices of the group as a response to a personal problem, rather than a decision that the normative behavior is wrong, can help diffuse others' anger about your choices. For example, I have had many people get upset when I insist on sticking to a vegetarian diet. Explaining that my choice is in response to a terrible family history of heart disease and that I understand that others may have different dietary needs tends to quell the anger. Conversely, relating the data on the consequences of a meat- versus plant-based diet tends to start a long protracted argument. While it can be tempting to extol the virtues of your new healthful habits and point out others' unhealthful habits, this is sure to lead to battles that may make it difficult to maintain your new practices. Admitting that you are different but not attempting to challenge or judge the group can help minimize social punishment.

The special case of drugs of abuse

Drug use and dependence can lead to weight gain and may underlie some people's weight problems or sabotage their attempts to lose weight. Substance use is one of the largest risk factors for eating disorders, including problems with binge eating. People with eating disorders have higher rates of substance use and substance use problems than matched individuals without these disorders (e.g. Krug et al., 2008), and it is likely that the substance use contributes to disordered eating behaviors. Moreover, there is growing evidence that substance use disorders and binge eating problems stem from shared underlying biology (e.g. Davis & Carter, 2009). Substance use problems can lead to weight gain or and may contribute to the maintenance of unhealthful habits. As you work to achieve and maintain a healthful weight, it can be useful to assess your use of alcohol and other illicit drugs, and to get help if you need it.

Alcohol is calorie rich and drinking may simply add to caloric intake. Moreover, it may encourage other reward seeking, and lead you to overeat when you drink. It may also lead to negative mood states that some may manage with food consumption.

Similarly, marijuana is one of the best known appetite stimulants. People (and laboratory animals) really do "get the munchies" after using marijuana. Chronic marijuana use can lead to weight gain and hurt efforts to lose weight. For example, a student of mine told me about a psychiatry client they were seeing who had been treated for nearly a decade for a binge eating disorder and had tried about every diet, medication, and behavioral treatment available, before it was discovered that she used marijuana four times per day. She and her doctor had never considered that her binge-eating problem might be caused by the fact that she was smoking a powerful appetite stimulant multiple times per day. Addressing the drug use helped her gain control of her eating patterns again.

Additionally, while quitting use of cigarettes has huge health benefits, smoking cessation does tend to result in weight gain. Still, those benefits far outweigh (no pun intended) the negative effects on weight. A recent study suggested that smoking cessation increased weight gain by 21 pounds over 5 years, once analyses controlled for differences between people who were successful versus unsuccessful in quitting smoking in clinical trials (Eisenberg & Quinn, 2006). Concerns about weight gain can be a problematic barrier to attempts to quit smoking, and thus a significant amount of research has been conducted to find ways of minimizing weight gain during smoking cessation attempts. Current evidence suggests that individualized interventions, very low calorie diets, cognitive behavioral therapy, and pharmacotherapies including bupropion, nicotine replacement therapy or fluoxetine may reduce weight gain during smoking cessation (Parsons et al., 2009). Proactively addressing the likelihood of weight gain during smoking cessation attempts can have significant benefits for long-term maintenance of a healthy weight.

Challenge #2: Enriching Your Life

Are you an ant or a grasshopper?

Realistically assess your biological drive for immediate gratification from food. Can you have dessert around without eating it? Can you fill your plate with yummy food and leave half of it there? Can you have a bad day and not empty the freezer of ice cream? If you find you are more like Aesop's fabled ant, and cannot help but store up all the food you encounter, a first step is to recognize this tendency and adjust your environment such that you encounter calorie-dense or excessive portions of food less often.

Shaping your environment to fit your biology

Portion control

Studies have confirmed that the more food someone is served the more they will eat (Rolls et al., 2002). For example, when researchers manipulated the amount of pasta served at a restaurant, without changing the price or the food itself, they found that customers ate 25% more calories during their meals, but did not report any difference in the appropriateness of the portion size or notice any difference in the portion size as compared to the amount they normally ate during a meal (Diliberti et al., 2004). This general effect of eating more when portions are larger without consciously being aware of the increased consumption is easy to replicate. With larger portions people of all sort reliably serve and consume between 20-50% more (Wansink & van Ittersum, 2007). Problematically, the concept of a standard portion has grown considerably in the last century. The surface area of the average dinner plate has increased 36% since 1960, and cookbooks have increased serving sizes. For example, entrée portions in the current *Joy of Cooking* are as much as 42% greater than the 1931 edition, and over-sized options at restaurants provide 2.5 times the portions of the standard meal. Knowing this, there are a few simple things you can do to improve your portion control and eat less without noticing:

1. Use smaller plates and dishware. When plates are smaller, people will put less on them. If you serve yourself food on a smaller plate, chances are you will eat less over time. Replacing large dishware with smaller versions can be a helpful weight loss intervention.

2. Do not even consider "all you can eat" options, "supersizing", or buying the "large" because it is cheaper by volume. Only expose yourself to meals or snacks that are appropriately sized. Select restaurants that provide reasonable portion sizes and do not go to ones that offer over-sized portions. As you start, you may need to look at the nutritional information sheets available at most restaurant chains to distinguish between those with reasonable versus excessive portion size. But once you become aware of the problematic restaurants and filter them from your list of possible meal sources, you will find it easier to lose weight.

3. Stock your kitchen only with healthful options in reasonable quantities. The garbage-bag-sized package of corn chips from Costco may be a great deal if you happen to run a taco truck, but it is a terrible thing to have in your personal kitchen. Purchase products in packages that provide appropriately small servings.

Reduce exposure to unhealthful food cues

While it is important to try to prevent yourself from learning false associations between food cues and other pleasures, most of us have already learned many associations that now overvalue and drive us to eat specific foods. Since these associations are difficult to unlearn, it can be extremely helpful to reduce your exposure to these cues and thereby avoid this habit-driven eating. While you will likely benefit from developing plans to steer clear of food cues that cause you the most difficulty, there are a few techniques for avoiding food cues that help most people:

1. Turn off your TV. Reduce your exposure to advertising. Many of the most effective interventions to prevent weight gain or encourage weight loss in children involve reducing television time. As we have described, the prefrontal brain regions take longer to develop. Children, like the "ants" among us, tend to have stronger drive for immediate gratification than the average adult because of their continuing brain development. If you tend to eat when food is offered, exposing yourself to the most persuasive food ads that high-paid advertising experts can devise to lure you to their product is not a good idea. If not watching TV is unthinkable to you, at least consider watching videos, recording shows or viewing online so that commercials are somewhat more controllable.

2. Do not go to the grocery store without a clear plan. Letting yourself impulse shop can leave you with a kitchen full of calorie rich treats. Grocery stores have learned to carefully place and highlight impulse items to encourage you to purchase them in times of weakness. For example, it is no coincidence that the candy is right beside the news and tabloids. With media headlines to arouse or stress you while you are captive in line, you are much more likely to reach for the chocolate bar. If it is available in your area, consider local produce delivery. Having a big box of vegetables show up on your doorstep can help you feel compelled to eat them, and discourage trips to the grocery store. Write yourself a clear and complete shopping list before you go to the store, and search only for those items on the list. Withdraw only as much cash as will cover the items on the list and leave your credit cards at home. Do not let any additional items sneak into your cart.

How can I enrich my life? Increasing healthful opportunities.

Improving social skills and social engagement and adding enrichment activities

Not all weight loss efforts need to be focused on food and exercise. The more that we find approval, relief, and solutions to our stressors from those around us, the less we will turn to food for pleasure and consolation. Making general efforts to increase access to rewarding opportunities in your life should reduce impulsive eating and help you lose weight. Honestly take stock of your social abilities. Are you able to elicit help from others when you need it? When you interact with others, is everyone generally satisfied with the outcome or do some win and others lose? Use the social skills exercises in Chapter 2.2 to find ways of having more positive interactions with people. Then get out and interact! Use your new social skills as you add new hobbies or activities to your life. Join an interest group, an exercise group, a support group, a religious community, or a learning group such as a class or book club. Volunteer on community projects. This can be a great way to both practice positive social skills and benefit from the immediate gratification of doing something that solves a community problem. While these activities may not seem directly related to a weight loss goal, social engagement and support has been shown to be related to recovery from all sorts of addictive behaviors and mood disorders. Being a valued part of a local community may dampen your need for immediate gratification, and allow you to think twice before eating a whole bag of cookies.

Progressive behavioral shaping

When you set a goal for yourself, how often do you fail? If you fail frequently, there is a good chance that your goals themselves may be the problem. They may be too big, too vague, or too difficult to put into action or too far in the future to be achievable. As an extreme example, while working with homeless poly-substance users, I have had multiple clients state that their plan to improve their life is to "get on Oprah" and in doing so immediately become famous and rich. While saying you want to lose 15 pounds may sound a bit more realistic than the "get discovered by Oprah" plan, these goals are similar in that they are very long-term, and require a wide variety of behaviors over a long period of time to achieve. Learning to break down your long-term goals into small doable steps can greatly increase your success and move you forward toward your bigger life goals. To lose weight, you will need to break your end goal into achievable pieces. If you want to make it formal, get a small notebook and a stopwatch. Write yourself a doable goal for the next four-hour period. For example, an initial goal could be to have a small bowl of whole grain oats for breakfast. This is much more immediate and achievable than losing 15 pounds, and is a helpful first step along the way. If you eat the oats, you can note your success, and then come up with a new goal for later in the day. For a second goal, you could ask your scheduled lunch date if she would be willing to walk to the café down the road instead of driving. For your third goal, you could try cooking up the dino kale you made yourself buy at the grocery store, and resolve to eat it even if you think it tastes funny at first. As a last goal for the day, you could plan to reconnect with a good friend that you have not talked to in a while instead of turning on the TV after dinner. If you manage to complete each of these, you will have successfully achieved four goals in one day, each of which involves doing a behavior that fosters a lifestyle where you could reasonably lose 15 pounds and keep it off. If it helps you recognize your success, chart your achievements with gold stars in your notebook. While you may feel a little silly, it may help keep you going and remind you of all the progress you have made toward your long-term goal. If you are not completing your four-hour goals, do not quit or give up hope. Instead, make your immediate goals easier so that you can achieve them. Reaching your long-term goals requires completing lots of little behaviors in the right direction, not a few big ones. Keep trying until you find the little behaviors that work for you.

Plan healthful responses to your inevitable exposure to "opportunities for relief"

For many of us, eating can become an automatic response to unpleasant feelings or distress. For example, you may eat when you are tired, hurt, angry, stressed, or nervous. When you feel bad you create an opportunity for immediate relief, and food is immediately rewarding. Consider the situations where you tend to eat in response to negative feelings. Is there another way to find quick relief that would be more in line with your weight loss goal? For some, practicing other ways of responding to distress can have a huge impact on food consumption. Sit down and pre-plan a healthful way of finding relief and then set yourself up so that alternative is consistently available to you.

As an example, I (J.T.) will start searching for food when I am anxious, tired and overwhelmed, and this can be problematic at work and at home. I find tea at least as soothing as food, and it has no calories. So I keep an electric teapot in my office and another in my home kitchen along with a large and varied stock of tea. I can make myself a cup within three minutes without leaving my desk, and the warm, fragrant liquid makes me feel better when things get a little crazy. Another response that makes me feel better without intaking additional calories is fidgeting. A brief burst of movement can help me shed my anxious energy and feel like I am escaping from my overwhelming situation. At work, this may just consist of running down the hall to check my mail, talk with a colleague, or use the restroom. If I am stuck on a conference call in my office, I might shuffle through the paper on my desk or clean things during the discussion.

Notably, letting myself fidget is not only a helpful diversion to keep me from running to the refrigerator when stressed, it may also encourage weight loss in its own right. One study compared the non-exercise-related movement patterns of lean versus mildly overweight self-described "couch potatoes" and found that the lean group spent a full 152 minutes per day longer upright, while the overweight group sat more consistently (Levine et al., 2005). The differences in holding still accounted for a 350 calorie difference each day! Another study looked at daily energy expenditure in 177 people while they were confined in a small, office-like, chamber. They found huge variation in the amount of energy individuals used, with fidgeting, or spontaneous physical activity, accounting for the majority of the difference (a full 100-800 calories/day!) (Ravussin et al., 1986).

Other ideas for providing quick relief include breathing practices, snuggling with a pet, or a short diversion, like checking e-mail or reading a quote from a humor book. If chewing on something is a hard-wired response to distress, you could make sure you have consistent access to sugar-free gum or celery or another safe option. We are all driven to make ourselves feel better during difficult moments. Making sure you can find relief in something other than cookies can make a big difference for long-term weight loss.

Challenge #3: Stress Resiliency

Chronic stress is a substantial contributor to obesity, making stress resiliency a key skill for preventing obesity and maintaining weight loss. For example, the Whitehall study looked at the impact of stress at work at four time points during a 19-year longitudinal study of nearly 6900 men and 3500 women on subsequent obesity. They found that work stress independently predicted later obesity, with those reporting stress at three time points having 173% the chance of becoming obese as those who reported stress at no time points (Brunner et al., 2007). Learning strategies for preventing stress and relaxing when you start to get tense is important for weight loss as well as mental health. Physical health and emotional health are interlinked in endless ways. Getting formal or informal help when you are having trouble emotionally is an important starting point when you are trying to improve your physical health.

Pacing, scheduling and self-care

Maintaining a regular eating schedule is crucial for keeping caloric intact stable and appropriate. Skipping meals is physically stressful. This stress, combined with true hunger, tends to lead to binge eating and caloric consumption well beyond that skipped in the last meal. Meal skipping can have substantial negative effects on weight gain over time. For example, middle-aged American men who consistently ate breakfast were nearly 25% less likely to gain eleven or more pounds over the next ten years than their breakfast-skipping peers (van der Heijden et al., 2007). Likewise, getting enough rest is crucial for preventing obesity. Short sleep duration has been associated with current and future obesity in both cross-sectional and longitudinal studies (Patel & Hu, 2008). In a population-based study, women who got less than six hours of sleep per night were nearly twice as likely to be obese and over three times as likely to be extremely obese as compared to women who slept between 7 and 8 hours per night (Anic et al., 2010). An important first step toward a healthful weight is to work out a consistent schedule with regular meals and adequate sleep and then stick to it.

Pre-planning and problem-solving

It is important to identify your stress triggers and plan solutions to them in advance of their occurrence so that you can prevent yourself from responding immediately to instant gratification (e.g. eating food) and can instead implement your pre-planned responses (e.g. tea and fidgeting). Make note of situations in which you tend to eat in response to stress, and preplan what you will do instead. If you tend to eat available snacks in high-stress meetings, you might plan on eating something healthful immediately beforehand. If you tend to eat your pushy mother-in-law's high-caloric meals to appease her, you may offer to cook a meal for her to both offer her a rest and provide a healthful alternative.

Relaxation

Exercise may be particularly promising for both reducing stress and increasing stress management and helping to increase metabolism and weight loss. Yoga, Tai Chi and similar wellness-focused exercise programs directly target stress management and may be ideal for those trying to improve stress resiliency and increase activity levels. Take a few classes and see if they work for you. If you have already learned physical activities or sports that helped you manage stress in the past, adding these to your daily or weekly plans can be useful. For example, maybe a run helps you clear your head or thirty minutes of gardening helps you forget the stress of the day. Give yourself time and permission to do these activities.

Challenge #4: Training Good Habits

Identifying and mastering your new behaviors

As we keep mentioning, losing weight requires consistent repetition of a lot of small pro-weight-loss behaviors. Identify these small behaviors. Learn, practice and become confident in your ability to do them and then keep at them until they become old habits. Observe and talk to others who do these behaviors, visualize and role-play, get a mentor or coach, and address your fears or concerns about a behavior by talking to someone with experience or a health professional.

Some habits that may help you lose or maintain weight:

1) Drink water before you start your meal.
2) Chew slowly and fully before swallowing.
3) Eat your vegetables first.

4) Park at the back of the parking lot.
5) Include the stairs in your normal travel routes.
6) Pack healthful snacks and a lunch in the morning.
7) Eat something healthful every 3-4 hours.
8) Rest when you are tired.
9) Ask food-preparers to hold the butter, mayonnaise and cheese or put it on the side.
10) Eat breakfast.
11) Change positions regularly.
12) Go for a walk after meals.
13) Ignore the processed food aisles at the grocery store.
14) Say "no thank you" when others offer you food.
15) Drink water or tea instead of soda or juice.
16) Associate unhealthful food with things you find disgusting or non-appealing (e.g. associate sausage with dog poop).
17) Brush your teeth right after eating to discourage going back for more.

These are just some examples to get you started. Brainstorm ideas that might work for you, and practice until they become automatic!

Reinforcing your new behaviors

Social reinforcement

Having someone to praise or share your successes and help catch you when you are having trouble can be extremely helpful for reinforcing new habits and preventing relapse to old ones. Try recruiting a friend or family member to join you in your attempt to change your habits to lose weight. If that does not work, consider joining a group that shares your goal, such as a Weight Watchers or Overeaters Anonymous group. Time spent with a community of people working on the same problems is extremely valuable for weight loss and maintenance efforts.

Monitoring and feedback

As we mentioned before, people who have had long-term success with weight loss tend to track what they eat and how much they weigh daily. This regular monitoring and feedback can help correct problems quickly and reinforce good behaviors. Weight Watchers, one of the few weight loss programs that has data to back up its effectiveness (Truby et al., 2006), has formalized this monitoring and feedback strategy. But anyone can follow this same strategy through judicious use of (1) measuring cups or a postage scale and (2) the calorie and food content information on food labels or available in calorie tables for standard ingredients available online.

Creating immediate contingencies for health behavior

Finding natural rewards in some behaviors can be difficult, at least at the start. Turning down dessert or opting for water at dinner can be hard to reframe in a positive light when everyone else is indulging. In these cases, it may be helpful to set up plans to reward yourself for your good work. For example, you could keep a log of the costs saved on all the desserts and drinks you did not buy and let yourself spend it on a non-caloric treat at the end of the week or month. The thought of the new clothes, massage, book, artwork, trip to the new science museum, night of babysitting or whatever treat you had in mind may make the dessert or drinks easier to avoid.

Challenge #5: Improving Problem-Solving

Novelty and new experiences

Most people approach dieting by trying to restrict themselves to eating less of their normal diet, or only a subset of the foods that they currently eat. This can leave you feeling deprived, and feeling deprived can lead you to relapse back to your old eating patterns. Choosing instead to adopt a new novel diet including different ingredients, different recipes, and different restaurants than those in your normal diet can be an easier way to improve your nutrition and reduce your calorie intake. Novelty has many benefits. First, novelty increases the brain's valuation of a reward; in this case, reminding your brain that this is good food and you should eat it again if you can, thus increasing your estimation of how good it is. Next, novelty challenges your brain to learn something new and will encourage growth of your cortical and limbic brain circuits. This may improve your general ability to problem-solve and hold back a habit, which will be helpful the next time you are tempted by a treat. Lastly, by eating something new, you avoid the need to stop your old habits before making decisions about what to eat. If I have eaten at McDonald's for years, it will take some mental effort not to order a burger before I remember my weight loss goal and consider a salad. If I try the new restaurant down the street, I will at least have to read the menu and consider my options before I am drawn to order. So consider a weight loss attempt as a foray into new eating habits, rather than a constraint on your current ones, and enjoy some exciting new foods.

Pre-planning for difficult situations

Pack yourself healthful food, or at least plan out what you are going to eat for the day at breakfast, rather than just waiting to see what you come across. If you have a plan for food consumption for the day, you are less likely to skip meals, or make poor choices out of hunger, stress, or temptation in the moment.

Ask or observe respected role models

Interview friends or family who have lost weight to see how they did it. They may be able to link you into local programs or networks that can help, or give you specific tips on how to lose weight given the realities of your local environment. Moreover, the practical tips and modeling of effective behaviors will make it easier for you to learn and adopt new behaviors. The experience of successful people who share your local environment can be extremely helpful.

Researchers have studied people who were successful at losing weight and keeping it off for a long time. While some of the basic findings are not surprising, such as that these people tend to eat relatively low calorie diets and exercise more than normal (McGuire et al., 1998), other findings may be less obvious (Kruger et al., 2006). Compared to unsuccessful dieters, those successful at weight loss and maintenance are less likely to use over-the-counter diet products. They are more likely to prepare their own food, not eat out frequently, plan meals, and report cooking and baking for fun. They are more likely to regularly monitor their behavior and success by tracking calorie and fat consumption, measuring the amount of food they eat and weighing themselves daily. They are more likely to lift weights, and therefore build energy-demanding muscle mass. Being more involved with your food tends to help rather than hinder weight loss attempts. Model your weight loss plans after those that were successful and you will increase your chance of success.

Play!

Perhaps the most important aspect of developing a weight loss or maintenance plan is making it fun! Your new behaviors must become self-reinforcing if you are going to keep them up. Find active things you like to do and do them more. Learn to play with food, cook, experiment and try new things. Indulge yourself in healthful treats on a regular basis. Spend more time with happy people with healthful habits, and do not let yourself be pulled down by others' criticism or excuses for stale, old, unhealthful routines. Give yourself permission to take care of yourself and rest. Regardless of public perceptions, effective people do not deprive themselves of sleep, fun and stress-relief, or they would cease to be effective quickly. Get up, try new things, and engage in life actively and with passion, and behavior change will become easier and even habitual itself. Get out and play!

Exercise: Is your Prefrontal Cortex Pulling its Weight in your Weight Loss Efforts?

Various regions of your prefrontal cortex are necessary for enacting strategies to improve eating or other health behaviors. Practicing these strategies may not only help with weight maintenance, but may also strengthen these areas of the prefrontal cortex and develop new skills with benefits across multiple domains. Moreover, being sure to engage all these regions of your prefrontal cortex in your efforts to improve weight management may make your attempts less sensitive to lapses when one type of strategy fails. Below we provide a checklist of common weight control strategies that engage each key region of the prefrontal cortex. Go through the checklist and mark each strategy or element that is true for you. When you are done, sum up the number of elements that you marked for each brain region. Compare these numbers. Are there regions of the prefrontal cortex that you are using less than others? If so, consider adopting some of the strategies within that domain. When it comes to extra pounds and your prefrontal cortex, you have to use it to lose it.

Dorsolateral Prefrontal Cortex (DLP, Daily Life Planning): Planning and Flexibility To Pursue Goals

__1. I have specific, measurable, long-term health goals.

__2. I am monitoring my weight and other health goals on a regular basis.

__3. I am able to flexibly revise the plans I have to include new healthful choices.

__4. I have developed a schedule to incorporate sufficient physical activity to achieve or maintain a healthy weight.

__5. I have identified physical activities that I can do on a daily basis.

__6. I have a flexible way of switching from one physical activity to another if one form is not available.

__7. I have informed myself of the health risks associated with weight gain.

__8. I have developed a way to track my progress on a regular basis.

__9. I have developed a way to reinstate healthy eating after relapses.

__10. I am able to regulate what I eat on weekends or in social settings.

Total for Dorsolateral Prefrontal Cortex ____________

Anterior Cingulate Gyrus (ACG, Action Control Guide): Motivational Commitment

__1. I am committed to initiating behaviors that lead to long-term goals.

__2. I am committed to maintaining behaviors that lead to long-term goals.

__3. I am able to stay with my program even when it is hard to resist eating.

__4. I stay motivated when I experience a lapse or relapse.

__5. I stay motivated after I have been successful in reaching a goal.

__6. I stay motivated even if I go on an occasional binge.

__7. I have remained motivated to remain on program for at least a year.

__8. I believe it is worth the effort in the future to stick with my plan.

__9. Overall, I remain motivated, in spite of negative moods or apathy.

__10. I am willing to stick with my plan indefinitely.

Total for Anterior Cingulate Gyrus ____________

Ventromedial Prefrontal Cortex (VMP, Valued Momentary Pleasures): Emotion-Driven Eating

__1. I am able to sense if I am making a poor eating choice.

__2. I am usually able to resist nutritionally poor, comfort foods.

__3. I am able to distinguish between being full versus emotionally fulfilled by food.

__4. I listen to my gut level emotions to avoid making bad eating choices.

__5. I am usually able to resist impulse buying when shopping.

__6. I do not tend to overeat when I am sad.

__7. I do not tend to overeat when I am angry.

__8. I do not tend to overeat when I am lonely.

__9. I do not tend to overeat when I am celebrating a success.

__10. I do not tend to overeat when I am tired.

Total for Ventromedial Prefrontal Cortex ____________

Orbitofrontal Cortex (OFC, One's Friends and Confidants): Social Eating

__1. I can taste something really good without having to eat more.

__2. I can sense when not to take even the first bite of something very enticing.

__3. I accept that others can eat things that I cannot.

__4. I am able to identify how eating too much could harm myself and thereby also be a source of distress to others close to me.

__5. I can resist overeating on Thanksgiving and other such occasions.

__6. I have developed an effective way to communicate my eating preferences to those close to me.

__7. I can resist eating unwholesome food served by others.

__8. I have been able to recruit others to help me stick with my program.

__9. I usually make good nutritional choices while eating socially.

__10. I can communicate my needs in a way that leads to meaningful dietary change.

Total for Orbitofrontal Cortex ____________

Appendices

Appendix 1: An Introduction to Basic Brain Circuits Involved in the Five Challenges

Meet the cast: A brief introduction to the neuroanatomical players in the book

In discussing the brain processes involved in changing health behavior, we have mentioned the brain regions involved. Connecting the jobs and functions involved in the processes with a few of the key brain regions that control them can help us decipher neurobiological research studies, and the effects of disorders and treatments that change these brain regions.

In understanding how the brain makes decisions and how to shape them, it is primarily important to understand the functional processes involved in the decisions. Neuroscientists and psychologists have done a lot of work to determine how decisions are made and the processes occur. They have also tried to determine which brain regions are involved in carrying out these processes. The difficulty here is that our brains use very distributed networks to complete most functions. It is rare that there is a single localized brain area responsible for any important function. Circuits are spread out and redundant. Additionally, our brains never waste real estate. Any given region of the brain or cluster of neurons is almost always used for multiple purposes. Brain regions will be involved in multiple processes. Therefore, it is not possible to create a one-to-one map of neural form to function. For the brain regions discussed in this book, trying to explain all of the functions and processes in which they are involved would be a monumental task and a giant tangent from our goal of understanding how to modify health behaviors. Instead, we have broken the basic functions of circuits discussed in this book into key components or roles, and will briefly describe key parts of the brain that contribute to these functions and how they interact with each other.

Role 1: Your Agent – Someone to find and alert you to opportunities to improve your well-being.

Your brain has a highly automated system that scans your environment while considering your skills. Its function is to alert you to opportunities that you could avail yourself of to improve your well-being. The extended *amygdala* and *ventral tegmental area (VTA)* are key brain regions involved in this function. These regions primarily look for opportunities to make your life better in the here and now. This may be an opportunity to get something nice, an opportunity to solve a problem that is bugging you, or an opportunity to escape a threat. These regions evaluate such opportunities based on all the information they can gather from their extensive networks. They give special attention to your prior experiences with the opportunity. For example, if a particular person has been particularly attentive and helpful to you in the past (perhaps they comforted you when you were lost and anxious in a new city, guided you to a nice meal, and then taught you how to navigate the subway system), then a chance to interact with that person again would be identified as a highly valuable opportunity. The extended amygdala and VTA generate reports on how much you stand to gain from taking an opportunity, and send these reports to the nucleus accumbens in the form of dopamine neuron firing. A copy of this report is also sent to the prefrontal cortex to be used for long-term decision-making (Hampton et al., 2007). The prefrontal cortex has some ability to modify the report based on additional information it has about competing goals, special contexts or other more nuanced concerns. The extended amygdala also generates emotional reactions to these opportunities and creates logs or memories of your experience with prior opportunities, but these jobs will be less of a focus of this book.

The extended amygdala and VTA seek opportunities that may be beneficial for you and brings them to your attention. They tend to look in places where they have found opportunities before, and tend to determine the value based on their previous experiences with similar opportunities in the past.

Role 2: Your Short-Term Financial Advisor– Someone to guide you regarding how to spend your effort (e.g. work or money) to help you in the here and now.

Your brain also has a system to help direct your energy, work or resources to maximize immediate benefits to your well-being. This system makes recommendations about how much money or work to spend on trying to obtain each opportunity that your Agent identifies. Your *nucleus accumbens* (located in your ventral striatum) is a key brain region involved in this function. The nucleus accumbens weighs your Agent's estimates of the potential value of an opportunity and considers your need for rapid gain versus long-term stability. The nucleus accumbens gets constant information about opportunities for immediate gratification from your Agent, and uses this information to calculate how much work you should be willing to do to (i.e. how much you would be willing to pay) to take advantage of that opportunity. Should you be making investments now? Is this opportunity really worth putting your work or money into? Do you really need to be working to improve your state right now?

Unfortunately, your nucleus accumbens only considers a very short time horizon (e.g. seconds to hours) in making its recommendation. It is kind of an extreme version of those financial advisors who might try to convince you that buying a house with a variable rate mortgage that you will only reasonably be able to afford for the next two years is a good idea. The immediate benefits are considered strongly, but a separate system considers the long-term consequences. Your nucleus accumbens will help you consider your need for housing and the immediate costs and benefits of taking out that mortgage (e.g. the how nice the house is, the cost this month). Other systems, such as circuits involving the prefrontal cortex, consider the longer-term impact of the decision and these have veto power over this circuit centered on the nucleus accumbens.

Your Short-Term Financial Advisor listens to: 1) the extended amygdala to find out about opportunities (Role 1), 2) the medial prefrontal cortex to find out about our overall financial outlook: Can I keep the opportunities coming? Do I feel in control of my environment? Do I have the ability to find resources when I need them? (Role 7), 3) the prefrontal cortex to make sure that there are not any rules against going after that immediate reward (Role 6), and 4) the dorsal raphe nucleus to find out about our current needs: Are all our body parts well fed and happy? Are we being threatened by outside invaders? Are there any environmental crises? (Role 4). It then talks to circuits that know how to carry out the work (see Role 3) and tells them how much and what to do.

Role 3: Your Well-Trained Laborer or Professional Athlete – Someone to carry out the complex, highly trained work or behaviors necessary to obtain the identified benefits.

Your brain has highly developed systems to guide your brain and body through the complex movements and reactions needed to successfully perform work toward a goal. The *striatum*, *caudate* and *basal ganglia* are key brain regions involved in this function. This system learns motor patterns following intensive practice. It can carry out complex behaviors without requiring focused attention. Like a professional athlete, it can do very difficult behaviors because it has practiced them extensively. However, it is not highly involved in making choices about when to do these behaviors. It needs a coach to tell it what behavior to do and how much energy to put into the behavior at any given time. In these situations, the nucleus accumbens provides the coaching advice. The nucleus accumbens may tell it to "do play C this time", "go hard on this one", "or use that new move that we practiced", and these brain regions will do their best to carry out these instructions.

Role 4: Your Watchdog or Sensational Journalist – Someone to alert you to the threats around and within you and sound warnings.

Having an alarm system to alert you about danger is crucial for survival. Thus, the brain system that provide this function evolved early and have been conserved. Your brain has a highly developed alarm system that warns you about threats and triggers emergency responses. The *dorsal raphe nucleus*, located deep in the brain, is the key region of this system.

The dorsal raphe nucleus gets constant information about possible threats of all sorts and transmits warnings all over the brain. It pays attention to potential problems with our internal state as well as potential threats from our environment or others. It then publicizes information about any detected threats by sending an alert to systems all over the brain. For example, it checks whether our cells are healthy. If not, it might issue headlines such as "Muscle Cells Hungry in the Arm" or "Freezing Temperatures in the Fingers". It checks whether we are being threatened by outside invaders. If so, it might issue headlines such as "Mosquito Stings Mid-back, Immune Fighters Initiate Swelling", "Boss Gives Us the Evil Eye After Comment in Meeting" or "Bad Bacteria Invade Stomach Riding on Chicken Sandwich". It checks whether we are endangered by environmental crises. If so, it might issue headlines such as "Extremely High Levels of Caffeine Found in Water Supply" or "Loud Noises Disrupt Sleep". It sends out alerts about any and all potentially dangerous situations that it observes and encourages the rest of the brain to initiate stress responses to deal with the threat immediately. It plays the important role of alerting us to possible dangers, although sometimes its suggestions may be alarmist and extreme.

This watchdog sends information to your agent (Role 1) and your short-term financial advisor (Role 2) suggesting that they amplify estimates of the benefits of and put more work or resources into opportunities for escape or immediate gratification. Thus, your watchdog encourages your brain to focus on the short-term when it thinks you are threatened or stressed. The watchdog also sends information to the executive system (Roles 5-7) to assess the threat and plan a response, helping focus attention on the threat so that the brain can use its problem-solving skills to ensure your safety and well-being.

Role 5: Your Management Executives – Someone to set priorities and determine where to focus effort.

At any given time, your brain is receiving information about many possibilities and concerns in your internal and external environment that you may want to pursue. Obviously, the brain cannot address them all at once. For example, you cannot behave to address a need for sleep, an opportunity for a meal, an upset child, and a chance to improve your housing all at the same time. Your brain needs management executives to set priorities and focus effort to efficiently and effectively address your needs and avail yourself of opportunities. This relatively complicated function is performed by highly integrated cortical circuits.

The *dorsolateral prefrontal cortex* and the *anterior cingulate cortex* appear to work together to help determine where to focus effort. They monitor goals, punishments, failures and rewards and decide which tasks to prioritize at any given moment. They may inhibit tasks given low priority and enhance attention and effort on tasks given high priority. We include them together because it is not clear exactly what each area is doing (Mansouri et al., 2009); they seem to act as partners on many tasks. Together, they manage the many tasks being conducted by the brain at any time, making sure that everything gets done safely, efficiently and in a timely manner.

Role 6: Your Strategist – Someone to let you know when it is time to change strategy and forge a new course.

Most of the time, the best response to a problem is to do what worked well in the past. Thus, our brains have a tendency to recycle responses when we encounter similar situations. This leads to the general behavioral truism that "past behavior is the best predictor of future behavior". However, sometime situations change and it is necessary to alter strategies and devise new responses to optimize our behavior and maximize the benefits we obtain. Our brains have thus developed a strategist to identify when new responses are needed and shake us out of our behavioral ruts.

Your *orbitofrontal cortex* tells you when it is time to make a change. It lets you know when you need to try something different than your stale old routine. The orbitofrontal cortex tells the rest of the brain things like "I know that worked the other time, but conditions have changed" or "Last time we tried that it failed miserably. We need to try a new strategy." Its job is to help us notice when the outcomes of our behavior are not positive in our current situation, even when that same behavior may have benefited us in another situation. It notices when contingencies change and makes sure that we change our behavior in response.

Role 7: Your Executive Press Secretary – Someone to quell panic and restore calm when potentially concerning situations are under control.

While it is important to have a highly sensitive alarm system or vigilant watchdog, it is equally important to have a smart, rational, calm overseer to assess whether identified threats really pose an immediate danger before initiating emergency responses. Clearly, it would be wasteful and potentially harmful to call in the National Guard every time the watchdog barks. Thus, our brain needs a clear focus to assess the situation and distinguish between threats on which we already have a handle and threats that are immediate, potentially harmful, and without an existing solution. Our brain needs an Executive Press Secretary to filter through the headlines, guide decisions about how to respond, and issue statements to calm the rest of the brain when emergency responses are not necessary.

A portion of the *ventromedial prefrontal cortex* is key for performing this function. The vetromedial prefrontal cortex keeps a close eye on identified potential threats, assesses the actual threat based on our past experience, and issues announcements when the situation is under control. It lets the rest of our brain know when we do not need to worry about potential threats because we know from experience that we can handle them. The ventromedial prefrontal cortex calms the rest of the brain when threats are discovered, stopping the brain from panicking and triggering all sorts of protective defense systems (i.e. our stress response). Like most defense systems, our stress response system conducts immediate actions that may rapidly resolve the threat, but are highly costly and often cause additional long-term problems. The ventromedial prefrontal cortex pays attention to the sensational media warnings, checks with advisors when necessary, and issues statements instructing the rest of the brain to "stand-down" and avoid over-responding to the threat. In other words, the ventromedial prefrontal cortex tells us when "the situation is under control".

Limbic versus executive roles

Roles 1-3 are primary functions of the brain's limbic reward circuit. Here, basically, your agent identifies opportunities and estimates the benefits of each. He sends that information to your short-term financial advisor and to your executive system so that they can determine how much and what sort of effort one should expend towards each opportunity. Your short-term financial advisor manages your well-trained laborer who performs the behaviors as planned. Role 4 is a component of the automatic maintenance systems that are housed in the midbrain and brainstem, the lower part of your brain that connects with the spinal cord. Your watchdog sounds the alarm to both your limbic reward circuit and your executive system when possible threats are detected. Roles 5-7 are components of the executive system led by parts of the prefrontal, frontal and limbic cortices. Here, your management executive prioritizes attention and behavior using information from your agent, as well as about your long-term goals, longer-term consequences and detailed context. Your strategist monitors outcomes of your choices and changes course when things are working. Your executive press secretary assesses and puts out potential fires, to help avoid unnecessary panic and maintain the calm necessary for optimal management and strategic decisions.

In understanding some of the characteristics and limitations of our neural actors, it can be useful to consider our limbic reward circuit versus our executive functions as a whole.

Characteristics of the limbic reward circuit

Your limbic reward circuit is involved in a number of important functions including the formation of new habits. In addition, it plays a crucial role in forming associations between cues and rewarding events. We believe that the limbic reward circuit plays a key role not only in addictions to cocaine and amphetamines, opiates, nicotine, marijuana and alcohol, but also addictive-like properties associated with eating disorders. Further, we believe that healthy addictions, including stimulating physical activity (e.g. moderately intense exercise), mental activity (e.g. listening to music) and social activity (e.g. getting approval or affection from a friend), as well as combinations of these (e.g. sexuality), also engage the limbic reward circuit.

Your limbic reward circuit is a series of brain structures that work together to help guide you through your day-to-day world. Its main job is to automatically select well-learned behaviors to optimize short-term improvements in your overall condition. It chooses between your habits to find the one most likely to make your life better in the next few minutes. To illustrate, your limbic reward circuit may currently be weighing the options of continuing to read, taking a nap, taking a bathroom break, preparing yourself a snack, or checking your phone for messages.

The reward system monitors our internal and external environment for opportunities to improve our well-being and ward off threats. It directs our well-trained behaviors to respond to these opportunities to provide immediate reward or relief without distracting ourselves from our other goals or focuses. For example, this is the system that helps us successfully eat a whole box of popcorn without missing a bit of the movie we are watching. We do not need to consciously attend to the popcorn, contemplate whether to eat each piece, or think about putting the popcorn in our mouth and chewing. Our reward system can notice the popcorn and decide to trigger eating behaviors depending on our need to relieve hunger or enjoy a salty treat, while we focus on the action in the movie.

Your limbic reward circuit is highly efficient and does not require conscious effort to make its decisions. In some ways, it might be considered your behavioral autopilot system. For example, it can direct you to eat a whole bag of chips while you watch TV, smoke a cigarette while you talk with a friend, comfort your child while you cook dinner, drive to work while you plan your day, or jog while you enjoy music. It plays back standard behavioral habits that have worked well in situations you have experienced before. For example, if pouting got you sympathy and care when you felt tired previously, your limbic reward circuit will encourage you to pout the next time you are tired. Furthermore, your limbic reward circuit will guide your behavioral choices unless it is overridden by the conscious control of your executive system.

Your limbic reward circuit's choices are limited to things that you have already learned and mastered. It cannot generate new behaviors or help make different choices than the ones you previously learned in similar situations. Your limbic reward circuit is also shortsighted. It cannot consider the long-term consequences of its choices, but rather picks what will work best to alleviate or improve your current immediate situation. However, this does not imply that the limbic reward circuit's decisions are haphazard, simple or rash. They are very carefully chosen based upon a broad consideration of known elements in your current environment, your lifelong experience in your world, and the behaviors you know how to do. This circuit receives a complicated mix of information collected from all over the brain. It uses this diverse information to guide its decisions. It also uses an elegant learning process both to learn when different behaviors are beneficial and also to constantly update your knowledge of opportunities in your world.

Your limbic reward circuit uses a consistent and relatively simple logic to make decisions about whether to carry out habits to gain relief from an unpleasant situation or gain benefit from an opportunity. When rewards or relief are achieved, the system will favor repeating that behavior again in the future. However, it does not involve multi-step planning or consideration of the effects downstream. The limbic reward circuit relies on the executive system both to plan for the future and to veto its plans when they may have undesirable longer-term consequences.

Characteristics of the executive system

The executive system is composed of prefrontal and frontal cortical circuits. The prefrontal cortex is a collection of brain structures found on the surface of the brain just behind your forehead as well as deep cortical structures that are in the prefrontal region. This part of the brain is evolutionarily new; humans have an abnormally large prefrontal cortex compared to most other animals. We are consciously aware of mental processing that occurs in our prefrontal cortex, and we are generally able to describe the logic used during prefrontal-cortex-driven decisions. The prefrontal cortex includes a number of more specific subregions, such as the orbitofrontal cortex (OFC), the dorsolateral prefrontal cortex (dlPFC), the anterior cingulate cortex (ACC), and the ventromedial prefrontal cortex (vmPFC). The functions of these subregions are key to the processes described in this book.

The prefrontal cortex considers our values, beliefs, long-term goals, unique situational factors, expectations, social context and other more complex concepts in making decisions about how to behave. It can both turn on or hold back our habitual behaviors, as well as choose to try a new behavior that has not yet been mastered. While the prefrontal cortex does not always make choices that are good for us in the long-term, it at least has the ability to consider long-term effects in its decision-making process. Moreover, we are generally conscious of the decisions our prefrontal cortex is making. This awareness can be helpful when we are trying to find ways to change our behavior patterns.

The balance and interplay between the influence of our limbic reward circuit and our executive prefrontal cortex will help determine whether our choices tend to be impulsive versus deliberate. Our training and experience will determine whether the habits driven by our reward system are healthful or not. Our beliefs, goals and social networks will determine whether our prefrontal cortex biases us toward healthful or unhealthful behaviors, and immediate rewards versus long-term goals. Training new habits and changing our beliefs, goals and social networks can help us alter our health behaviors.

The prefrontal cortex works to prioritize goals and focus our attention and effort on our current priorities. It assesses the success of our decisions and develops and redirects strategy when things are not going well. The prefrontal cortex oversees and overrides our behavioral autopilot when necessary. It watches other people interact with the world and learns from their experiences, even when these experiences are relayed second-hand. The prefrontal cortex uses sophisticated logic and complicated analysis of data collected from a wide variety of sources to make decisions. This helps the prefrontal cortex make balanced decisions in complicated circumstances, but also makes the prefrontal cortex relatively slow. All that analysis takes a long time. While the prefrontal cortex can make executive decisions even when life gets confusing it cannot do so quickly, leaving your behavior under the control of your autopilot in the meantime. If your autopilot is badly programmed, these lags can be a problem.

How our brain actors work together to make health-related decisions

In our model, decisions about how to behave are controlled by two main brain circuits, the limbic reward system and the executive system. The limbic reward system can make decisions quickly, efficiently, and without conscious effort; however, it can only consider the short-term effects of choices. The executive system can make decisions after considering many options and the short- and long-term consequences of the behavior; however, since this process is more flexible and complex, it generally takes longer to make a decision. Both systems are crucially important for guiding health behaviors.

Effects of psychiatric disorders and treatments on these key brain structures

Some clinicians find it easier to understand and remember brain anatomy and circuits in terms of the effects they have when they dysfunction. Thus, now that we have explained how these brain structures and processes interact during normal function, we provide a description of these key brain regions as they have been found to contribute to psychiatric or behavioral disorders and their treatment. As we noted before, almost all brain regions are involved in multiple functions so there is a caveat to this section: the problems resulting from damage of these key brain regions are substantially greater than loss of the key functions we focus on in our model and this book.

<u>Limbic and motor systems</u>

Striatum: The striatum includes several large structures located behind the frontal lobes and deep to the cortex. Clients with damage to the striatum (e.g. Huntington's disease) exhibit many different forms of frontal-lobe pathologies, or symptoms seen in patients with damage to the frontal lobe, in part because the connections between striatum and the frontal lobe have been impaired. Further, these clients exhibit automatic, habitual movements known as chorea. The chorea may be suppressed for a while by intentional effort, but without ongoing suppression by the striatum circuits, these habitual movements will return. Damage to the striatum releases all sorts of trained-in habitual movement patterns. Generally, because all of these behaviors are released simultaneously, this appears as undirected movements rather than specific habit behaviors.

Basal ganglia: Once habits are trained and stored in the basal ganglia, these habits can be performed without conscious awareness or the need for conscious memory centers. If we have undamaged basal ganglia, we will not forget how to ride a bicycle or to brush our teeth even if we lose conscious memories. Clients with damage to the hippocampus or other parts of the brain that form conscious new memories, develop severe deficits of short-term memory. They are not able to consciously remember things that they have learned or experienced. But they can still learn procedures and acquire habits as long as the basal ganglia are intact. But habit learning by the basal ganglia requires programming, specifically through practice of the behavior in conjunction with activation of the reward system.

Clinical improvement in clients with obsessive-compulsive disorder has been associated with a reduction of activity in parts of the basal ganglia. Specifically, clients with obsessive-compulsive disorder treated with either cognitive behavioral therapy or selective serotonin reuptake inhibitors (SSRIs) showed a significant decrease in activity in the right caudate (Linden, 2006; Benazon, et al., 2003). The basal ganglia, in particular the caudate, receive outputs from the three regions of the frontal lobes described below. These key frontal lobe centers may be able to modify activity in the basal ganglia and thus influence habits through these connections.

Amygdala: The amygdala comprises two almond-shaped structures located deep in the brain, each on one side of the head. People with damage to their amygdala lose the ability to assess the importance or salience of emotional cues. Several clients with selective bilateral damage to the amygdala have been studied and their behavior described (Adolphs et al., 2007). For example, SM was found to have a normal range of emotion, but was extremely dispassionate, particularly when describing traumatic experiences, and lacked a normal sense of distrust or danger (Tranel et al., 2006). She could not really tell when music was scary, sad, or calming, even though she was able to perceive the music and identify when music was happy (Gosselin et al., 2007). Clients with amygdala damage did not display an aversion to loss in gambling tasks (De Martino et al., 2010). They are generally able to recognize and respond to emotion cues, but these cues do not induce the same fear, anxiety, caution, and avoidance as individuals with intact amygdala.

Clinical improvements in clients with anxiety and mood disorders have been associated with changes in activity in the amygdala. In studies for PTSD, phobias and major depression, individuals that responded to cognitive behavioral therapy showed a reduction of activity in the amygdala (Bryant, et al., 2008; Schienle et al., 2007; Siegle et al., 2006).

Executive systems

Orbitofrontal cortex: This region is located behind the top of the bony orbits of your eye sockets. Damage to this region impairs social intelligence and reward assessment. People with damage to this region exhibit disinhibition; in other words, they demonstrate a lack of social judgment, tactlessness, limited insight, and other aspects of impoverished social intelligence. People with this damage also neglect personal care (Cummings & Mega, 2003).

What underlies the impairment of social intelligence? One possibility is that since the orbitofrontal cortex is necessary to change strategy in new situations, people with damage to this region cannot help but carry out their standard responses even in situations where such behavior is inappropriate.

The orbitofrontal cortex is in an active conversation with reward centers of the brain. Whereas the reward centers quickly compute the short-term benefits of an action, biased toward immediate gratification, the orbitofrontal cortex is able to delay habitual responses and collaborate with other executive system regions to come up with a more nuanced response. Again, it can block a trained habit to try a new behavior. Clients with obsessive-compulsive disorder (OCD) get stuck repeating certain behaviors. When these clients are treated with cognitive behavioral therapy, they have a better response to therapy when there is increased activity in the left orbitofrontal cortex (Porto et al, 2009). Similarly, in clients phobically afraid of spiders, those who gained long-term benefits from cognitive behavioral therapy (i.e. reversing their habitual emotional response to spider cues) also showed greater activation of the orbitofrontal cortex (Schienle et al., 2009).

Dorsolateral frontal cortex: This region is located in the area of the frontal lobes behind the forehead and above the orbital area. Damage to this region impairs executive functions, leading to difficulty coming up with a new action plan in response to changing events, difficulty in making plans, poor abstraction, and impaired ability to generate strategies for problem-solving.

From these findings, it can be inferred that this part of the brain helps a person make health-related decisions about what behaviors to change and how to change them, after receiving input from the orbitofrontal cortex suggesting that a new strategy is needed. The ability to identify and respond to problems (e.g. following an obstacle to or cessation of a healthy behavior) requires effective use of the dorsolateral frontal cortex. Doing the same maladaptive behavior over and over again is an example of perseveration. Being creative, flexible and developing a backup plan requires a healthful dorsolateral frontal cortex. These actions can help maintain and reinstate behaviors following relapse.

Modification of activity in the dorsolateral prefrontal cortex has been associated with treatment-related improvement in a number of mental health disorders. These changes have been seen in the dorsolateral prefrontal cortex of clients who received antidepressant therapy (Fales et al., 2009). Although cognitive behavioral therapy is not consistently effective in treating clients with schizophrenia, improvement in these clients was associated with greater activity in the dorsolateral prefrontal cortex (Kumari et al., 2009). In major depression, there are indications that people who respond to cognitive behavioral therapy have activation of the dorsolateral frontal cortex as well as selected structures in the limbic system, such as the hippocampus (Seminowicz et al., 2004). However, it is not easy to map which regions of the frontal cortex are most likely to be responsible for the benefits of cognitive behavioral therapy, since other structures are involved including the orbitofrontal cortex and anterior cingulate gyrus (Kennedy et al., 2007).

Anterior cingulate gyrus: This region is located close to the middle of the frontal lobe of each hemisphere. People with damage to this area exhibit impaired motivation including reduced interest, poor initiation of behaviors, reduced activity and reduced concern. People with damage to this region have difficulty prioritizing an action to motivate its completion. In the extreme case, a client with damage to each side of the anterior cingulate gyrus may develop a condition known as akinetic mutism, in which the person will speak only when spoken to and will not get up out of bed, even to go to the bathroom. They show no initiative whatsoever. The opposite occurs in people with intractable obsessive-compulsive disorder (OCD), for whom there is excessive motivation to repeat a specific set of events. Interestingly, one rather drastic treatment for OCD is the surgical destruction of part of the anterior cingulate gyrus.

People with mood disorders often have difficulty motivating or prioritizing behaviors. People with major depression who had the lowest activity in their anterior cingulate gyrus showed the greatest clinical improvement following cognitive behavioral therapy (Siegle et al., 2006). Also, lower activity in the anterior cingulate gyrus in response to fear cues predicted better clinical response to cognitive behavioral therapy for posttraumatic stress disorder (PTSD) (Bryant et al., 2008). Presumably, people with PTSD who had decreased response to fearful stimuli were better able to dampen anxious responses with the help of treatment.

Appendix 2: How the Brain Changes Itself: A Brief Introduction to Neuroplasticity

In order to understand how your brain learns and changes it is helpful to understand some basics about how the brain communicates and how it changes with experience. We briefly describe how neurons talk to one another and create useful connections to get things done.

Languages of the brain

Brain regions talk to one another using chemical signals transmitted by the neurons. These chemical signals have two main functions: 1) neurotransmitters send information through existing circuits to deliver information and produce responses, and 2) neuromodulators change existing circuits. Our overly efficient brains often use the same chemicals as both neurotransmitters and neuromodulators, which can make it difficult to explain brain function in simple terms. However, as a rule, the brain uses relatively simple or easy-to-produce chemicals primarily as neurotransmitters, and relatively complex or more difficult-to-produce chemicals primarily as neuromodulators. For convenience, we will classify these chemicals with regards to these primary roles.

Neurotransmitters

Some of these chemical signals are simple commands where one neuron tells another how to respond immediately. Examples of neurotransmitters are glutamate and GABA. These chemicals are simple amino acids, which are basic in structure and easy to supply. Neurotransmitters primarily send information through existing circuits, which allows them to rapidly drive responses.

Neuromodulators

Other chemical signals change the relationship between neurons or brain regions, or change the personality of the neurons involved. These are called neuromodulators. They might make neurons more or less receptive or more or less reactive to another neuron or set of neurons. Examples of neuromodulators are dopamine, serotonin and peptides (i.e. strings of amino acids such as enkephalin or oxytocin).

Most neurons contain multiple neurotransmitters and neuromodulators and they may release them together or separately. Often a neuron will release only neurotransmitters when it is transmitting a weak or low frequency signal, but then release both neurotransmitters and neuromodulators when transmitting a stronger or higher frequency signal. This allows the neurons to pass on messages using existing networks when standard information is being passed along (e.g. using neurotransmitters only) and modify the networks themselves when new information or associations are identified within ourselves or our environment. For example, because you already know how to read, your brain will primarily use neurotransmitters and existing networks to identify and decode the words on this page. When you encounter a new word of which you do not know the meaning, your brain will need to alter its connections to encode the word within its networks. In order to learn this new term, your neurons will release both neurotransmitters and neuromodulators; the neuromodulators will change how your neurons talk to one another so that the next time you see this word you will remember what it means.

Excitability and plasticity

Excitability describes how easy it is to get a neuron to pass on a signal. If a neuron fires and sends a neurotransmitter message to a connected neuron, how likely is it that the second neuron will fire and send a neurotransmitter message to its connections? In a way, excitability can be thought of as a measure of the extent to which a neuron gossips. If it is told something, does it pass the message along? How reliably? Increasing excitability of a neuron means that information is more likely to get passed on through a circuit, the same way you know telling something to your most gossiping neighbor ensures that everyone in your neighborhood will soon know the news. Increasing excitability of neurons makes it more likely that whatever thought, behavior, or calculation that those neurons are trying to trigger will occur. The greater the excitability, the more consistent the desired outcome.

Increasing the excitability of a neuron refers to making the neuron more likely to continue to pass on a signal. Decreasing the excitability of a neuron refers to making the neuron less likely to respond to a signal. Neuromodulators help us shape circuits to better filter information and change what we respond to over time. Plasticity refers to your ability to change the excitability of your neurons. A brain that can modify the excitability of neurons quickly and efficiently in response to change is considered very plastic. A very plastic brain learns quickly.

Getting your brain to work optimally requires training your neuronal networks so that important messages are successfully delivered and unimportant ones are dropped. For example, we hope that when someone finds a fire in a building that message is successfully passed on to everyone else in the building, the fire department and the police. However, when someone sends an e-mail scam, we hope that the message is deleted and not passed to others. In the brain, learning involves building up neuron excitability so that messages that have some importance to you are delivered to all relevant parts of the brain and body while those that are not important are ignored. We must learn which pieces of the information available to us deserve our attention and only send these along through our networks.

Enhancing connections: Changing the efficiency of neuronal communication

Neurons do not directly touch each other but connect to each other at the gaps between them called synapses. These synapses are specialized structures where two neurons communicate. The first neuron has an axon terminal from which neurotransmitters and neuromodulators are released and the second neuron has a post-synaptic density (i.e. a special cell structure to which signaling machinery can be attached) that holds receptors and signaling systems to respond to the transmitted signals. You can think of this being analogous to the mouth of one person and the ear of another. The axon terminal, like the mouth, transmits a signal to be detected by another neuron, and the post-synaptic density, like the ear, collects the signal and processes it to be interpreted by the second neuron. Most neurons, like our heads, have both "mouths" and "ears" and can both send and receive messages. However, a single neuron typically has thousands of "mouths" and communicates to thousands of "ears" located on neighboring neurons, with multiple languages (neurotransmitters and neuromodulators) and volume (excitability) that are modified on an ongoing basis.

The efficiency or strength of a connection refers to how well or how reliably the synapse can send signals from one neuron to another. To continue our analogy, a strong connection would be one where the second neuron consistently "hears" the message being sent correctly. A weak connection would be one where the second neuron does not notice things that the first neuron "said" or "hears" them incompletely. A connection can be strengthened either by making the first neuron "louder", or improving the second neuron's ability to "listen". Neurons have many strategies for improving connections. For example, the first neuron can release more neurotransmitters (i.e. yell louder), it can reshape itself to send a more focused signal (i.e. use a megaphone), or reposition itself to better reach the post-synaptic density (i.e. turn toward its target). The second neuron can make more receptors (i.e. amplify the sound, as with a microphone) or move the receptors around to better collect the message (i.e. turn toward the speaker). Neurons strengthen their connections when connections are used frequently, thereby developing networks of neurons that communicate efficiently to complete a function.

Appendix 3: A Conceptualization of Three Loops that Modify Habits

We are what we repeatedly do.
Excellence, then, is not an act, but a habit.

Aristotle

Introduction

During much of our waking lives, we act in accord with our habits. They shape our behavior, health, interactions, hopes and fears. They are manifested as skilled movements, mannerisms, cravings, customs, rituals, habitual speech patterns, automatic thoughts, obsessions and compulsions (Grabiel, 2008). As we have proposed in this book, a basic understanding of the underlying neurobiology is useful to help inform and inspire health-related behavior change. However, this Appendix is for those who seek a deeper, more nuanced understanding of the ways in which the prefrontal cortex can instigate or modify the habits of the basal ganglia. Although some material may recapitulate information presented elsewhere in the book, I (W.G.) hope this section will provide a greater understanding of the cortico-subcortical loops involved in the formation and retrieval of habits.

The prefrontal cortex, constituting a third of cerebral cortex, is critically involved in the formation of new habits. Most of the activity within the prefrontal cortex is implicit, that is, removed from our consciousness. For example, when you meet someone for the first time, your prefrontal cortex rapidly and almost automatically makes cognitive and moral judgments such as likeability, and social and sexual attraction or repulsion (Forbes & Graffman, 2010). By contrast, explicit, conscious activity of the prefrontal cortex is more limited and includes our ability to redirect our focus and to plan; in essence, to invent our future.

The formation of new habits and the transformation of old habits rely in large part on three key areas of the prefrontal cortex and their connections to the basal ganglia. The three prefrontal regions I will discuss are in constant communication so it is difficult to say that any habit relies on only one of the regions.

The three prefrontal areas each have loops as described below, which are illustrated in the Figure on the next page.
1. *The lower loop:* The orbitofrontal cortex, situated behind the bony orbits of the eye sockets, is critically involved in reward-based behavior.
2. *The middle loop:* The anterior cingulate gyrus, located near the middle of the frontal region, is critically involved in enabling us to focus attention, as well as in obsessions and compulsions.
3. *The upper loop:* The dorsolateral prefrontal cortex, located on the sides of the frontal region, engages in executive planning, organizing and creating.

FIGURE: Three loops involved in modifying habits

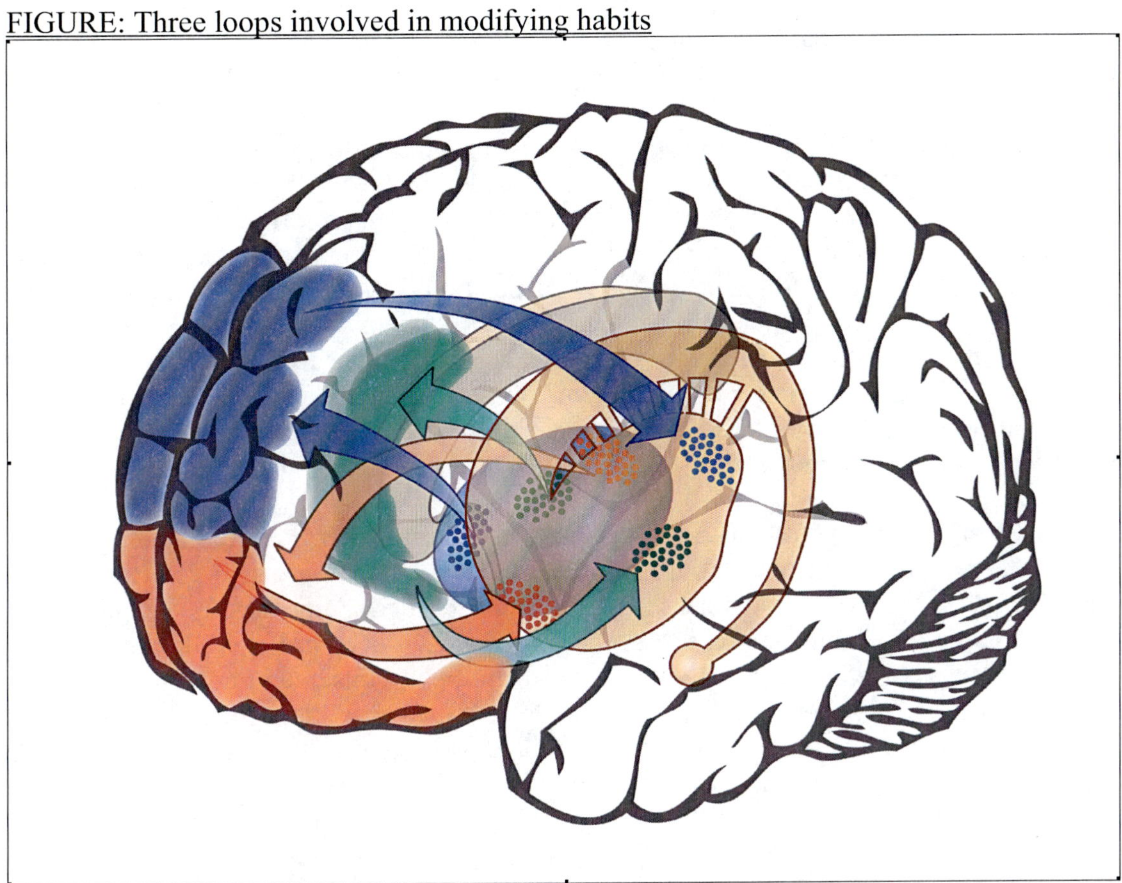

Legend: The lower loop (orange) includes a medial view of part of the orbitofrontal cortex, its projection on the caudate nucleus, and its return from the thalamus back to the prefrontal cortex.

The middle loop (green) depicts part of the anterior cingulate, deep to the surface of the brain, including a region that curves below the corpus callosum (in gray), known as the subcallosal cingulate.

The upper loop (blue) shows the upper part of the dorsolateral frontal cortex, its projection onto the head of the caudate nucleus, and its return by means of the thalamus to the dorsolateral prefrontal cortex.

Each of these three loops is involved in the organization of complex and specialized forms of information processing and especially the formation of habits based on rewards (lower loop), redirection of attention (middle loop) and executive functions (upper loop).

These prefrontal regions send one-way messages to different areas of the basal ganglia, including a fetal-looking structure with an oversized head and a long tail, the caudate nucleus. What is the purpose of the connections between the prefrontal cortex and the basal ganglia? The answer might lie in the finding that the caudate and adjacent structures of the basal ganglia are instrumental in storing and retrieving learned behavioral, emotional and cognitive habits. Further, these habits are likely to be critically involved in what is described as higher cognitive processes.

The loops connecting the prefrontal regions with the basal ganglia and then back to the same prefrontal regions, provide important clues to understanding how the prefrontal regions program new habits within the basal ganglia and how maladaptive habits can be restrained or retrained. The study of these loops has assumed an increasingly important role in characterizing neuropsychiatric disorders, their anatomy and successful treatments as described in the *Annual Review of Medicine* (Taber et al., 2010).

The functions controlled by these loops require that the entire system is intact. Thus, cortical or subcortical damage to the structures within the loops will produce similar functional impairments. In other words, disorders of the prefrontal cortex produce symptoms similar to those resulting from damage to the subcortical structures to which they connect. This explains why so many of the functions commonly attributed to the prefrontal cortex can be impaired by damage to the loops that connect to the striatum and thalamus and why patterns of abnormal cortical and subcortical metabolism coexist for the same disorders. For example, patients with Huntington's disease initially have degeneration of the head of the caudate nucleus and exhibit massive deficits similar to those that occur with large prefrontal lesions.

Advances in the brain and behavioral sciences have led to a critical distinction between memories that arise from conscious, autobiographic recollection and memories that are habit-based. Conscious memories have been termed "episodic", "explicit" or "autobiographic." Habit memories have been termed "procedural". Following damage to the regions of the brain necessary to form new conscious memories (i.e. the hippocampus and adjacent medial temporal lobe structures) the patient can still learn procedures, such as repeated patterns of skilled movements, yet will not remember learning them. They can also learn key activities of daily living. Procedural memory may also enable people to find their way from one place to another, although the hippocampus normally helps with this task by creating a mental map. The sparing of habit memories enables people with Alzheimer's disease with profound impairment of short-term memory to practice well-rehearsed rituals; for example, in the context of religious traditions, and to sing familiar songs (Vance et al., 2008).

I now describe features of the three loops, their anatomy, functional characteristics and how they are involved in the formation of healthful and pathological habits.

1. LOWER LOOP

The lower loop, embodying the orbitofrontal cortex, is critically involved in habits relating to reward-seeking and social restraint. The orbitofrontal cortex is situated behind the eye sockets, forming the floor of the prefrontal cortex and extending upward in the middle of the anterior frontal region. It has inputs from other areas of the prefrontal cortex, regions of the temporal lobe that are involved in the formation of emotional memories (e.g. the amygdala), and sensory areas, including those involved in smell and taste. The orbitofrontal cortex has a major output to the lower middle part of the head of the caudate nucleus and, via the globus pallidus, to the thalamus, where it projects back to the orbitofrontal cortex, thereby forming a loop.

Works devoted to the understanding of the orbitofrontal cortex (see Zald & Rauch, 2006), describe a highly complex system whose functional regions are still being revealed. Remarkably, a patient who suffers the loss of the orbitofrontal cortex may not show impairment on a standardized test of intelligence, yet will exhibit markedly abnormal social conduct and social awareness.

In addition, the lower loop is vitally important for regulating reward-based behaviors, ranging from those affecting appetite and cravings for food, caffeine, nicotine, alcohol, and illegal substances. As discussed previously, reward expectancies and their associated cues to these behaviors are strongly influenced by dopamine. Dopamine projections include the brainstem's ventral tegmental area, the nucleus accumbens and adjacent amygdala, the caudate nucleus and putamen, and the prefrontal cortex regions involved in each of the three loops.

Effects of lesions to regions in the lower loop

Hyperphagia: Excessive eating follows certain forms of damage to the orbitofrontal cortex. The right side of the orbitofrontal cortex is preferentially activated by smells and tastes (Kringelbach, 2010) and, in collaboration with the limbic rewards circuit, the orbitofrontal cortex contributes to estimates of the reward value of food and other habits.

Social disinhibition: Orbitofrontal lesions generally produce dramatic changes in social behavior, characterized by disinhibition (Cummings & Mega, 2003), impaired empathy, blunted moral judgment and risky decision-making (Fuster, 2008). Patients exhibit poor social judgment, make tactless and inappropriate remarks, commit antisocial acts, make inane humor, and engage in inappropriate sexual or social behaviors.

Acquired sociopathy: Damage to portions of the orbitofrontal cortex of both hemispheres has been termed "acquired sociopathy" (Damasio, 1994). People with this disorder are unable to experience "gut" level information and, as a result, make risky choices. Reportedly, bilateral damage to the middle aspect of the orbitofrontal cortex impairs the ability of the person to experience their own emotions, and, by extension, identify how others might feel. The orbitofrontal cortex helps us use our emotions to make decisions.

Fronto-temporal dementia: Many patients with fronto-temporal dementia have degeneration of the orbitofrontal cortex that is associated with social and behavioral abnormalities such as those described above. In contrast, the prefrontal cortex is usually spared early in Alzheimer's disease and social impairments typically develop as secondary symptoms only after the prefrontal regions are affected.

Data from imaging studies

Food reward appraisal

When healthy individuals receive fMRI scans that are capable of evaluating metabolic activity, the orbitofrontal regions light up when the person is given a small amount of chocolate. As more chocolate is provided, it no longer is rewarding. At the point of satiety, the orbitofrontal cortex no longer shows the increased metabolic activity (O'Doherty et al., 2006).

Substance use disorders
Abnormal metabolic activity in the orbitofrontal region can be detected in drug-dependent patients experiencing craving and binging. Reductions in the gray matter in the middle and sides of the orbitofrontal cortex have been documented in abstinent cocaine addicts (Goldstein et al., 2006).

2. MIDDLE LOOP

The anterior cingulate cortex is involved in maintaining attention. The cingulate extends from the parietal lobe forward to the frontal lobe as a long rainbow-shaped structure. The functions and divisions of the cingulate are not well known, but recent findings have provided important insights concerning the role of the anterior cingulate in compulsive behaviors.

The anterior cingulate receives projections from many key cortical fields including the parietal and temporal lobes and the hippocampus. It sends a one-way projection onto the dorsal striatum, where it returns to the anterior cingulate after passing through the globus pallidus and thalamus to form the middle loop.

Effects of naturally occurring lesions to structures in the middle loop

Apathy: Patients with damage to the anterior cingulate exhibit a reduction of motivation and goal-directed activities and loss of concern. There is reduced curiosity, loss of interest in usual activities (social, professional, recreational) and a lack of interest in learning and new experiences. Their normal response to errors is blunted, as is the response to an unexpected reward.

Hypokinesia and akinesia: Naturally occurring lesions that include bilateral involvement of the anterior cingulate can produce a profound loss of concern and may also be accompanied by reduction of movement (i.e. akinesia). An extreme manifestation, akinetic mutism, occurs in patients with apathy, immobility and lack of speech. Patients will eat if fed, urinate or defecate if taken to the toilet, and speak or move occasionally when prompted, but otherwise there is a profound inhibition of self-directed behavior.

Effects of anterior cingulotomy for obsessive-compulsive disorders (OCD)

The most common symptoms of OCD include recurrent thoughts of contamination, doubt, aggression or sex, and recurrent compulsions to wash, check, hoard, count or engage in other rituals. These symptoms can usually be treated with psychological and pharmacological therapies. However, a small group of patients, resistant to these treatments and suffering from disabling OCD, have been shown to benefit from the surgical destruction or disconnection of the anterior cingulate (see Cummings & Mega, 2003). In other words, surgically-induced apathy may effectively counter the obsessions and compulsions of this disorder.

Data from imaging studies

Obsessive-compulsive disorders (OCD)
People with OCD tend to have heightened metabolic activity in the anterior cingulate and its subcortical projections. Meta-analyses of brain volume changes in OCD indicate a

significant reduction of the anterior cingulate and orbitofrontal cortices. The abnormalities were interpreted as a disruption of the frontal neostriatal circuit (Rotge et al., 2009).

OCD spectrum disorders
Abnormalities of metabolic activity of the middle loop have also been reported in people with OCD spectrum disorders (Saxena, 2008). In these conditions, disproportionate attention is often directed toward somatic concerns; for example, dysmorphic disorder (preoccupation with an imagined defect in appearance), hypochrondriasis (preoccupation with somatic symptoms), compulsive hair pulling and compulsive skin picking.

Tourette syndrome
In this disorder characterized by multiple motor or vocal tics and stereotypies and complex repetitive and unwanted behavioral patterns, an abnormality of metabolic activity has been linked to the anterior cingulate and its subcortical projections (Muller-Vahl et al., 2009). The metabolic activity has been hypothesized to do with activation of dopamine circuits. Cocaine, which increases dopamine activity, can also induce tics. Reduced cingulate cortical thickness has been reported in people with Tourette syndrome (Worbe et al., 2010).

3. UPPER LOOP
The upper loop, composed of the dorsolateral (upper, side) region of the prefrontal cortex, is associated with executive functions including planning and decision-making.

The dorsolateral prefrontal cortex has reciprocal inputs from orbitofrontal and anterior cingulate areas as well as from the posterior association cortices of the parietal and temporal lobes. The dorsolateral area projects onto the head of the caudate nucleus and projects back to the same prefrontal area from the thalamus.

Effects of damage to regions in the upper loop
Perseveration: Patients with pathology affecting the upper loop have a tendency to repeat a response that had initially been rewarded, even though it is no longer rewarded. Difficulty in switching strategies is exemplified by the commands in the game, "Simon Says", where the person has to inhibit a response to a motor command based on whether or not the command includes the words "Simon says".

Impaired planning: The dorsolateral prefrontal cortex is capable of forming plans of action. Patients with damage to this region have substantial difficulty prioritizing, using time wisely, and remaining focused on an objective. The future is constructed based on expectations and plans. However, in people with damage to the dorsolateral prefrontal regions, there is impairment in "memory of the future" in the sense that these patients exhibit a failure to foresee contingencies, prioritize and execute plans that are flexible and proactive. Various neuropsychological tests, but not intelligence tests, are sensitive to the defects of dorsolateral lesions (see Cummings & Mega, 2003).

Moreover, the dorsolateral cortex is primarily involved in tasks that require the integration of spatially and temporally discontiguous elements of cognition, requiring the organization of activities in time and place to execute plans. The "executive functions" of the upper loop are likely to involve forms of top-down thinking that are separate from the emotional and reward-based, present-centered reasoning of the lower loop.

Impaired retrieval and fluid intelligence
Long-term memory retrieval can be impaired in patients with damage to the dorsolateral prefrontal cortex. Verbal retrieval, such as the ability to think of the names of objects in a given category, is more impaired when the hemisphere specialized for language, usually the left, is damaged, and non-verbal retrieval is more sensitive to right hemisphere damage. Similarly, patients with dorsolateral prefrontal damage do not generate many ideas in tests of creativity and exhibit excessive concreteness in their approach to problem-solving.

Broca's aphasia
The neurologist Paul Broca reported that damage to a region of the language-dominant hemisphere located in the lower aspect of the dorsolateral prefrontal cortex next to the motor strip for speech impaired fluent language. The impairment was termed, Broca's aphasia. In these patients, there is not only an impairment of verbal retrieval, but also loss of fluency and brief, grammatically-impoverished utterances. Although the ability to sing and use habitual phrases and automatic speech, such as curse words, remains intact, the patient with damage to Broca's area typically has subcortical lesions to the basal ganglia (Ulman, 2006).

4. MULTISYSTEM DISORDERS
Most neuropsychiatric disorders are thought involve a complex interplay of the three loops described above. In order to illustrate, several conditions are reviewed.

Disorders of attention
The analysis that follows relies on the conceptual scheme of Joaquin Fuster (2008), a leading expert in the study of the prefrontal cortex. Essentially all patients with prefrontal impairments have defective attention; however, there are three different kinds of attention. The upper loop is considered to be most important in maintaining an object of intention, the lower loop is involved in exclusion (i.e. the ability to suppress extraneous thoughts) and the middle loop helps to maintain the intention to focus.

For example, if you attempt to focus on your breath, a form of meditation, the upper loop is more critical for focusing on the breathing itself, the lower loop for suppressing unrelated thoughts and the middle loop, after attention is momentarily diverted, for restoring the focus back to one's breathing.

Attention deficit disorders probably involve all three forms of attention. In addition, impairments of the middle loop have been associated with reduction of movement (i.e. akinesia). By extrapolation, excessive movement (i.e. hyperkinesia) may follow excessive stimulation of the middle loop. Note that disorders of attention are very common in people with Tourette syndrome, also involving the middle loop. The standard pharmacological treatment of ADHD involves psychostimulants, which in turn activate the dopamine circuits. It is also of interest that that prefrontal cortex, especially the dorsolateral prefrontal region, is one of the last cortical fields to mature, and maturation does not occur prior to the second or third decades of life. Therefore, many people with ADHD will outgrow their disorder (Fuster, 2008). More neuroimaging research is needed to distinguish ADHD in youth from adult forms.

Major depression

There is convincing evidence that all three prefrontal regions are involved in major depression. The lower loop affects awareness of the mood state and the expectation of negative reinforcement. The middle loop probably governs the field of attention to those circumstances that are associated with the mood disorder. The upper loop involves defective processing of information, including rumination (i.e. an example of perseveration) and the kinds of cognitive distortions that are treatable with cognitive behavioral therapy.

In patients who remain unresponsive to antidepressants, psychological therapies, electroconvulsive therapy, transcranial magnetic stimulation and other standard treatments for major depression, deep brain stimulation has produced enduring benefits in over half of all patients who undergo the procedure (Mayberg, 2009). Helen Mayberg, a neurologist, has been instrumental in mapping the regions of the brain that respond to deep brain stimulation. To date, the area of greatest interest has been the subcallosal cingulate cortex, the tip of the anterior cingulate cortex buried beneath the corpus, also known as area 25.

When healthy people are asked to think depressed thoughts, imaging studies indicate that area 25 becomes metabolically active. Excessive metabolic activity in area 25 also occurs in people who are depressed until they respond to antidepressants or cognitive therapy. The regions of the frontal lobe that respond to antidepressants are different than those responsive to cognitive behavioral therapy, though each affect area 25. In addition, dorsolateral prefrontal activity is reported when cognitive behavioral therapy is implemented.

Deep brain stimulation is administered to a small group of patients in whom no other treatment has been successful. The stimulator is implanted in the area of the subcallosal cingulate cortex and provides continuous stimulation. The people that successfully respond to deep brain stimulation report a profound lifting of the mood state and show a reduction of hypermetabolic activity of area 25. Although deep brain stimulation does not cure the depressive disorders, as there are many social and cognitive hurdles to overcome, patients report being able to take part in their own recovery.

Eating disorders

We have described that damage to the orbitofrontal cortex can impair the ability to restrain eating, drinking, smoking or using other drugs that engage the cortical and subcortical dopamine reward circuits. The motivation and concern to attend to healthy eating or to avoid unhealthy addiction probably depends on the integrity of the middle loop. The ability to devise long-term plans to modify eating-related behaviors is consistent with the capabilities of the upper loop.

A successful plan to develop healthy eating habits is likely to engage all three loops including sustainable systems of social support, environmental contingencies, food replacement strategies, awareness of visceral and emotional states surrounding food (lower loop), systems of reminders and motivators to maintain or reinstate focus (middle loop) and the organizational mastery of goals and contingency planning (upper loop).

5. HABIT SUBSTITUTION AND HABIT HIERARCHIES

Habits may be changed individually or may be subject to comprehensive lifestyle modification in which master habits can be developed to help regulate subordinate habits.

Habit substitution

The aphorism, "It takes a thief to catch a thief," may be restated as, "It takes a habit to alter a habit." If you wish to change a habit that engages the lower loop such as avoiding the tendency to interrupt when discussing a matter that provokes intense emotions, it may be helpful to acquire a competing habit such as taking a deep breath before interrupting. The habit of taking a deep breath can counter and inhibit the habit of making impulsive remarks. By delaying a response, you have time to engage the wisdom of your prefrontal regions to frame a response in ways that are more likely to lead to conflict resolution.

Master habits

Although this discussion is conjectural, I believe it is likely that some master habits control secondary habits. One might prefer to think of master habits as skills or tactical plans, but I am suggesting that there is a hierarchy of habits, with certain critical ones capable of facilitating subordinate habits. Below are three examples of master habits:

Developing and revising your life plan

Be true to what you value, cherish and believe in by developing a habitual method to remind you of your long-term goals. If you live an authentic life and seek to optimize your health and wellness and the health and wellness of others, you may want to write down your long-term objectives. Dare to dream. It is your life and the opportunities to fulfill it occur only in one lifetime. You can engage the upper loop to invent your future and revise your dreams as needed. View your long-term objectives on a daily basis as a work of art, as the embodiment of your potential. By displaying your goals in verbal or pictorial form, you can habitually remind yourself of your intended path and its destinations.

Reviewing your successes and setbacks

Careful attention to the circumstances that led to a problem can provide key insights in terms of prevention. It is itself a worthy habit to pay attention to what you did correctly and acknowledge your triumphs in habit formation. Adapt what works, but do not perseverate when a strategy continuously fails. An accurate account also avoids an exaggerated view of setbacks. In sum, documenting the circumstances that led to a lapse, for example, in healthy eating, social discourse or physical activity, can reduce errors of inclusion, exclusion or intent that limit sustained attention.

Proactive thinking one day at a time

Making intensive lifestyle changes can be linked to maintaining multiple coexisting habits. If you construct a to-do list that is revised on a daily basis, it enables you to engage all three prefrontal regions, including the capacity to plan, sustain motivation and seek the right kinds of rewards including healthy pleasures.

Concluding remarks

The lower loop is rooted in the "here and now" with rich sensory and emotional connotations and reward-related expectations. The middle loop is rooted in the domain of attention and intention, regaining focus, enabling one to continue in spite of distractions and unhealthy attractions. The upper loop is able to imagine and realize the future, more rational than emotional. Still, we make decisions based on all three of these systems. Success in school, in one's profession, and in close relationships involves networks of the loops.

References Cited

Abler B, Walter H, Erk S, Kammerer H, Spitzer M. Prediction error as a linear function of reward probability is coded in human nucleus accumbens. Neuroimage. 2006; 31(2):790-5.

Abumaria N, Rygula R, Havemann-Reinecke U, Rüther E, Bodemer W, Roos C, Flügge G. Identification of genes regulated by chronic social stress in the rat dorsal raphe nucleus. Cell Mol Neurobiol. 2006; 26(2):145-62.

Adolphs R. Looking at other people: mechanisms for social perception revealed in subjects with focal amygdala damage. Novartis Found Symp. 2007; 278:146-59.

Aharon I, Etcoff N, Ariely D, Chabris CF, O'Connor E, Breiter HC. Beautiful faces have variable reward value: fMRI and behavioral evidence. Neuron. 2001; 32(3):537-51.

Allen SM, Shah AC, Nezu AM, Nezu CM, Ciambrone D, Hogan J, Mor V. A problem-solving approach to stress reduction among younger women with breast carcinoma: a randomized controlled trial. Cancer. 2002; 94(12):3089-100.

Allport G, Vernon, PE, Lindzey G. Study of values: a scale for measuring the dominant interests in personality (3rd edition). Boston: Houghton Mifflin, 1970.

Anic GM, Titus-Ernstoff L, Newcomb PA, Trentham-Dietz A, Egan KM. Sleep duration and obesity in a population-based study. Sleep Med. 2010; 11(5):447-51.

Antony MM, Swinson RP. Shyness & social anxiety workbook. Oakland: New Harbinger Publications, Inc., 2008.

Banasr M, Duman RS. Regulation of neurogenesis and gliogenesis by stress and antidepressant treatment. CNS Neurol Disord Drug Targets. 2007; 6(5):311-20.

Bandura A. Self-efficacy: the exercise of control. W.H. Freeman and Company: United States, 1997.

Baran SE, Campbell AM, Kleen JK, Foltz CH, Wright RL, Diamond DM, Conrad CD. Combination of high fat diet and chronic stress retracts hippocampal dendrites. Neuroreport. 2005; 16(1):39-43.

Barbieri L, Boggian I, Falloon I, Lamonaca D; Centro Diurno 5 (CD5) collaborators. Problem-solving skills for cognitive rehabilitation among persons with chronic psychotic disorders in Italy. Psychiatr Serv. 2006; 57(2):172-4.

Bardo MT. Neuropharmacological mechanisms of drug reward: beyond dopamine in the nucleus accumbens. Crit Rev Neurobiol. 1998; 12(1-2):37-67.

Bechara A, Tranel D, Damasio H. Characterization of the decision-making deficit of patients with ventromedial prefrontal cortex lesions. Brain. 2000; 123(Pt 11):2189-202.

Beck AT. Cognitive therapy and the emotional disorders. New York: Penguin Books, 1976.

Benazon NR, Moore GJ, Rosenberg DR. Neurochemical analyses in pediatric obsessive-compulsive disorder in patients treated with cognitive-behavioral therapy. J Am Acad Child Adolesc Psychiatry. 2003; 42(11):1279-85.

Benedetti F. Placebo effects: understanding the mechanisms in health and disease. New York: Oxford University Press, 2008.

Blakeslee S, Blakeslee M. The body has a mind of its own: how body maps in your brain help you do (almost) everything better. New York: Random House, 2007.

Brady KT, Killeen TK, Brewerton T, Lucerini S. Comorbidity of psychiatric disorders and posttraumatic stress disorder. J Clin Psychiatry. 2000; 61 Suppl 7:22-32.

Brake WG, Zhang TY, Diorio J, Meaney MJ, Gratton A. Influence of early postnatal rearing conditions on mesocorticolimbic dopamine and behavioural responses to psychostimulants and stressors in adult rats. Eur J Neurosci. 2004; 19(7):1863-74.

Braun K, Lange E, Metzger M, Poeggel G. Maternal separation followed by early social deprivation affects the development of monoaminergic fiber systems in the medial prefrontal cortex of Octodon degus. Neuroscience. 2000; 95(1):309-18.

Bray S, O'Doherty J. Neural coding of reward-prediction error signals during classical conditioning with attractive faces. J Neurophysiol. 2007; 97(4):3036-45.

Bremner JD, Elzinga B, Schmahl C, Vermetten E. Structural and functional plasticity of the human brain in posttraumatic stress disorder. Prog Brain Res. 2008; 167:171-86.

Brunner EJ, Chandola T, Marmot MG. Prospective effect of job strain on general and central obesity in the Whitehall II Study. Am J Epidemiol. 2007; 165(7):828-37.

Bryant RA, Felmingham K, Kemp A, Das P, Hughes G, Peduto A, Williams L. Amygdala and ventral anterior cingulate activation predicts treatment response to cognitive behaviour therapy for post-traumatic stress disorder. Psychol Med. 2008; 38(4):555-61.

Buckworth J, Sears L. Increasing and maintaining physical activity in clinical populations. In: Best practices in the behavioral management of chronic disease: volume 2 other medical disorders. Trafton JA, Gordon WP (eds.), Los Altos: Institute for Brain Potential, 2008.

Burns D. The feeling good handbook. New York: William Morrow and Company, Inc., 1989.

Butler RN, Forette F, Greengross BS. Maintaining cognitive health in an ageing society. J R Soc Health. 2004; 124(3):119-21.

Castrén E, Rantamäki T. The role of BDNF and its receptors in depression and antidepressant drug action: Reactivation of developmental plasticity. Dev Neurobiol. 2010; 70(5):289-97.

Champagne F, Meaney MJ. Like mother, like daughter: evidence for non-genomic transmission of parental behavior and stress responsivity. Prog Brain Res. 2001; 133:287-302.

Chein JM, Schneider W. Neuroimaging studies of practice-related change: fMRI and meta-analytic evidence of a domain-general control network for learning. Cognitive Brain Res. 2005; 25(3): 607-623.

Chernoff RA, Davison GC. An evaluation of a brief HIV/AIDS prevention intervention for college students using normative feedback and goal setting. AIDS Educ Prev. 2005; 17(2):91-104.

Christakis NA, Fowler JH. The spread of obesity in a large social network over 32 years. N Engl J Med. 2007; 357(4):370-9.

Christakis NA, Fowler JH. The collective dynamics of smoking in a large social network. N Engl J Med. 2008; 358(21): 2249-58.

Christiansen BA, Smith DT, Roehling PV, Goldman MS. Using alcohol expectancies to predict adolescent drinking behavior after one year. J Consult Clini Psychol 1989; 57(1): 93-99.

Christiansen BA, Goldman MS. Alcohol-related expectancies versus demographic/ background variables in the prediction of adolescent drinking. J Consult Clin Pschol 1983; 51: 249-257.

Christianson JP, Paul ED, Irani M, Thompson BM, Kubala KH, Yirmiya R, Watkins LR, Maier SF. The role of prior stressor controllability and the dorsal raphé nucleus in sucrose preference and social exploration. Behav Brain Res. 2008; 193(1):87-93.

Cohen DA. Neurophysiological pathways to obesity: below awareness and beyond individual control. Diabetes. 2008; 57(7):1768-73.

Colloca L, Benedetti F. Placebo analgesia induced by social observational learning. Pain. 2009; 144(1-2):28-34.

Colman RJ, Anderson RM, Johnson SC, Kastman EK, Kosmatka KJ, Beasley TM, Allison DB, Cruzen C, Simmons HA, Kemnitz JW, Weindruch R. Caloric restriction delays disease onset and mortality in rhesus monkeys. Science. 2009; 325(5937):201-4.

Comalli PE Jr, Wapner S, Werner H. Interference effects of Stroop color-word test in childhood, adulthood, and aging. J Genet Psychol. 1962; 100:47-53.

Cooper MA, McIntyre KE, Huhman KL. Activation of 5-HT1A autoreceptors in the dorsal raphe nucleus reduces the behavioral consequences of social defeat. Psychoneuroendocrinology. 2008; Oct;33(9):1236-47.

Costa G. The impact of shift and night work on health. Applied Ergonomics. 1996; 27(1): 9-16.

Côté S, Bouchard S. Documenting the efficacy of virtual reality exposure with psychophysiological and information processing measures. Appl Psychophysiol Biofeedback. 2005; 30(3):217-32.

Cummings JL, Mega JS. Neuropsychiatry and behavioral neuroscience. New York: Oxford University Press, 2003.

Czéh B, Müller-Keuker JI, Rygula R, Abumaria N, Hiemke C, Domenici E, Fuchs E. Chronic social stress inhibits cell proliferation in the adult medial prefrontal cortex: hemispheric asymmetry and reversal by fluoxetine treatment. Neuropsychopharmacology. 2007; 32(7):1490-503.

Daley A. Exercise and depression: a review of reviews. J Clin Psychol Med Settings. 2008; 15(2):140-7.

Damasio A. Descartes' error: emotion, reason, and the human brain. New York: G.P. Putnam's Sons, 1994.

Darkes J, Goldman MS. Expectancy challenge and drinking reduction: experimental evidence for a mediational process. J Consult Clin Psychol. 1993; 61(2):344-53.

Darkes J, Goldman MS. Expectancy challenge and drinking reduction: process and structure in the alcohol expectancy network. Exp Clin Psychopharmacol. 1998; 6:64-76.

Davis C, Carter JC. Compulsive overeating as an addiction disorder. A review of theory and evidence. Appetite. 2009; Aug;53(1):1-8.

DeBusk RF, Miller NH, Superko HR, Dennis CA, Thomas RJ, Lew HT, Berger WE 3rd, Heller RS, Rompf J, Gee D, Kraemer HC, Bandura A, Ghandour G, Clark M, Shah RV, Fisher L, Taylor CB. A case-management system for coronary risk factor modification after acute myocardial infarction. Ann Intern Med. 1994; 120(9):721-9.

Defrin R, Ginzburg K, Solomon Z, Polad E, Bloch M, Govezensky M, Schreiber S. Quantitative testing of pain perception in subjects with PTSD--implications for the mechanism of the coexistence between PTSD and chronic pain. Pain. 2008; 138(2):450-9.

De Martino B, Camerer CF, Adolphs R. Amygdala damage eliminates monetary loss aversion. Proc Natl Acad Sci U S A. 2010; 107(8):3788-92.

de Quervain DJ, Fischbacher U, Treyer V, Schellhammer M, Schnyder U, Buck A, Fehr E. The neural basis of altruistic punishment. Science. 2004; 305(5688):1246-7.

Del Arco A, Mora F. Prefrontal cortex-nucleus accumbens interaction: in vivo modulation by dopamine and glutamate in the prefrontal cortex. Pharmacol Biochem Behav. 2008; 90(2):226-35.

Delsignore A, Schnyder U. Control expectancies as predictors of psychotherapy outcome: a systematic review. Br J Clin Psychol. 2007; 46(Pt 4):467-83.

Diliberti N, Bordi PL, Conklin MT, Roe LS, Rolls BJ. Increased portion size leads to increased energy intake in a restaurant meal. Obes Res. 2004; 12(3):562-8.

Dilk MN, Bond GR. Meta-analytic evaluation of skills training research for individuals with severe mental illness. J Consult Clin Psychol. 1996; 64(6):1337-1346.

Dominey PF, Inui T. Cortico-striatal function in sentence comprehension: insights from neurophysiology and modeling. Cortex. 2009; 45(8):1012-8.

Dong Y, Green T, Saal D, Marie H, Neve R, Nestler EJ, Malenka RC. CREB modulates excitability of nucleus accumbens neurons. Nat Neurosci. 2006; 9(4):475-7.

Eisenberg D, Quinn BC. Estimating the effect of smoking cessation on weight gain: an instrumental variable approach. Health Serv Res. 2006; 41(6):2255-66.

Embry DD, Flannery DJ, Vazsonyi AT, Powell KE, Atha H. Peacebuilders: a theoretically driven, school-based model for early violence prevention. Am J Prev Med. 1996; 12(5 Suppl):91-100.

Eyberg SM, Boggs SR, Algina J. Parent-child interaction therapy: a psychosocial model for the treatment of young children with conduct problem behavior and their families. Psychopharmacol Bull. 1995; 31(1):83-91.

Fales CL, Barch DM, Rundle MM, Mintun MA, Mathews J, Snyder AZ, Sheline YI. Antidepressant treatment normalizes hypoactivity in dorsolateral prefrontal cortex during emotional interference processing in major depression. J Affect Disord. 2009;112(1-3):206-11.

Féart C, Samieri C, Rondeau V, Amieva H, Portet F, Dartigues JF, Scarmeas N, Barberger-Gateau P. Adherence to a Mediterranean diet, cognitive decline, and risk of dementia. JAMA. 2009; 302(6):638-48.

Fillit HM, Butler RN, O'Connell AW, Albert MS, Birren JE, Cotman CW, Greenough WT, Gold PE, Kramer AF, Kuller LH, Perls TT, Sahagan BG, Tully T. Achieving and maintaining cognitive vitality with aging. Mayo Clin Proc. 2002; 77(7):681-96.

Flannery DJ, Vazsonyi AT, Liau AK, Guo S, Powell KE, Atha H, Vesterdal W, Embry D. Initial behavior outcomes for the peacebuilders universal school-based violence prevention program. Dev Psychol. 2003; 39(2):292-308.

Flor H, Lutzenberger W, Knost B. Spouse presence alters brain response to pain. Society for Neuroscience abstracts, 2002, Orlando, FL.

Forbes, CE, Grafman, J. The role of the human prefrontal cortex in social cognition and moral judgment. Ann Rev. Neurosci. 2010; 33: 299-324.

Fowler JH, Christakis NA. Dynamic spread of happiness in a large social network: longitudinal analysis over 20 years in the Framingham Heart Study. BMJ. 2008; 337: a2338.

Francis DD, Kuhar MJ. Frequency of maternal licking and grooming correlates negatively with vulnerability to cocaine and alcohol use in rats. Pharmacol Biochem Behav. 2008; 90(3):497-500.

Francis DD, Diorio J, Plotsky PM, Meaney MJ. Environmental enrichment reverses the effects of maternal separation on stress reactivity. J Neurosci. 2002; 22(18):7840-3.

French SA, Story M, Jeffery RW. Environmental influences on eating and physical activity. Ann Rev Public Health. 2001; 22: 309-35.

Fuster, J. The prefrontal cortex (4th edition). Academic Press, 2008.

Gander P, Purnell H, Garden A, Woodward A. Work patterns and fatigue-related risk among junior doctors. Occup Environ Med. 2007; 64(11):733-8.

Gangwisch JE, Heymsfield SB, Boden-Albala B, Buijs RM, Kreier F, Pickering TG, Rundle AG, Zammit GK, Malaspina D. Sleep duration as a risk factor for diabetes incidence in a large U.S. sample. Sleep. 2007; 30(12):1667-73.

Gardner KL, Thrivikraman KV, Lightman SL, Plotsky PM, Lowry CA. Early life experience alters behavior during social defeat: focus on serotonergic systems. Neuroscience. 2005; 136(1):181-91.

George SZ, Zeppieri G Jr, Cere AL, Cere MR, Borut MS, Hodges MJ, Reed DM, Valencia C, Robinson ME. A randomized trial of behavioral physical therapy interventions for acute and sub-acute low back pain (NCT00373867). Pain. 2008; 140(1):145-57.

Gitterman A, Schulman L (eds.). Mutual aid groups, vulnerable and resilient populations, and the life cycle. New York: Columbia University Press, 2005.

Goldstein, RZ, Alia-Klein, N, Cottone, LA, Volkow, ND. The orbitofrontal cortex in drug addiction (pp. 481-522). In: Zald, DH, Rauch, SL (eds.). The orbitofrontal cortex. New York: Oxford University Press, 2006.

Gosselin N, Peretz I, Johnsen E, Adolphs R. Amygdala damage impairs emotion recognition from music. Neuropsychologia. 2007; 45(2):236-44.

Grabiel, AM. Habits, rituals, and the evaluative brain. Annu. Rev. Neurosci. 2008; 31: 359-87.

Grace AA, Floresco SB, Goto Y, Lodge DJ. Regulation of firing of dopaminergic neurons and control of goal-directed behaviors. Trends Neurosci. 2007; 30(5):220-7.

Graybeil AM. Habits, rituals and the evaluative brain. Annu Rev Neurosci. 2008; 31:359-87.

Hagemann N, Strauss B, Busch D. The complex problem-solving competence of team coaches. Psychology of Sport and Exercise. 2008; 9(3): 301-317.

Hampton AN, Adolphs R, Tyszka MJ, O'Doherty JP. Contributions of the amygdala to reward expectancy and choice signals in human prefrontal cortex. Neuron. 2007; 55(4): 545-55.

Hayes SC, Strosahl KD, Wilson KG. Acceptance and commitment therapy: an experiential approach to behavior change. New York: Guilford Press, 1999.

Helmeke C, Ovtscharoff W Jr, Poeggel G, Braun K. Imbalance of immunohisto-chemically characterized interneuron populations in the adolescent and adult rodent medial prefrontal cortex after repeated exposure to neonatal separation stress. Neuroscience. 2008; 152(1):18-28.

Hester R, Garavan H. Executive dysfunction in cocaine addiction: evidence for discordant frontal, cingulate, and cerebellar activity. J Neurosci. 2004; 24(49):11017-22.

Higgins ST, Petry NM. Contingency management. Incentives for sobriety. Alcohol Res Health. 1999; 23(2): 122-7.

Hollon SD, Steward MO, Strunk D. Enduring effects for cognitive behavioral therapy in the treatment of depression and anxiety. Annual Review of Psychology. 2006; 57: 285-315.

Hölzl R, Kleinböhl D, Huse E. Implicit operant learning of pain sensitization. Pain. 2005; 115(1-2):12-20.

Huizenga HM, Crone EA, Jansen BJ. Decision-making in healthy children, adolescents and adults explained by the use of increasingly complex proportional reasoning rules. Dev Sci. 2007; 10(6): 814-25.

Hull JG, Bond CF Jr. Social and behavioral consequences of alcohol consumption and expectancy: a meta-analysis. Psychol Bull. 1986; 99(3):347-60.

Humphreys K. Circles of recovery. New York: Cambridge University Press, 2004.

Huot RL, Gonzalez ME, Ladd CO, Thrivikraman KV, Plotsky PM. Foster litters prevent hypothalamic-pituitary-adrenal axis sensitization mediated by neonatal maternal separation. Psychoneuroendocrinology. 2004; 29(2):279-89.

Hurley KM, Black MM, Papas MA, Caulfield LE. Maternal symptoms of stress, depression, and anxiety are related to nonresponsive feeding styles in a statewide sample of WIC participants. J Nutr. 2008; 138(4):799-805.

Iacoboni M. Imitation, empathy, and mirror neurons. Annu Rev Psychol. 2009; 60:653-70.

Ipser J, Seedat S, Stein DJ. Pharmacotherapy for post-traumatic stress disorder - a systematic review and meta-analysis. S Afr Med J. 2006; 96(10):1088-96.

Jason LA, O'Donnell WT Jr. Behavioral interventions to reduce youth exposure to unhealthful media. In: Best practices in the behavioral management of chronic disease: volume 3 from preconception to adolescence, Trafton JA, Gordon WP (eds.), Los Altos: Institute for Brain Potential, 2008.

Jolliffe CD, Nicholas MK. Verbally reinforcing pain reports: an experimental test of the operant model of chronic pain. Pain. 2004; 107(1-2):167-75.

Jones K, Daley D, Hutchings J, Bywater T, Eames C. Efficacy of the Incredible Years Programme as an early intervention for children with conduct problems and ADHD: long-term follow-up. Child Care Health Dev. 2008; 34(3):380-90.

Jones K, Daley D, Hutchings J, Bywater T, Eames C. Efficacy of the Incredible Years Basic parent training programme as an early intervention for children with conduct problems and ADHD. Child Care Health Dev. 2007; 33(6):749-56.

Kazdin AE, Siegel TC, Bass D. Cognitive problem-solving skills training and parent management training in the treatment of antisocial behavior in children. J Consult Clin Psychol. 1992; 60(5):733-47.

Keltikangas-Järvinen L, Pulkki-Råback L, Elovainio M, Raitakari OT, Viikari J, Lehtimäki T. DRD2 C32806T modifies the effect of child-rearing environment on adulthood novelty seeking. Am J Med Genet B Neuropsychiatr Genet. 2009; 150B(3):389-94.

Kennedy SH, Konarski JZ, Segal ZV, Lau MA, Bieling PJ, McIntyre RS, Mayberg HS. Differences in brain glucose metabolism between responders to CBT and venlafaxine in a 16-week randomized controlled trial. Am J Psychiatry. 2007; 164(5):778-88.

Killgore WD, Balkin TJ, Wesensten NJ. Impaired decision making following 49 h of sleep deprivation. J Sleep Res. 2006; 15(1):7-13.

Killgore WD, Lipizzi EL, Kamimori GH, Balkin TJ. Caffeine effects on risky decision making after 75 hours of sleep deprivation. Aviat Space Environ Med. 2007;78(10):957-62.

Kirby LG, Pan YZ, Freeman-Daniels E, Rani S, Nunan JD, Akanwa A, Beck SG. Cellular effects of swim stress in the dorsal raphe nucleus. Psychoneuroendocrinology. 2007; 32(6):712-23.

Kjellgren A, Bood SA, Axelsson K, Norlander T, Saatcioglu F. Wellness through a comprehensive yogic breathing program - a controlled pilot trial. BMC Complement Altern Med. 2007; 7:43

Knutson B, Rick S, Wimmer GE, Prelec D, Loewenstein G. Neural predictors of purchases. Neuron. 2007; 53(1):147-56.

Knutson KL, Van Cauter E. Associations between sleep loss and increased risk of obesity and diabetes. Ann N Y Acad Sci. 2008; 1129:287-304.

Koran LM, Bullock KD, Hartston HJ, Elliott MA, D'Andrea V. Citalopram treatment of compulsive shopping: an open-label study. J Clin Psychiatry. 2002; 63(8):704-8.

Koyama T, McHaffie JG, Laurienti PJ, Coghill RC. The subjective experience of pain: where expectations become reality. Proc Natl Acad Sci U S A. 2005; 102(36):12950-5.

Kringelbach, ML. The hedonic brain: a functional neuroanatomy of human pleasure. In: Kringelbach, ML, Berridge, KC. Pleasures of the brain. New York: Oxford University Press, 2010.

Kroeze W, Oenema A, Dagnelie PC, Brug J. Examining the minimal required elements of a computer-tailored intervention aimed at dietary fat reduction: results of a randomized controlled dismantling study. Health Educ Res. 2008; 23(5):880-91.

Krug EG, Brener ND, Dahlberg LL, Ryan GW, Powell KE. The impact of an elementary school-based violence prevention program on visits to the school nurse. Am J Prev Med. 1997; 13(6):459-63.

Krug I, Treasure J, Anderluh M, Bellodi L, Cellini E, di Bernardo M, Granero R, Karwautz A, Nacmias B, Penelo E, Ricca V, Sorbi S, Tchanturia K, Wagner G, Collier D, Fernández-Aranda F. Present and lifetime comorbidity of tobacco, alcohol and drug use in eating disorders: a European multicenter study. Drug Alcohol Depend. 2008; 97(1-2):169-79.

Kruger J, Blanck HM, Gillespie C. Dietary and physical activity behaviors among adults successful at weight loss maintenance. Int J Behav Nutr Phys Act. 2006; 3:17.

Kumari V, Peters ER, Fannon D, Antonova E, Premkumar P, Anilkumar AP, Williams SC, Kuipers E. Dorsolateral prefrontal cortex activity predicts responsiveness to cognitive-behavioral therapy in schizophrenia. Biol Psychiatry. 2009;66(6):594-602.

Lally P, van Jaarsveld CHM, Potts HWW, Wardle J. How are habits formed: modelling habit formation in the real world. Eur J Social Psychol. 2010; 46(6):998-1009.

Larsson B, Fossum S, Clifford G, Drugli MB, Handegård BH, Mørch WT. Treatment of oppositional defiant and conduct problems in young Norwegian children: results of a randomized controlled trial. Eur Child Adolesc Psychiatry. 2009; 18(1):42-52.

Lau-Barraco C, Dunn ME. Evaluation of a single-session expectancy challenge intervention to reduce alcohol use among college students. Psychol Addict Behav. 2008; 22(2):168-75.

Lee JY, Kim JM, Kim JW, Cho J, Lee WY, Kim HJ, Jeon BS. Association between the dose of dopaminergic medication and the behavioral disturbances in Parkinson disease. Parkinsonism Relat Disord. 2010; 16(3):202-7.

Leeuw M, Goossens ME, van Breukelen GJ, de Jong JR, Heuts PH, Smeets RJ, Köke AJ, Vlaeyen JW. Exposure in vivo versus operant graded activity in chronic low back pain patients: results of a randomized controlled trial. Pain. 2008; 138(1):192-207.

Levine JA, Lanningham-Foster LM, McCrady SK, Krizan AC, Olson LR, Kane PH, Jensen MD, Clark MM. Interindividual variation in posture allocation: possible role in human obesity. Science. 2005; 307(5709):584-6.

Liberzon I, Britton JC, Phan KL. Neural correlates of traumatic recall in posttraumatic stress disorder. Stress. 2003; 6(3):151-6.

Liberman RP, Eckman TA, Marder SR. Training in social problem-solving among persons with schizophrenia. Psychiatric Services. 2001; 52:31–33.

Lillis J, Hayes SC, Bunting K and Masuda A. Teaching acceptance and mindfulness to improve the lives of the obese: a preliminary test of a theoretical model. Annals of Behavioral Medicine. 2009; 37(1): 58-69.

Linden DE. How psychotherapy changes the brain--the contribution of functional neuroimaging. Mol Psychiatry. 2006; 11(6):528-38.

Lockley SW, Barger LK, Ayas NT, Rothschild JM, Czeisler CA, Landrigan CP; Harvard Work Hours, Health and Safety Group. Effects of health care provider work hours and sleep deprivation on safety and performance. Jt Comm J Qual Patient Saf. 2007; 33(11 Suppl):7-18.

Maier, SF, Amat J, Baratta MV, Watkins LR. Behavioral control, the medial prefrontal cortex, and resilience. Discourses in Clinical Neuroscience. 2006; 8: 397-407.

Mandyam CD, Wee S, Eisch AJ, Richardson HN, Koob GF. Methamphetamine self-administration and voluntary exercise have opposing effects on medial prefrontal cortex gliogenesis. J Neurosci. 2007; 27(42):11442-50.

Mansouri FA, Tanaka K, Buckley MJ. Conflict-induced behavioural adjustment: a clue to the executive functions of the prefrontal cortex. Nature Reviews Neuroscience 2009; 10:141-152.

Marcus CL, Loughlin GM. Effect of sleep deprivation on driving safety in housestaff. Sleep. 1996; 19(10):763-6.

Marmot MG, Shipley MJ, Rose G. Inequalities in death--specific explanations of a general pattern? Lancet. 1984; 1(8384):1003-6.

Marosits MJ. Improving financial and patient outcomes: the future of demand management. Healthc Financ Manage. 1997; 51(8):43-4.

Marshall NS, Glozier N, Grunstein RR. Is sleep duration related to obesity? A critical review of the epidemiological evidence. Sleep Med Rev. 2008; 12(4):289-98.

Martell BA, O'Connor PG, Kerns RD, Becker WC, Morales KH, Kosten TR, Fiellin DA. Systematic review: opioid treatment for chronic back pain: prevalence, efficacy, and association with addiction. Ann Intern Med. 2007; 146(2):116-27.

Martín-Sánchez E, Furukawa TA, Taylor J, Martin JL. Systematic review and meta-analysis of cannabis treatment for chronic pain. Pain Med. 2009; 10(8):1353-68.

Matsumoto M, Smith JC. Progressive muscle relaxation, breathing exercises, and ABC relaxation theory. J Clin Psychol. 200; 57(12):1551-7.

Mayberg, HS. Targeted electrode-based modulation of neural circuits for depression. J. Clin Invest. 2009; 119 (4) 717-725.

McCrady B, Stout R, Noel N. Effectiveness of three types of spouse-involved alcohol treatment: outcomes 18 months after treatment. Br J Addict. 1991; 86(11):1415-1424.

McEwen BS. Stress and hippocampal plasticity. Annu Rev Neurosci. 1999; 22:105-22.

McGinnis JM, Foege WH. Actual causes of death in the United States. JAMA. 1993; 270(18):2207-12.

McGuire MT, Wing RR, Klem ML, Seagle HM, Hill JO. Long-term maintenance of weight loss: do people who lose weight through various weight loss methods use different behaviors to maintain their weight? Int J Obes Relat Metab Disord. 1998; 22(6):572-7.

McKellar JM. Increasing Self-Efficacy for Health Behavior Change: A Review of Self-Management Interventions. In: Trafton J, Gordon W (eds.), Best Practices in the Behavioral Management of Chronic Disease, Volume I: Neuropsychiatric Disorders. Los Altos: Institute for Brain Potential, 2010.

McLean N, Griffin S, Toney K, Hardeman W. Family involvement in weight control, weight maintenance and weight-loss interventions: a systematic review of randomised trials. Int J Obes Relat Metab Disord. 2003; 27(9):987-1005.

Meloni EG, Reedy CL, Cohen BM, Carlezon WA Jr. Activation of raphe efferents to the medial prefrontal cortex by corticotropin-releasing factor: correlation with anxiety-like behavior. Biol Psychiatry. 2008;63(9):832-9.

Michaels CC, Holtzman SG. Early postnatal stress alters place conditioning to both mu- and kappa-opioid agonists. J Pharmacol Exp Ther. 2008; 325(1):313-8.

Millder BL, Cummings JL (eds). The human frontal lobes: functions and disorders (2nd edition). New York: Guilford Press, 2007.

Miller WR, Rollnick S. Motivational interviewing: preparing people for change (2nd edition). New York: Guilford Press, 2002.

Mladenovic Djordjevic A, Perovic M, Tesic V, Tanic N, Rakic L, Ruzdijic S, Kanazir S. Long-term dietary restriction modulates the level of presynaptic proteins in the cortex and hippocampus of the aging rat. Neurochem Int. 2010; 56(2):250-5.

Mokdad AH, Marks JS, Stroup DF, Gerberding JL. Actual causes of death in the United States, 2000. JAMA 2004; 291(10): 1238-1245.

Moffett MC, Vicentic A, Kozel M, Plotsky P, Francis DD, Kuhar MJ. Maternal separation alters drug intake patterns in adulthood in rats. Biochem Pharmacol. 2007; 73(3):321-30.

Moreira MT, Smith LA, Foxcroft D. Social norms interventions to reduce alcohol misuse in university or college students. Cochrane Database Syst Rev. 2009; (3):CD006748.

Morgan D, Grant KA, Gage HD, Mach RH, Kaplan JR, Prioleau O, Nader SH, Buchheimer N, Ehrenkaufer RL, Nader MA. Social dominance in monkeys: dopamine D2 receptors and cocaine self-administration. Nat Neurosci. 2002; 5(2):169-74.

Morgenthaler T, Kramer M, Alessi C, Friedman L, Boehlecke B, Brown T, Coleman J, Kapur V, Lee-Chiong T, Owens J, Pancer J, Swick T; American Academy of Sleep Medicine. Practice parameters for the psychological and behavioral treatment of insomnia: an update. An american academy of sleep medicine report. Sleep. 2006; 29(11):1415-9.

Morin CM, Espie CA. Insomnia: a clinician's guide to assessment and treatment. New York: Springer, 2003.

Müller-Vahl KR, Kaufmann J, Grosskreutz J, Dengler R, Emrich HM, Peschel T, O'Doherty, JP, Dolan, RJ. The role of human orbitofrontal cortex in reward prediction and behavioral choice: insights from neuroimaging (pp. 265-283). In: Zald, DH, Rauch, SL (eds.). The orbitofrontal cortex. New York: Oxford University Press, 2006.

National Institute of Health and the friends of the National Library of Medicine. PTSD: A Growing Epidemic. NIH Medline Plus. 2009; 4(1):10-14.

Nixon RD, Sweeney L, Erickson DB, Touyz SW. Parent-child interaction therapy: one- and two-year follow-up of standard and abbreviated treatments for oppositional preschoolers. J Abnorm Child Psychol. 2004; 32(3):263-71.
Nixon RD, Sweeney L, Erickson DB, Touyz SW. Parent-child interaction therapy: a comparison of standard and abbreviated treatments for oppositional defiant preschoolers. J Consult Clin Psychol. 2003; 71(2):251-60.

Olson AK, Eadie BD, Ernst C, Christie BR. Environmental enrichment and voluntary exercise massively increase neurogenesis in the adult hippocampus via dissociable pathways. Hippocampus. 2006; 16(3): 250-60.

O'Farrell TJ. Behavioral couples therapy for alcohol and drug use. Psychiatric Times, 1999: XVI (4), available at: http://www.psychosocial.com/addiction/bct.html.

O'Farrell TJ, Cutter HSG, Choquette KA. Behavioral marital therapy for male alcoholics: marital and drinking adjustment during the two years after treatment. Behavior Therapy. 1992; 23:529-549.

Park CL, Gaffey AE. Relationships between psychosocial factors and health behavior change in cancer survivors: an integrative review. Ann Behav Med. 2007; 34(2):115-34.

Park DC, Reuter-Lorenz P. The adaptive brain: aging and neurocognitive scaffolding. Annu Rev Psychol. 2009; 60:173-96.

Parsons AC, Shraim M, Inglis J, Aveyard P, Hajek P. Interventions for preventing weight gain after smoking cessation. Cochrane Database Syst Rev. 2009; (1):CD006219.

Patel SR, Hu FB. Short sleep duration and weight gain: a systematic review. Obesity. 2008; 16(3):643-53.

Pawlow LA, Jones GE. The impact of abbreviated progressive muscle relaxation on salivary cortisol. Biol Psychol. 2002; 60(1):1-16.

Pawlow LA, O'Neil PM, Malcolm RJ. Night eating syndrome: effects of brief relaxation training on stress, mood, hunger, and eating patterns. Int J Obes Relat Metab Disord. 2003; 27(8):970-8.

Perkonigg A, Owashi T, Stein MB, Kirschbaum C, Wittchen HU. Posttraumatic stress disorder and obesity: evidence for a risk association. Am J Prev Med. 2009; 36(1):1-8.

Petry NM. A comprehensive guide to the application of contingency management procedures in clinical settings. Drug Alcohol Depend. 2000; 58(1-2):9-25.

Porto PR, Oliveira L, Mari J, Volchan E, Figueira I, Ventura P. Does cognitive behavioral therapy change the brain? A systematic review of neuroimaging in anxiety disorders. J Neuropsychiatry Clin Neurosci. 2009; 21(2):114-25.

Ravussin E, Lillioja S, Anderson TE, Christin L, Bogardus C. Determinants of 24-hour energy expenditure in man. Methods and results using a respiratory chamber. J Clin Invest. 1986; 78(6):1568-78.

Read D, Van Leeuwen B. Predicting hunger: the effects of appetite and delay on choice. Organizational bchavior and human decision processes. 1998: 76(2): 189-205.

Reis HT, Rusbult CE (eds). Close relationships. New York: Psychology Press, 2004.

Rodriguez PF, Aron AR, Poldrack RA. Ventral-striatal/nucleus-accumbens sensitivity to prediction errors during classification learning. Hum Brain Mapp. 2006; 27(4):306-13.

Roesch MR, Olson CR. Neuronal activity related to reward value and motivation in primate frontal cortex. Science. 2004; 304(5668):307-10.

Rolls BJ, Morris EL, Roe LS. Portion size of food affects energy intake in normal-weight and overweight men and women. Am J Clin Nutr. 2002; 76(6):1207-13.

Roman E, Nylander I. The impact of emotional stress early in life on adult voluntary ethanol intake-results of maternal separation in rats. Stress. 2005; 8(3):157-74.

Romano JM, Turner JA, Jensen MP, Friedman LS, Bulcroft RA, Hops H, Wright SF. Chronic pain patient-spouse behavioral interactions predict patient disability. Pain. 1995; 63(3):353-60.

Rosenblum LA, Coplan JD, Freidman S, Bassoff T, Gorman JM, Andrews MW. Adverse early experiences affect noradrenergic and serotonergic functioning in adult primates. Biol Psycho. 1994; 35: 221-227.

Ross A, Thomas S. The health benefits of yoga and exercise: a review of comparison studies. J Altern Complement Med. 2010; 16(1): 3-12.

Rotge JY, Guehl D, Dilharreguy B, Tignol J, Bioulac B, Allard M, Burbaud P, Aouizerate B. Meta-analysis of brain volume changes in obsessive-compulsive disorder. Biol Psychiatry. 2009; Jan 1;65(1):75-83.

Rozeske RR, Der-Avakian A, Bland ST, Beckley JT, Watkins LR, Maier SF. The medial prefrontal cortex regulates the differential expression of morphine-conditioned place preference following a single exposure to controllable or uncontrollable stress. Neuropsychopharmacology. 2009; 34(4):834-43.

Rubak S, Sandbaek A, Lauritzen T, Christensen B. Motivational interviewing: a systematic review and meta-analysis. Br J Gen Pract. 2005; 55(513):305-12.

Saint-Exupery A. The little prince. Gaillimard, 1943.

Saling LL, Phillips JG. Automatic behaviour: efficient not mindless. Brain Res Bull. 2007; 73(1-3):1-20.

Sapolsky RM. Why zebras don't get ulcers (3rd edition). New York: Henry Holt and Company, 2004.

Sapolsky RM. Glucocorticoids, stress, and their adverse neurological effects: relevance to aging. Exp Gerontol. 1999; 34(6):721-32.

Saxena, S. Neurobiology and treatment of compulsive hoarding. CNS Spectrum. 2008; 13(9)14: 29-36.

Scarmeas N, Luchsinger JA, Schupf N, Brickman AM, Cosentino S, Tang MX, Stern Y. Physical activity, diet, and risk of Alzheimer disease. JAMA. 2009; 302(6):627-37.

Schienle A, Schäfer A, Hermann A, Rohrmann S, Vaitl D. Symptom provocation and reduction in patients suffering from spider phobia: an fMRI study on exposure therapy. Eur Arch Psychiatry Clin Neurosci. 2007; 257(8):486-93.

Schneider W, Chein JM. Controlled & automatic processing: behavior, theory, and biological mechanisms, Cognitive Science: A Multidisciplinary Journal. 2003; 27:3,525-559.

Schultz W. Predictive reward signal of dopamine neurons. J Neurophysiol. 1998; 80(1):1-27.

Scott DJ, Stohler CS, Egnatuk CM, Wang H, Koeppe RA, Zubieta JK. Individual differences in reward responding explain placebo-induced expectations and effects. Neuron. 2007; 55(2):325-36.

Seminowicz DA, Mayberg HS, McIntosh AR, Goldapple K, Kennedy S, Segal Z, Rafi-Tari S. Limbic-frontal circuitry in major depression: a path modeling metanalysis. Neuroimage. 2004; 22(1):409-18.

Shin LM, Wright CI, Cannistraro PA, Wedig MM, McMullin K, Martis B, Macklin ML, Lasko NB, Cavanagh SR, Krangel TS, Orr SP, Pitman RK, Whalen PJ, Rauch SL. A functional magnetic resonance imaging study of amygdala and medial prefrontal cortex responses to overtly presented fearful faces in posttraumatic stress disorder. Arch Gen Psychiatry. 2005; 62(3):273-81.

Shipherd JC, Keyes M, Jovanovic T, Ready DJ, Baltzell D, Worley V, Gordon-Brown V, Hayslett C, Duncan E. Veterans seeking treatment for posttraumatic stress disorder: what about comorbid chronic pain? J Rehabil Res Dev. 2007; 44(2):153-66.

Shonkoff JP, Boyce WT, McEwen BS. Neuroscience, molecular biology, and the childhood roots of health disparities: building a new framework for health promotion and disease prevention. JAMA. 2009; 301(21):2252-9.

Siegle GJ, Carter CS, Thase ME. Use of FMRI to predict recovery from unipolar depression with cognitive behavior therapy. Am J Psychiatry. 2006; 163(4):735-8.

Smith-Coggins R, Howard SK, Mac DT, Wang C, Kwan S, Rosekind MR, Sowb Y, Balise R, Levis J, Gaba DM. Improving alertness and performance in emergency department physicians and nurses: the use of planned naps. Ann Emerg Med. 2006; 48(5):596-604.

Sorbi MJ, Peters ML, Kruise DA, Maas CJ, Kerssens JJ, Verhaak PF, Bensing JM. Electronic momentary assessment in chronic pain I: psychological pain responses as predictors of pain intensity. Clin J Pain. 2006; 22(1):55-66.

Sorrell JT, Trafton JA, McKellar, JD. Intergrated management of pain. Unpublished workbook: VA Palo Alto, 2005.

Spikmans FJ, Brug J, Doven MM, Kruizenga HM, Hofsteenge GH, van Bokhorst-van der Schueren MA. Why do diabetic patients not attend appointments with their dietitian? J Hum Nutr Diet. 2003; 16(3):151-8.

Stitzer M, Petry N. Contingency management for treatment of substance abuse. Annu Rev Clin Psychol. 2006; 2:411-34.

Stroop, JR. Studies of interference in serial verbal reactions. Journal of Experimental Psychology. 1935; 18: 643-662.

Taber KH, Hurley RA, Yudofsky. Diagnosis and treatment of neuropsychiatric disorders. Ann Rev of Med. 2010; 61:121-133.

Taha SA, Fields HL. Inhibitions of nucleus accumbens neurons encode a gating signal for reward-directed behavior. J Neurosci. 2006; 26(1):217-22.

Thomas R, Zimmer-Gembeck MJ. Behavioral outcomes of Parent-Child Interaction Therapy and Triple P-Positive Parenting Program: a review and meta-analysis. J Abnorm Child Psychol. 2007; 35(3):475-95.

Timko C, DeBenedetti A. A randomized controlled trial of intensive referral to 12-step self-help groups: one-year outcomes. Drug Alcohol Depend. 2007; 90(2-3):270-9.

Tobler PN, Fiorillo CD, Schultz W. Adaptive coding of reward value by dopamine neurons. Science. 2005; 307(5715):1642-5.

Trafton JA, Gifford EV. Behavioral reactivity and addiction: the adaptation of behavioral response to reward opportunities. J Neuropsychiatry Clin Neurosci. 2008; 20(1):23-35.

Trafton JA, Gordon W (eds.). Best practices in the behavioral management of chronic disease: volume 1 neuropsychiatric disorders. Los Altos: Institute for Brain Potential. 2008a.

Trafton JA, Gordon W (eds). Best practices in the behavioral management of chronic disease: volume 2 other medical disorders. Los Altos: Institute for Brain Potential, 2008b.

Tranel D, Gullickson G, Koch M, Adolphs R. Altered experience of emotion following bilateral amygdala damage. Cogn Neuropsychiatry. 2006; 11(3):219-32.

Truby H, Baic S, deLooy A, Fox KR, Livingstone MB, Logan CM, Macdonald IA, Morgan LM, Taylor MA, Millward DJ. Randomised controlled trial of four commercial weight loss programmes in the UK: initial findings from the BBC "diet trials". BMJ. 2006; 332(7553):1309-14.

Ulman, MT. Is Broca's area part of a basal ganglia thalamocortical circuit? Cortex. 2006; 42(4):480-5.

Umilta MA, Kohler E, Gallese V, Fogassi L, Fadiga L. I know what you are doing. A neurophysiological study. Neuron. 2001; 31: 155-65.

U.S. Department of Energy. Consumer energy tax incentives: what the American Recovery and Reinvestment Act means to you. Available at: http://www.energy.gov/taxbreaks.htm. Accessed 11/10/10.

van der Elst W, van Boxtel MP, van Breukelen GJ, Jolles J. The Stroop color-word test: influence of age, sex, and education; and normative data for a large sample across the adult age range. Assessment. 2006; 13(1):62-79.

van der Heijden AA, Hu FB, Rimm EB, van Dam RM. A prospective study of breakfast consumption and weight gain among U.S. men. Obesity (Silver Spring). 2007; 15(10):2463-9.

van Honk J, Hermans EJ, Putman P, Montagne B, Schutter DJ. Defective somatic markers in sub-clinical psychopathy. Neuroreport. 2002; 13(8):1025-7.

Vance DE, Moore BS, Farr KF, Struzick T. Prefrontal and anterior cingulate cortex abnormalities in Tourette Syndrome: evidence from voxel-based morphometry and magnetization transfer imaging. BMC Neurosci. 2009; May 12;10:47.

Venkatraman V, Chuah YM, Huettel SA, Chee MW. Sleep deprivation elevates expectation of gains and attenuates response to losses following risky decisions. Sleep. 2007; 30(5):603-9.

Vieweg WV, Julius DA, Bates J, Quinn JF 3rd, Fernandez A, Hasnain M, Pandurangi AK. Posttraumatic stress disorder as a risk factor for obesity among male military veterans. Acta Psychiatr Scand. 2007; 116(6):483-7.

Vlaeyen JW, de Jong J, Geilen M, Heuts PH, van Breukelen G. Graded exposure in vivo in the treatment of pain-related fear: a replicated single-case experimental design in four patients with chronic low back pain. Behav Res Ther. 2001; 39(2):151-66.

Volpp KG, John LK, Troxel AB, Norton L, Fassbender J, Loewenstein G. Financial incentive-based approaches for weight loss: a randomized trial. JAMA. 2008; 300(22): 2631-7.

Wager TD, Rilling JK, Smith EE, Sokolik A, Casey KL, Davidson RJ, Kosslyn SM, Rose RM, Cohen JD. Placebo-induced changes in FMRI in the anticipation and experience of pain. Science. 2004; 303(5661):1162-7.

Walch JM, Rabin BS, Day R, Williams JN, Choi K, Kang JD. The effect of sunlight on postoperative analgesic medication use: a prospective study of patients undergoing spinal surgery. Psychosomatic Medicine. 2005; 67: 156-163.

Wansink B, van Ittersum K. Portion size me: downsizing our consumption norms. J Am Diet Assoc. 2007; 107(7):1103-6.

Webber KH, Tate DF, Michael Bowling J. A randomized comparison of two motivationally enhanced Internet behavioral weight loss programs. Behav Res Ther. 2008; 46(9):1090-5.

Webster-Stratton C, Jamila Reid M, Stoolmiller M. Preventing conduct problems and improving school readiness: evaluation of the Incredible Years Teacher and Child Training Programs in high-risk schools. J Child Psychol Psychiatry. 2008; 49(5):471-88.

Weintraub D. Dopamine and impulse control disorders in Parkinson's disease. Ann Neurol. 2008; 64 Suppl 2:S93-100.

West DS, DiLillo V, Bursac Z, Gore SA, Greene PG. Motivational interviewing improves weight loss in women with type 2 diabetes. Diabetes Care. 2007; 30(5):1081-7.

White B, Sanders SH. The influence on patients' pain intensity ratings of antecedent reinforcement of pain talk or well talk. J Behav Ther Exp Psychiatry. 1986; 17(3):155-9.

Wikipedia. Employer transportation benefits in the United States. Available at: http://en.wikipedia.org/wiki/Employer_transportation_benefits_in_the_United_States. Accessed 11/10/10.

Wise RA, Bozarth MA. Brain mechanisms of drug reward and euphoria. Psychiatr Med. 1985; 3(4):445-60.

Woods MP, Asmundson GJ. Evaluating the efficacy of graded in vivo exposure for the treatment of fear in patients with chronic back pain: a randomized controlled clinical trial. Pain. 2008; 136(3): 271-80.

Worbe Y, Gerardin E, Hartmann A, Valabrégue R, Chupin M, Tremblay L, Vidailhet M, Colliot O, Lehéricy S. Distinct structural changes underpin clinical phenotypes in patients with Gilles de la Tourette syndrome. Brain. 2010; 133(Pt 12):3649-60.

Zack M, Poulos CX. A D2 antagonist enhances the rewarding and priming effects of a gambling episode in pathological gamblers. Neuropsychopharmacology. 2007; 32(8): 1678-86.

Use this page to list how you can benefit from applying the 5 brain challenges:

DISCLAIMER: Why You May Not Want To Read This Book

- **Changing health behaviors is not easy.** In any given year, only about 2% of people attempting to quit smoking manage to succeed; only one in five, using the best available programs, are able to lose 10% of their body weight for five years and about the same percentage are able to maintain a program of physical activity for five years.
- **Completing this book is not easy.** We provide you with the information and exercises that can facilitate meaningful change; however, it is fair to say that not more than one in five people starting the book will complete the exercises.
- **Applying the five principles is not easy**. The best available research strongly supports practicing key principles in order to develop and maintain skills. The odds of success in achieving healthful goals are greatly increased by completing the exercises. However, they require substantial thought and effort.
- **Continuing to apply the principles after relapse is not easy. Lapses and** relapses are a normal part of the cycle by which healthful habits and skills are compromised by unanticipated life events. It takes a daily focus and concentrated effort to reapply these principles to achieve your goals. Contrary to popular books in the field, our approach, while highly comprehensive and comprehensible, does not purport to be quick nor easy.

Why You May Want To Read This Book

- **Changing health behaviors can change your life, wellness and longevity.** We provide evidence-based recommendations from leading scientists who have provided Best Practice recommendations as part of the series of works published by IBP,
- **Completing this book is worth the effort.** Learn the five key brain challenges to be tackled in order to create meaningful change in the behaviors needed to optimize health-related habits and behaviors.
- **This is the only book of its kind that integrates study of brain function with the skills needed to make a meaningful and enduring change in health-related goals.** Apply the principles underlying the five key brain challenges by following a systematic and thought-provoking series of exercises at the end of each challenge.
- **We provide the knowledge and resources to overcome relapse and refine your skills as part of a lifelong quest to optimize your health and wellness.** Improve your skills as you overcome obstacles, setbacks, lapses, and relapses. Learn as you continually refine your health-related skills.

IBP is a leading providing of continuing education for health professionals concerning the brain and behavioral sciences. In addition, IBP publishes the most comprehensive evidence-based reviews focusing on the behavioral management of chronic conditions in a three-volume series entitled, Best Practices in the Behavioral Management of Chronic Disease.